BETTER THINGS

An Annotated Visual Essay of Photographs Interpreting the Collection of the Memorial Art Gallery of the University of Rochester.

DOUGLAS HOLLELEY

CLARELLEN

CLARELLEN
116 Elmwood Ave
Rochester NY 14611
www.clarellen.com

ISBN: 0–9707138–2–7

Printed in Hong Kong through Inter Press Limited.

ACKNOWLEDGMENTS

I WOULD like to acknowledge the assistance I received from the many wonderful and enthusiastic faculty and staff of the Memorial Art Gallery of the University of Rochester. Most importantly I would like to thank Dr. Grant Holcomb, The Mary W. and Donald R. Clark Director, for entrusting me with the task of interpreting the collection and providing me with the broadest and most generous of "briefs." His invitation to simply look and respond to the gallery and its collection was an inspiring challenge.

Additionally other Faculty and Staff assisted in many invaluable ways. Carolyn Buechel Wilson, the Director's Assistant, facilitated access to the collection and enabled me to meet with the right person at the right time as the project developed. Marjorie Searl, Chief Curator, helped with the identification and correct labeling of the images as well as providing invaluable editorial and proof reading assistance with the text.

Lu Harper, Librarian, assisted with copyright and reference image issues and Donna DeFord, Visitor Services Coordinator, helped by coordinating my visits with the security personnel and by just generally looking after me. Finally thanks to Kevin Gibson, Area Manager, University of Rochester Facilities and all the security personnel, who helped me roam safely through the gallery with my tripod and camera.

At the University of Rochester River Campus my research into the origins of the motto of the University was facilitated by Nancy Martin, the John M. and Barbara Keil University Archivist and Rochester Collections Librarian, Rush Rhees Library and Melissa Mead, Digital and Visual Resources Librarian, Rare Books & Special Collections.

For proof reading and editorial assistance I would like to acknowledge the help of Sally Goers Fox, Visiting Professor at the University of Buffalo and also faculty member at the University of Rochester. Professor David Pankow, Curator of the Melbert B. Cary Jr. Graphic Arts Collection, Rochester Institute of Technology was of great assistance with his comments and advice with respect to design and production issues.

Finally I would like to thank all of the artists, some of them anonymous, whose work I came to know on an intimate level. Special thanks to the art galleries, copyright organizations, estates, and artists who gave me permission to reproduce the artworks. (See the Index for details.) The reference images in the Index are from the archives of the Memorial Art Gallery with the exception of those referring to pages 10, 34, 47, 52, 54, 76, 77, 80, 84, 85, 91, and 94. These were made by the author.

Note: All possible efforts were made to correctly attribute and acknowledge copyright of the artworks. If for any reason an omission has occurred I would like to offer my sincere apologies.

COLOPHON

The images in this portfolio were made on a Nikon 990 digital camera. The works of art were photographed in situ and the light levels were often very low. As a result long exposure times were the order of the day. It is for this reason that I would like to thank the Director and the Security Staff for trusting me to mount the camera on a tripod.

The images were subsequently corrected in Adobe Photoshop. For the most part the images are printed as photographed other than corrections for color and contrast. The document was assembled in Adobe InDesign. The body text is set with Gill Sans, the Index with Arial and the italicized captions are set with Adobe Garamond.

Douglas Holleley

CONTENTS

PREFACE
Page v

INTRODUCTION
Pages 1 through 9

THE MAG
Pages 10 through 13

Chapter 1
ON READING
Pages 14 through 27

Chapter 2
ON MEN AND WOMEN
Pages 28 through 53

Chapter 3
ON THE LAND
Pages 54 through 69

Chapter 4
MELIORA
Pages 70 through 93

INDEX
Pages 94 through 119

Memorial Art Gallery
OF THE UNIVERSITY OF ROCHESTER

PREFACE

I HAD the privilege of first seeing an exhibition of photographs by Douglas Holleley in 2003. Haunting and provocative, he combined image and text to present a world of mystery, ambiguity and beauty that was both autobiographical and philosophical in nature. This exhibition was the catalyst for his keen eye, and equally keen mind, to view afresh the permanent collection of the Memorial Art Gallery.

Much as our previous book, "Voices in the Gallery,"[1] drew upon contemporary poets and novelists to respond to and "reinterpret" the collection, so, too, does "Better Things" offer both creative and original insights into many of the paintings, sculptures, decorative arts and even architectural details of the museum. What Holleley terms "interactive readings" provides the visitor, whether young or old, the opportunity to see the collection "afresh" from his or her own vantage point. The visitor is challenged to move beyond the formal conventions of museum practice and create their own museum experience. Indeed, the essence of Holleley's project is this personal, creative interaction with works of art.

Holleley is correct when he states that my initial proposal was broad and the "most generous of briefs." I did want him "to simply look and respond," to respond as an artist and certainly without any sense of administrative interference or micromanagement. What neither of us knew was that the initial concept of a small artist's book would result in a magnificent portfolio of photographs with text, an exhibition of the work and, as seen in this book, an imaginative, inspired approach to looking at art in a museum.

"Better Things" is true to the University's motto, "Meliora," as we do "see and appreciate better things." It is also true to the artist's intention. We see things better while "reading" the book.

Dr. Grant Holcomb, The Mary W. and Donald R. Clark Director.

[1] *Voices in the Gallery, Writers on Art* The University of Rochester Press. 2001.

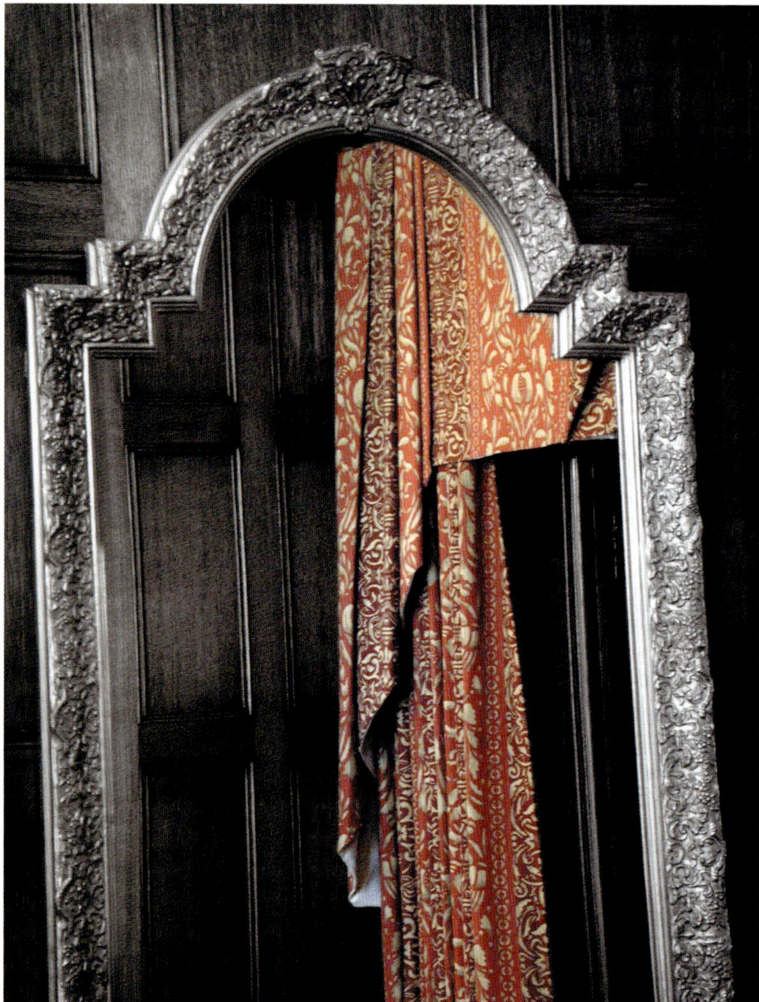

Mirror and curtain in the foyer of the M & T Ballroom, Cutler Union.

It is no coincidence that the art museum as we know it, and the medium of photography itself, developed almost simultaneously. Each share many characteristics and both emerged out of similar circumstances.

INTRODUCTION

The Art Museum

ART museums are so much a part of contemporary life that it is difficult to imagine the world without them. However, like their partner, (the medium of) photography, art museums are for the most part a nineteenth century invention and as such are a relatively recent phenomenon in the history of western culture and art. Until their inception artworks were tied to both their place of origin and ritualistic function. Religious works were housed in churches, portraits of royal families were displayed in palaces, and images of abundance were confined to the houses of the wealthy. However, with the advent of common, publicly accessible venues for the presentation of all these visual manifestations of value (either spiritual or material) the objêts d'art housed therein needed to be cataloged, classified and displayed. As a consequence a number of things occurred.

Firstly, the relationship of a work of art to its site, and its original, often ritualistic use, was severed. This process of secularization emphasized the perception of an image as an artifact. Malraux describes this process as "transforming the artist's visions into pictures as it transformed the gods into statues."[1] Even portraits changed in nature and became examples of an artist's oeuvre rather than the person depicted in the painting.

Additionally, the experience of art became more intellectualized. The art museum necessitated a classification system to contextualize what were necessarily fragments of a greater whole. Instead of the temple or church providing a "built-in" or more correctly a "built-around" framework of meaning, now labels and other supporting data became an essential part of the display. As Malraux observed, "in the art museum each exhibit is taken to mean something different from itself, this specific difference being its raison d'être and the justification for its presence there. In the past a Gothic statue was an integral part of the cathedral…and was never expected to consort with works of different mood and outlook. Every art collection is an anthology of contrasts."[2]

This need to categorize, collate and organize a collection is a double edged sword. It is necessary to make the collection accessible to the public but the process can sometimes limit our reading of the artworks. This can occur if we dwell too much on context rather than individual images. The risk exists that the works are evaluated and "read" by how well they "fit in" to a variety of categories and conventions. These categories include, but are not limited to, genre, medium, authorship, cultural significance and position within any art philosophy and/or movement. All of these things can subsequently combine to make us often look at the artwork on display as, in turn, a portrait, an etching, a Picasso, a Medieval religious work, an Impressionist work, etc. Thus specific images with specific messages can become instead exemplars of larger (often language-based, non visual) ideas. Rather than messages, they run the risk of being perceived and read as pigeon-holed "objects."

Early in the project photographs were made of the physical structure of the Gallery itself.

Below: Covered furniture in the M & T Ballroom of the Cutler Union.

Opposite: Spiral staircase to the tower of the Cutler Union.

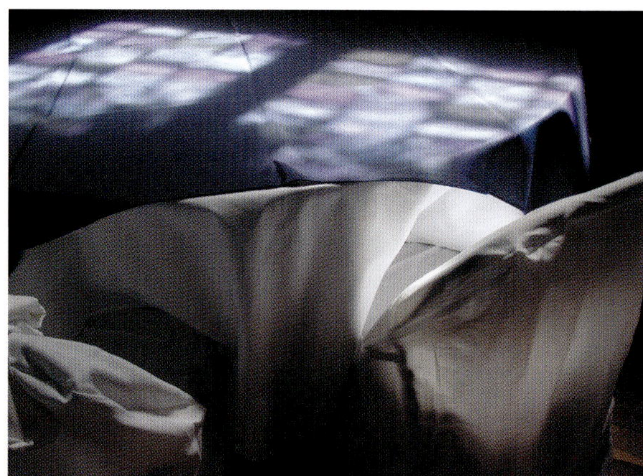

Conventional Photography of Art

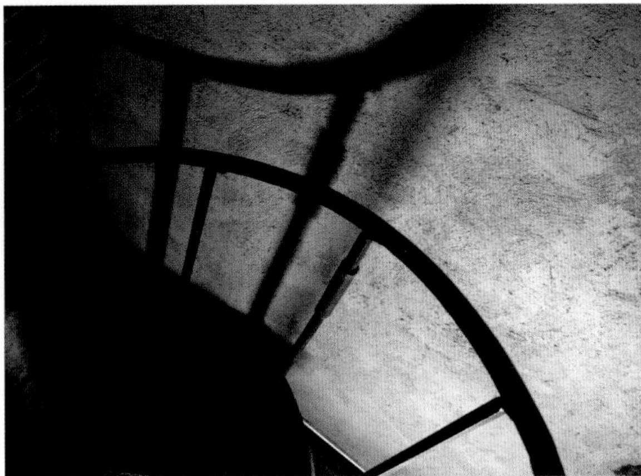

A DESCRIPTION of photography itself sounds very much like that of the art museum—the main difference being that of degree. Like the art museum, photography removes the work from its original context. A photograph of a painting can be sent easily to any part of the world. This seemingly simple act has a number of consequences. Probably the most significant is the fact that the original context and physical properties of the original works, what Walter Benjamin describes as their "aura," completely evaporate.[3]

Original works of art, no matter how far removed from their original context, always retain something of their aura—there is always a vestigial connection to the original ritualistic use of the object—even if this be as simple as the self evident proof of the object's survival through time.

Photographs on the other hand completely eliminate this connection. The painting or sculpture is stripped of its patina. The embedded brush marks, evidence of the original connection between the maker of the image and the image itself, disappear. The experience of seeing the original work, either in its original context or in the art museum, is replaced by the viewing of a printed reproduction which is not only different in tactile quality but is now able to be viewed in a handy "one size fits all" scale. Michelangelo's thirteen and a half foot high statue of David and a palm sized prehistoric votive sculpture both end up as an eight by ten inch print, and, like the art museum itself, words usually accompany the image to provide context. In the museum there is a wall label. In photography, there is the caption.

Much of this is due to the practices and assumptions of conventional photography. Normally when photographing works of art, supreme efforts are made, to as correctly as possible, render the "art object" in a way as to almost negate the fact that it is being photographed. Paintings are carefully removed from their position on the gallery wall, taken to a well equipped studio, and then evenly illuminated with dedicated studio lighting so that the ensuing photograph is as close a facsimile of the original as possible. This effort to maintain the integrity of the original work of art as an object or artifact has its place when cataloging a collection, but it has other consequences and meanings, most of them unintended.

In the past I have referred to this as the application of the "perpendicular proprietorial perspective" or "P^3." (See Figure 1.) In other words by placing the camera in a position of dominance over the object, the act of photography "takes possession" of the artwork, as much as it documents its appearance. This convention reinforces the perception of the artworks as objects and "things" rather than images with specific stories to tell. More importantly, it creates the impression that the photograph is the same as the original object. However, a photograph merely approximates an original work of art in the same way a map approximates a geographical reality—yet such is the power of photography, that this distinction is not often apparent.

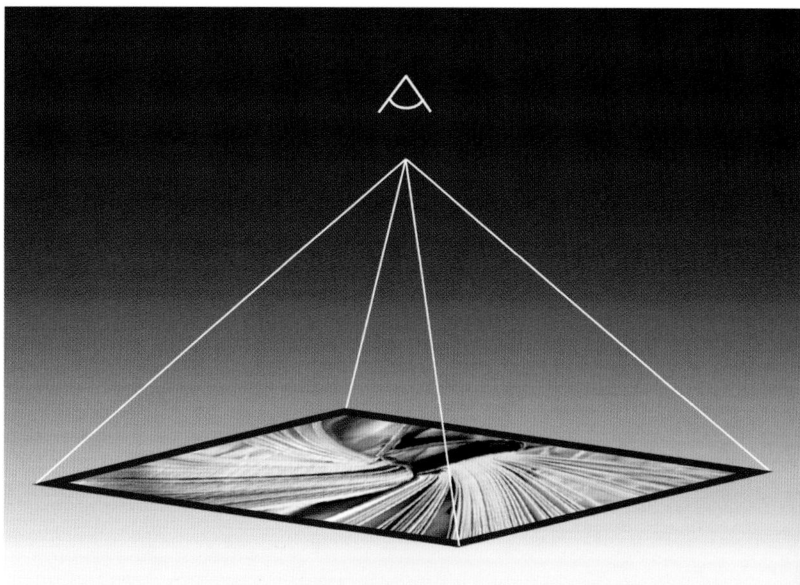

Figure 1. Conventional photographic practice centers the camera over the artwork in a position of dominance. The subsequent photograph often subtly reinforces our perception of the painting as an object rather than an image.

Alternative Methods of Photographing Works of Art

THE fundamental issue is of course that the original works of art in the Memorial Art Gallery, and the photographs of them in this book, are images—images with specific stories to tell, facts to display and nuances to appreciate. It is these messages, expressed directly and uncompromisingly as visual structure, that underpin the power of art. Thus the challenge is to devise a method of working that allows these messages to transcend the limitations of conventional (P^3) photography. To effect this I adopted an approach based on the premise that if it is legitimate for a photographer to roam through the world, selecting from a series of events to create a coherent perspective, so too can a photographer roam through an art gallery, or even an individual painting, and create a microcosmic visual reality that simultaneously draws from, comments upon, and adds to, the original reality.

I term this act "interactive reading," as the images so made represent a visual manifestation of the commonplace, yet highly complex, act of cognition we call "reading." Reading is not a passive act. When we read a book, not only are the eyes engaged but also the sense of touch as the book is cradled in the hands while the pages are turned. It can also be argued that the sense of hearing is similarly involved, in that the words and images on the page are also capable of conjuring up sound in the mind of the reader. However, the most important aspect of reading is that the mind of the reader must participate with the page in order to make sense of the marks printed thereon.

The photographs in this book are not expressions of "ownership" or even "documentation." Instead, by engaging in a (visual) dialog with the artworks, the photographs make visible not only the artwork as an object but also, through their framing and structure, the process of selective attention, personal identification, intellectual curiosity and judgment

I first employed the method of interactive reading when asked to photograph Dürer's "Hierin sind begriffen vier Bucher von menschlicher Proportion," his 1528 treatise on proportion as related to the human figure. In so doing I realized that such an activity could be more than a mere subjective act of interpretation but could also be a form of visual archaeology—in the sense that objective verifiable data could actually be extracted from the source rather than imposed upon it. In the case of the Dürer portfolio this methodology combined flexible image framing (not the P^3) with digital technology to introduce color into the black and white line drawings of Dürer's text. In so doing the figures, which in the original work functioned as somewhat secondary supporting illustrations, became instead prominent, almost three-dimensional, entities. These figures, when illuminated in this manner, manifested emotional, even sexual qualities, that were always "there" waiting to be read, but in their original form, were hidden beneath a veneer of pseudo-scientific objectivism.

In the case of the images in this portfolio, the argument that the images in their totality reveal an "objective truth" in the same way as those in the Dürer portfolio is more difficult to make. However, they do represent a truth—one of many truths—waiting to be read by a careful observer.

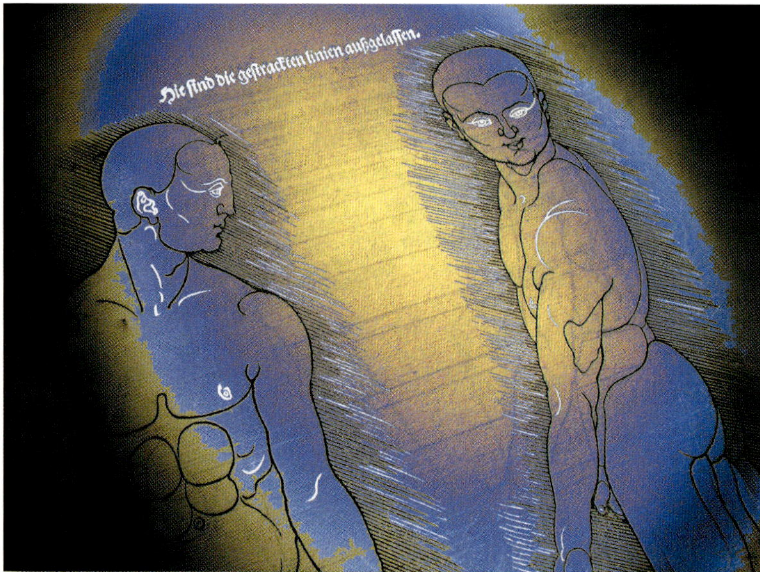

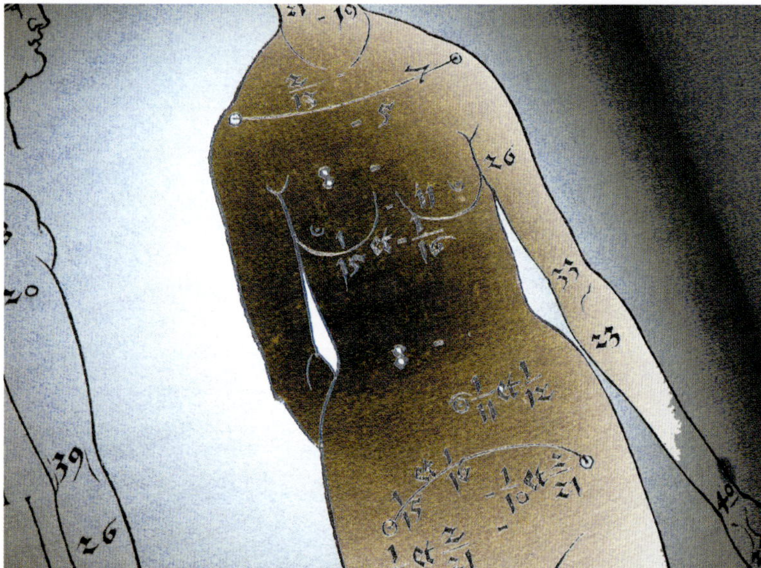

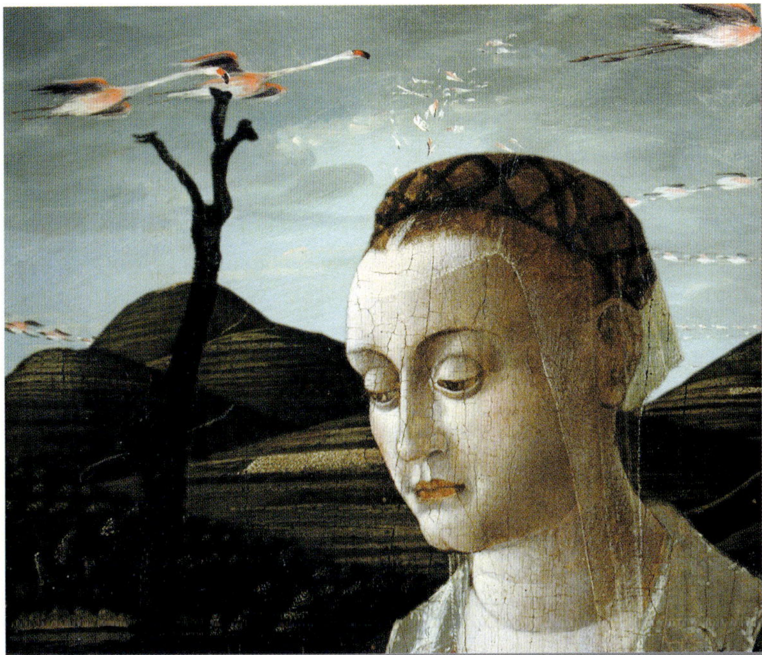

At an earlier stage in the work, paintings were not paired but instead, superimposed over each other. In this case a fifteenth century Italian Madonna is combined with a nineteenth century advertisement for the Colt Firearms Company. (Compare with pps. 58 and 59.)

that occurs constantly when we read and attempt to understand a text, an image or a collection of images.

The method I employed to achieve this was to regard the paintings as fields of choice and potential. In other words I concentrated on details rather than the whole image. A precedent for this seemingly arbitrary act is the notion of the "punctum." The French critic Roland Barthes[4] coined this term while engaged in an extended meditation on a photograph of his deceased mother. Barthes described the sometimes unbearable poignancy generated by a small, often initially unnoticed detail in the photograph. He sees the punctum not so much as a summation of the content of the image, but a minute yet significant structure that insistently calls the viewer back to view the image again and again.

Additionally, a small, but significant proportion of the photographs were either edited or enhanced digitally. Sometimes selected areas of the paintings would be "blocked out" so that relevant details could better reveal themselves. However, for the most part I made no alteration to the color(s) of the paintings. The photographs correlate as closely as possible with the original artworks. Exceptions to this are those paintings where the varnish had yellowed with age—these paintings have been digitally corrected to eliminate the color cast so formed. In only two cases were the colors modified substantially. (See Pages 60 and 90.)

AFTER trying various strategies (see Page 7), I decided the images were best arranged in pairs. The connections were based on purely visual criteria such as color, gesture and form. In this way their arrangement echoed my method of photography. In much the same way I engaged in a dialog with each of the individual works when photographing, so too the photographs subsequently engaged in a dialog with each other. This process quickly broke down barriers of time, space and category. Freed even further from their original context, characters and events could now speak directly to each other across geographical borders and even time itself.

As the work progressed connections extended, not just from photograph to photograph, but from pair to pair. Over time four distinct themes emerged as a result of this process. They are:

1. On Reading
2. On Men and Women
3. On the Land
4. Meliora

Other photographers and/or artists would, could, and most likely should, end up with a result different to this. Unlike the specific message communicated by the photographs of Dürer's book (Page 6), I cannot claim that these categories are intrinsically connected to the works of art. However, the organic way they emerged supports the claim that this methodology has validity, if not specificity of outcome. The process of interactive reading renders the collection in a coherent perspective. The fact that there may be other perspectives is not the point. Plenty of these exist already. They can be found in art history texts and in the layout of any one of the hundreds of museums of art across the country.

The real issue of course is that any and all of these perspectives emphasize the very need to have a perspective. When all is said and done the

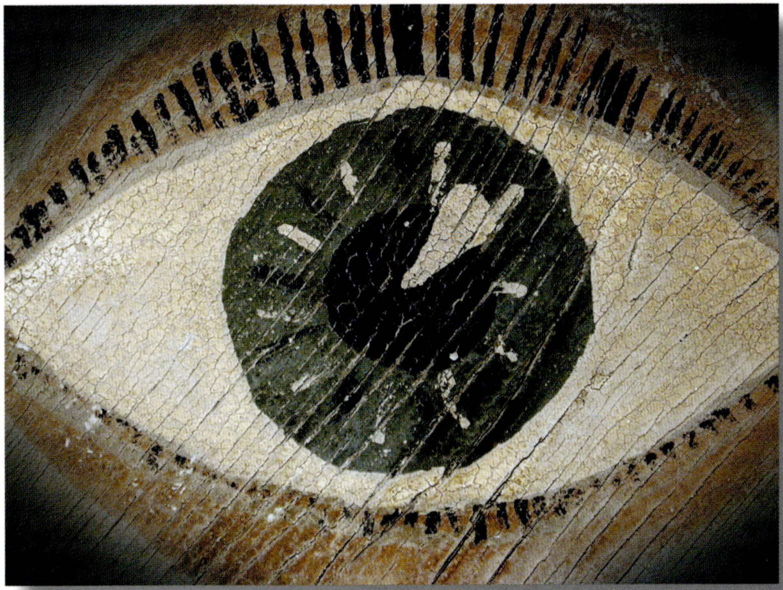

Detail of a nineteenth century commercial sign advertising the services of an optometrist.

message of these wonderful works of art stays eternally locked within their form. They are time capsules, not hidden away in some masonry wall to be unearthed in the distant future, but are instead right here, right now—and they call out their respective messages, many from centuries if not millennia ago, directly to the viewer in much the same way they did when first called into being. How we read them is up to us. But read them we must.

Footnotes:

[1] André Malraux *The Psychology of Art, Volume I: Museum Without Walls* New York: Pantheon Books, 1949.
[2] Malraux *op cit.*
[3] Walter Benjamin *The Work of Art in the Age of Mechanical Reproduction* London: Fontana Press, 1992.
[4] Roland Barthes *Camera Lucida, Reflections on Photography* Translation: Richard Howard. New York: Hill and Wang, 1981.
See also the author's portfolio, *Re-Reading the Book. A Photographic Analysis of Albrecht Dürer's Hierin sind begriffen vier Bucher von menschlicher Proportion.* Rochester, N.Y.: 2000. Reproduced courtesy of the Melbert B. Cary Jr. Graphic Arts Library, R.I.T.

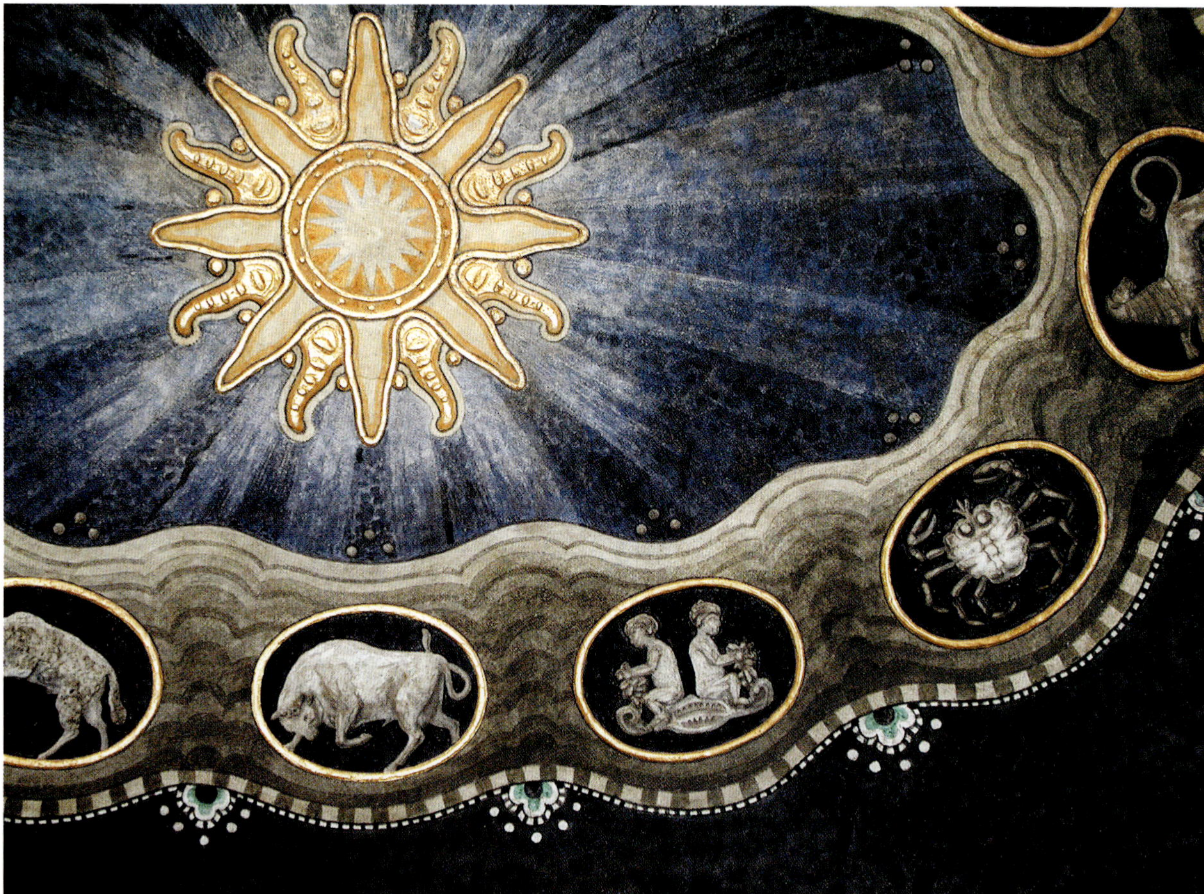

The zodiac mosaic inside the portico of the original building.

THE MAG

The Memorial Art Gallery, or "the mag," was built in 1913 with funds donated to the University of Rochester by Emily Sibley Watson, the daughter of Hiram Sibley, president of the Western Union telegraph company. Emily Watson wanted to perpetuate the memory of her son from her first marriage, James George Averell, who died of cholera at age 26.

The original structure was designed by the New York architects Foster and Gade. The building is based on a similar structure built in Rimini, Italy by the early Renaissance architect, Leon Battista Alberti. This "Renaissance jewel box" was enlarged in 1926 with the addition of the neo-classical Fountain Court at the rear.

The second major building that forms part of the gallery complex is the Cutler Union. This building, best described as "Collegiate Gothic" in style, was dedicated in 1933 as a union building for women students after the men left the Prince Street Campus for the River Campus in 1930. The building is named after James Cutler, a wealthy Rochesterian and patron of the University. Cutler made his fortune by designing the mail chute, found in most twentieth-century, multi-storied buildings. After the women students also left in 1955, the Cutler Union was used by the Eastman School of Music until 1987 at which time it became part of the MAG.

In 1968 the two buildings reached towards each other with a sympathetic and unobtrusive modernist wing designed by the Rochester architectural firm Waasdorp, Northrup and Kaelber. In 1987 a new entrance and welcoming space, the Vanden Brul Pavilion, designed by architect Frank Grosso, finally connected the two buildings.

Most museums are/were built to house an existing collection. This was not the case with the MAG. Instead, Emily Watson specifically made a gift of the building itself—hoping that its very presence would encourage community engagement in the development of the collection. She wanted art-minded citizens to make it "truly their own." This has proved to be the case and the collection has grown thanks to a variety of sources primarily from within the Rochester community. Undoubtedly this is the reason for the richness, variety and balance of the collection.

The source for this information is the highly detailed book, *Magnum Opus, The Story of the Memorial Art Gallery* by Rochester historian, Elizabeth Brayer, published in 1988 by the Memorial Art Gallery of the University of Rochester.

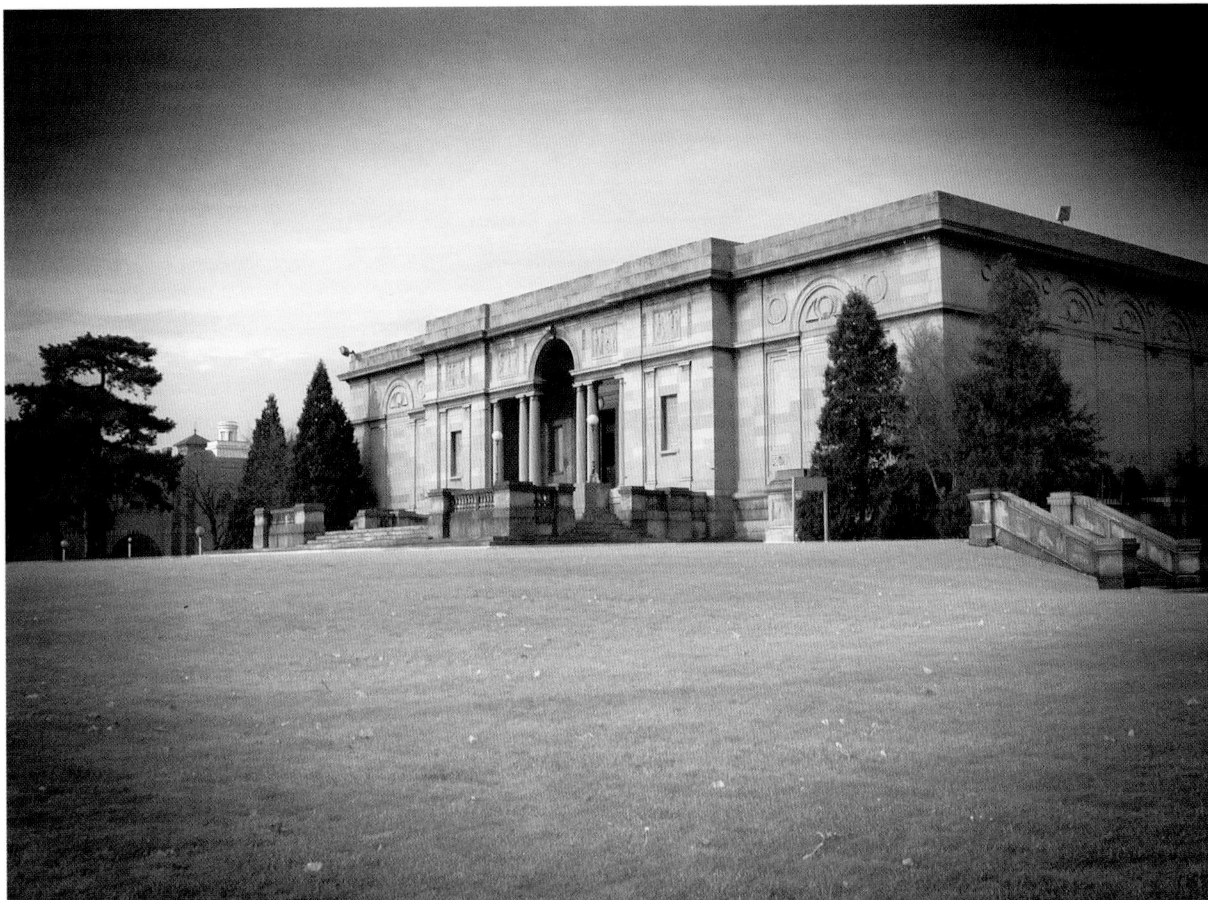

A view of the original building from the lawn adjacent to University Avenue.

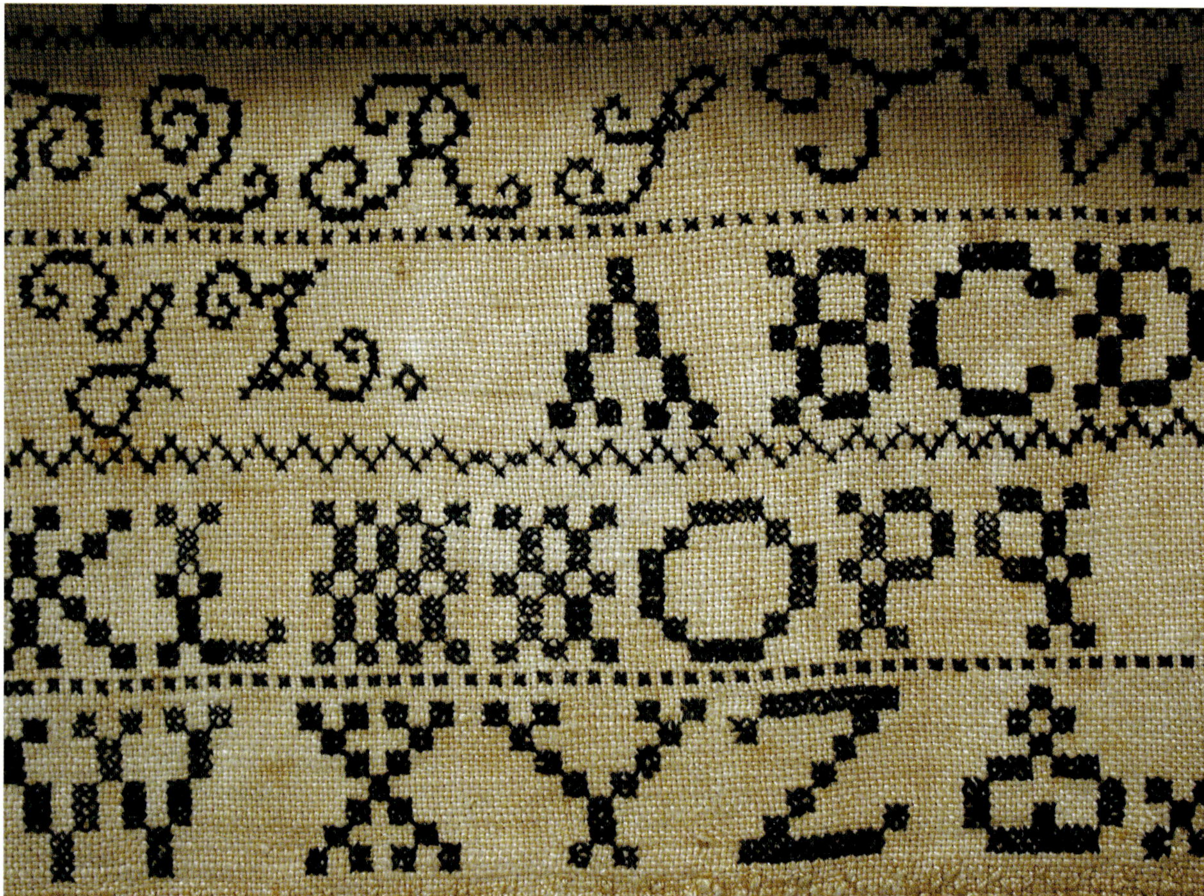

ON READING

To visit a museum is literally to enter a giant, three-dimensional book. However, no longer are the pages held safely in the hand or nestled on the sheets and covers of one's bed. Instead, with very little imagination, it is possible to visualize oneself as a Lilliputian reader surrounded by gigantic signs and symbols, each crying out waiting to be read and understood.

To read this "text" however, one cannot rely on the safety and order of the conventional codex. There is no identifiable sequence and no road map to steer you through the maze. Instead museums present a series of cultural or spatial cues. Hence the Medieval gallery, the Renaissance room, the Native Art display, the Twentieth Century Art section etc. These systems serve the vital function of making the collection accessible. However, they sometimes mask the fact that Medieval, Renaissance, Indigenous and Modern artists were people—people with more in common than not—despite differences in geographic location, cultural systems and place in time. All were born, had relationships, sometimes married, worked, had problems, experienced joys, faced death, sustained (and sometimes created) belief systems, and died.

These human experiences and values are manifested in most art in most cultures. Each culture in its own way, and in its own time, finds the means to give form to these simultaneously abstract but very real qualities and events. To share them at a personal level we need only shed the false comfort that comes with the cocoon of category. If we can hold back the urge to look at the works of art as "objects" or "symbols of culture," then we can allow the images to speak to us in their own voice, in their own time, and in their own way. Within this giant book, we can read these dramas and joys that reach out to touch us through time and space via the power of art and the sometimes almost cruel specificity of visual depiction.

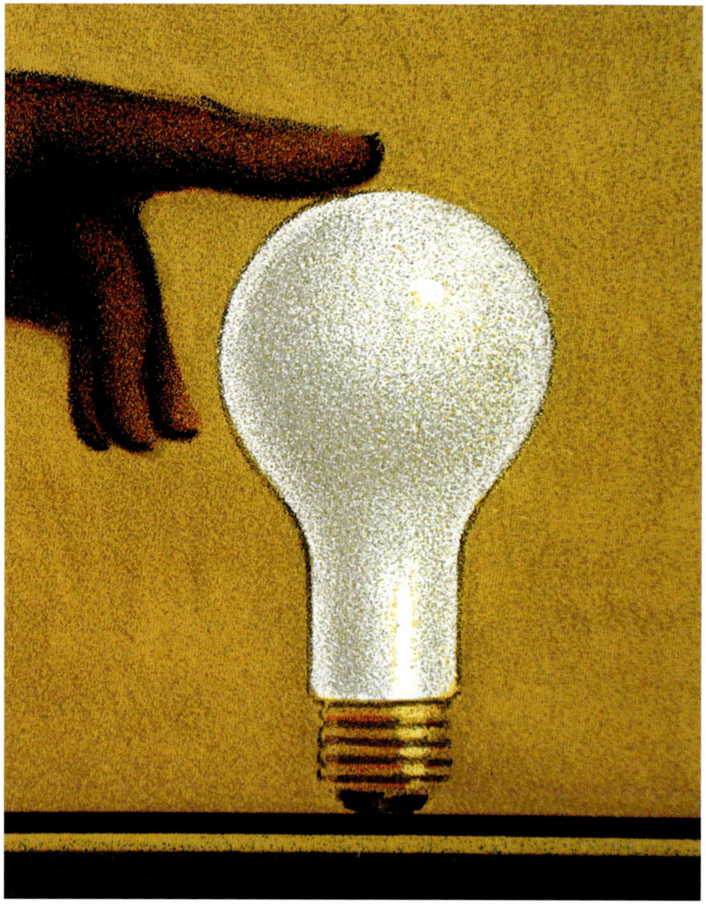

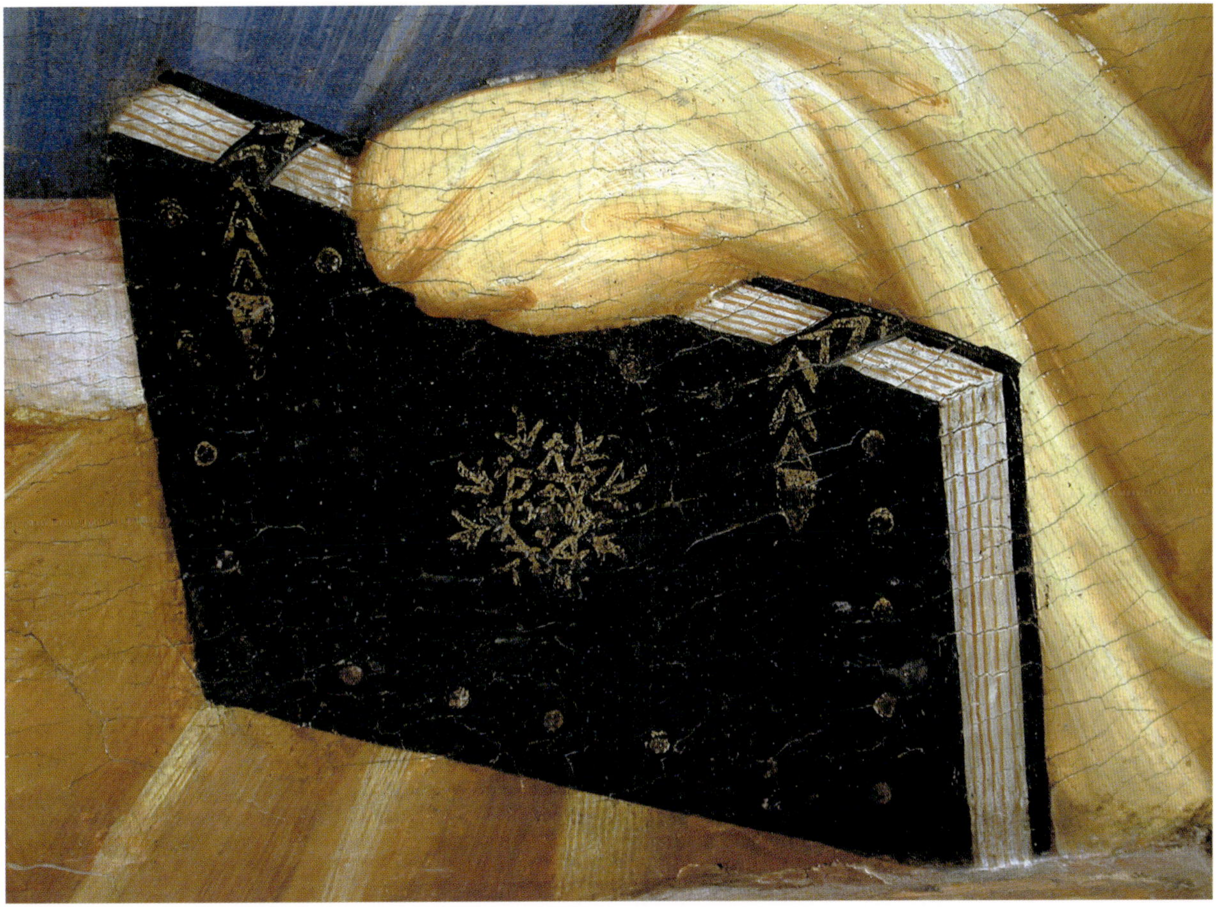

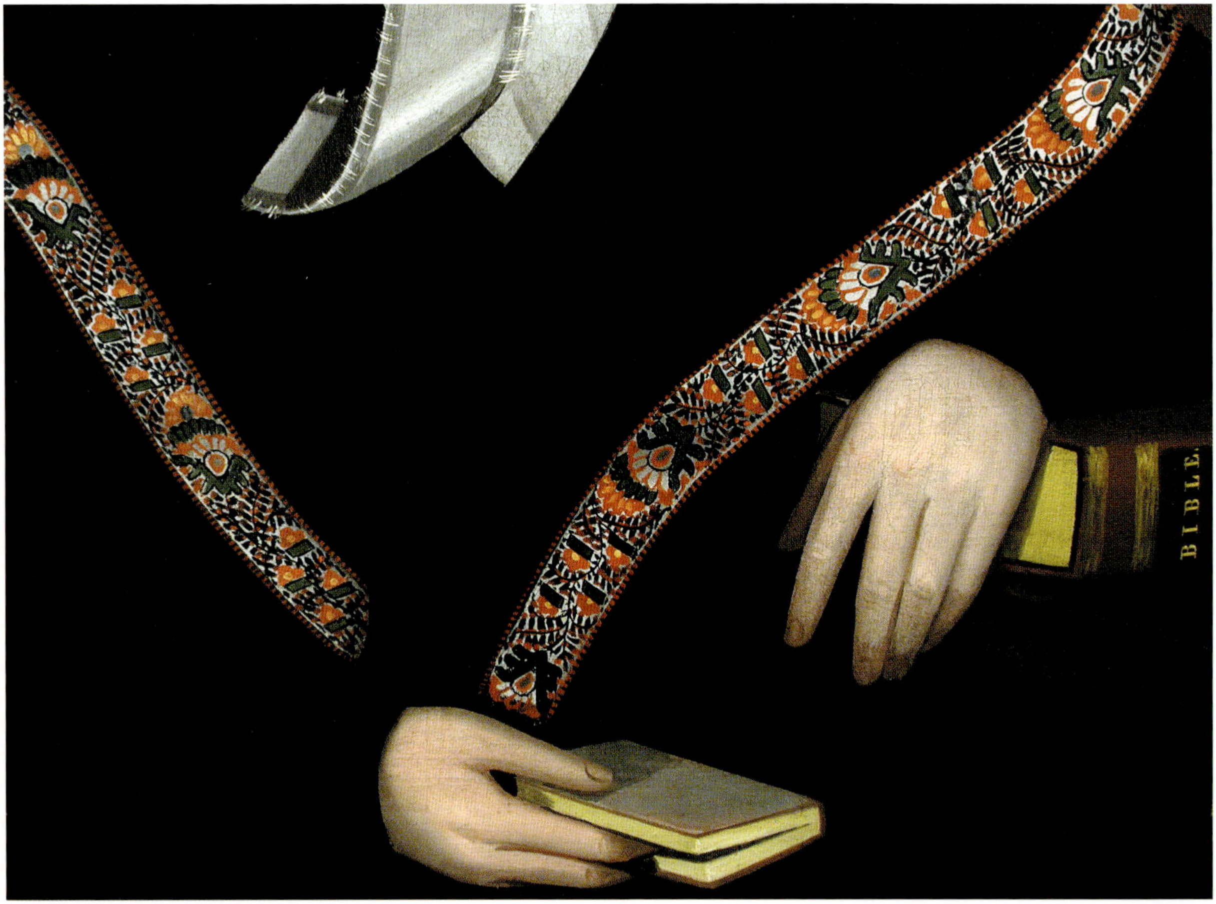
BIBLE

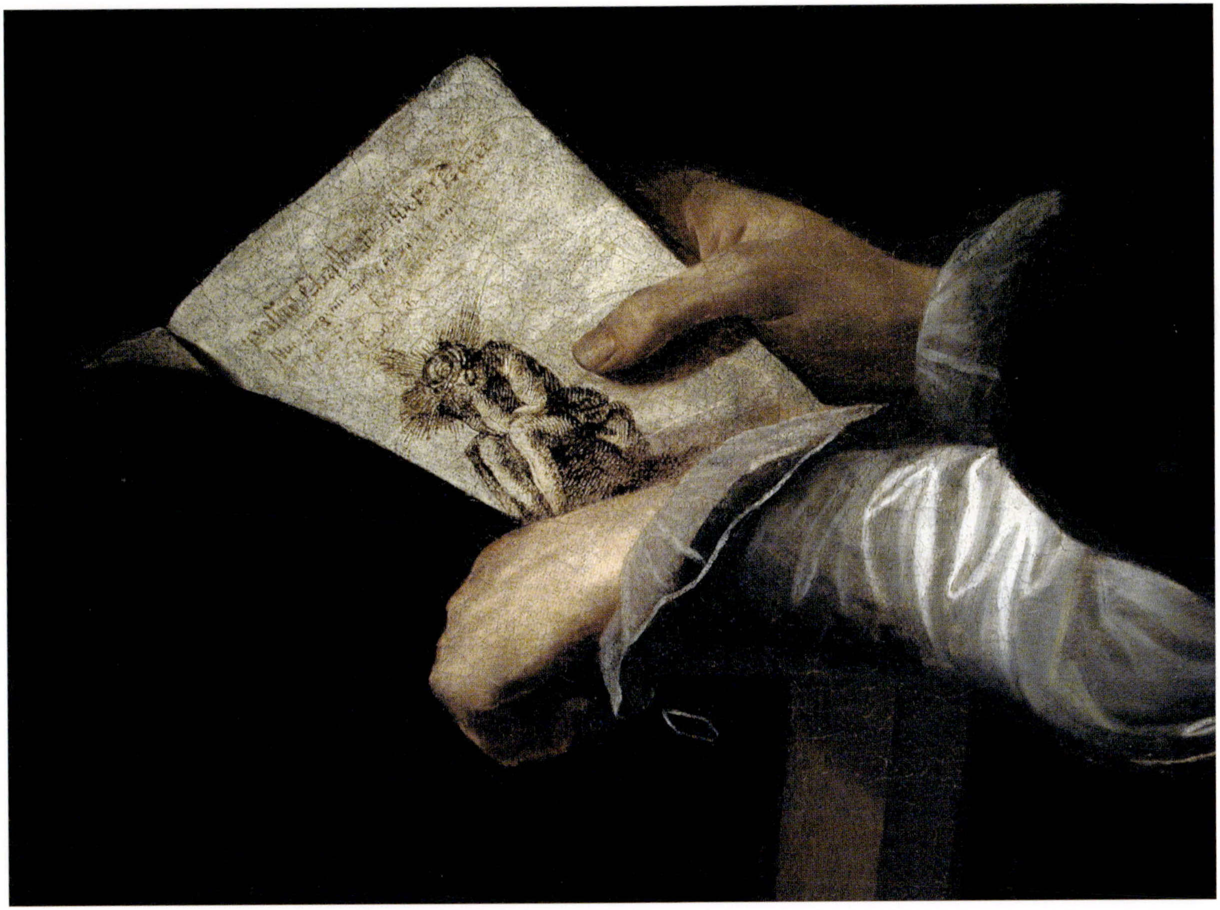

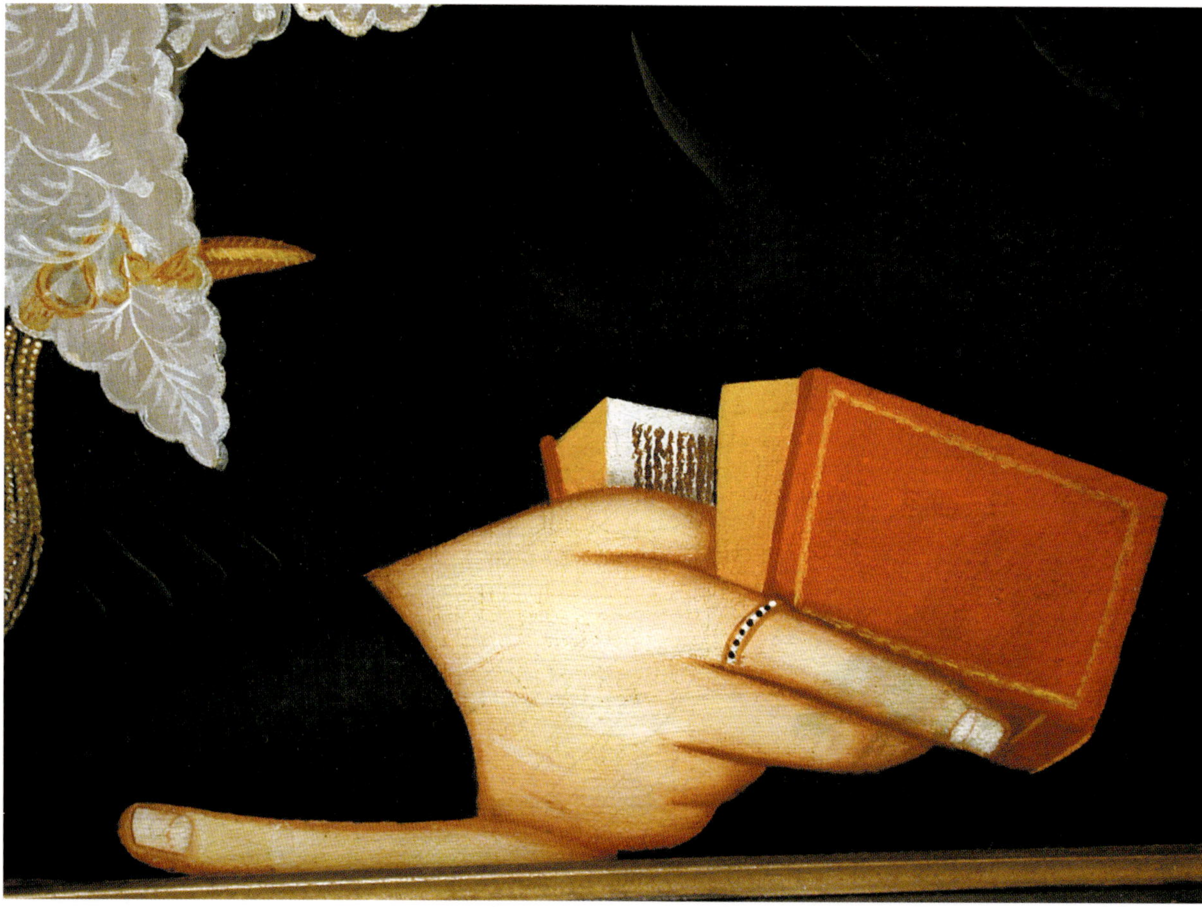

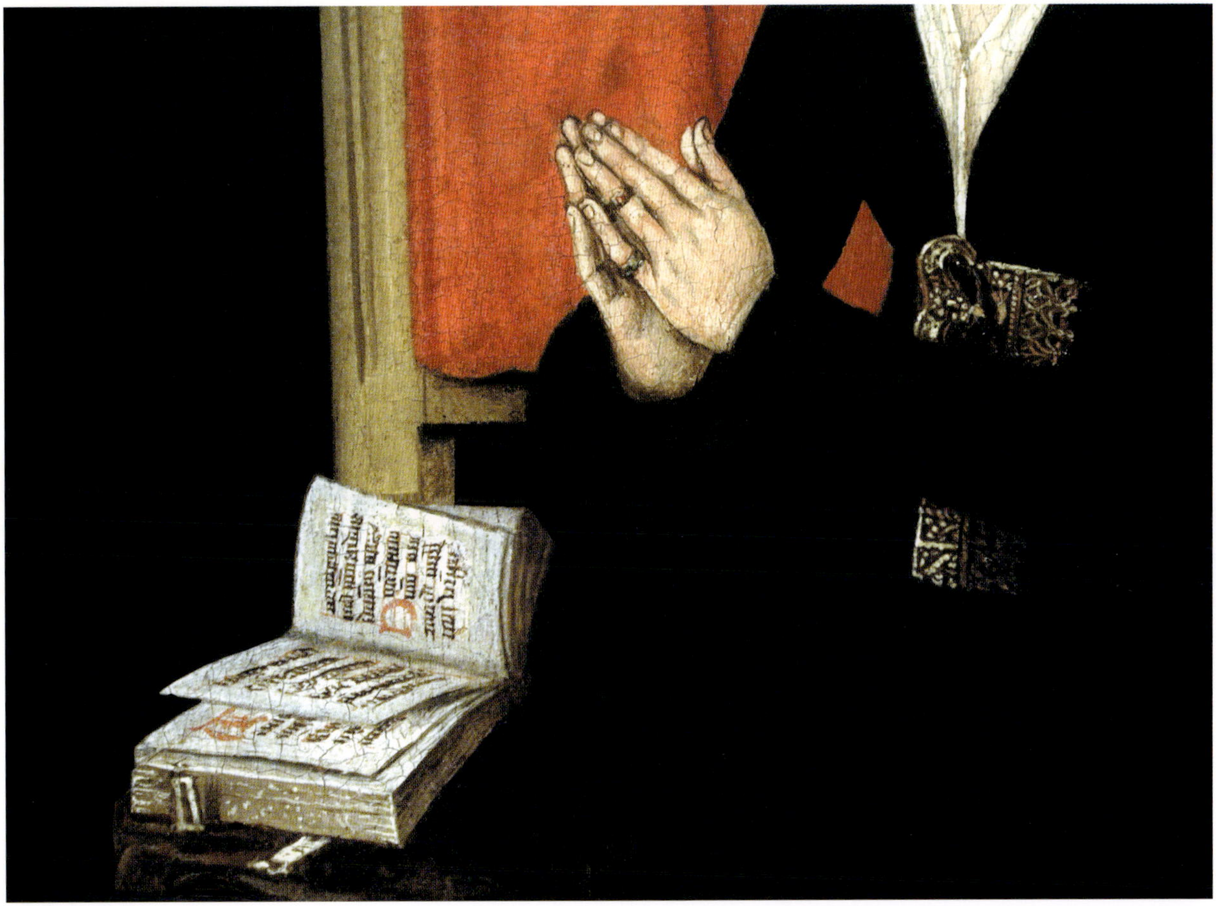

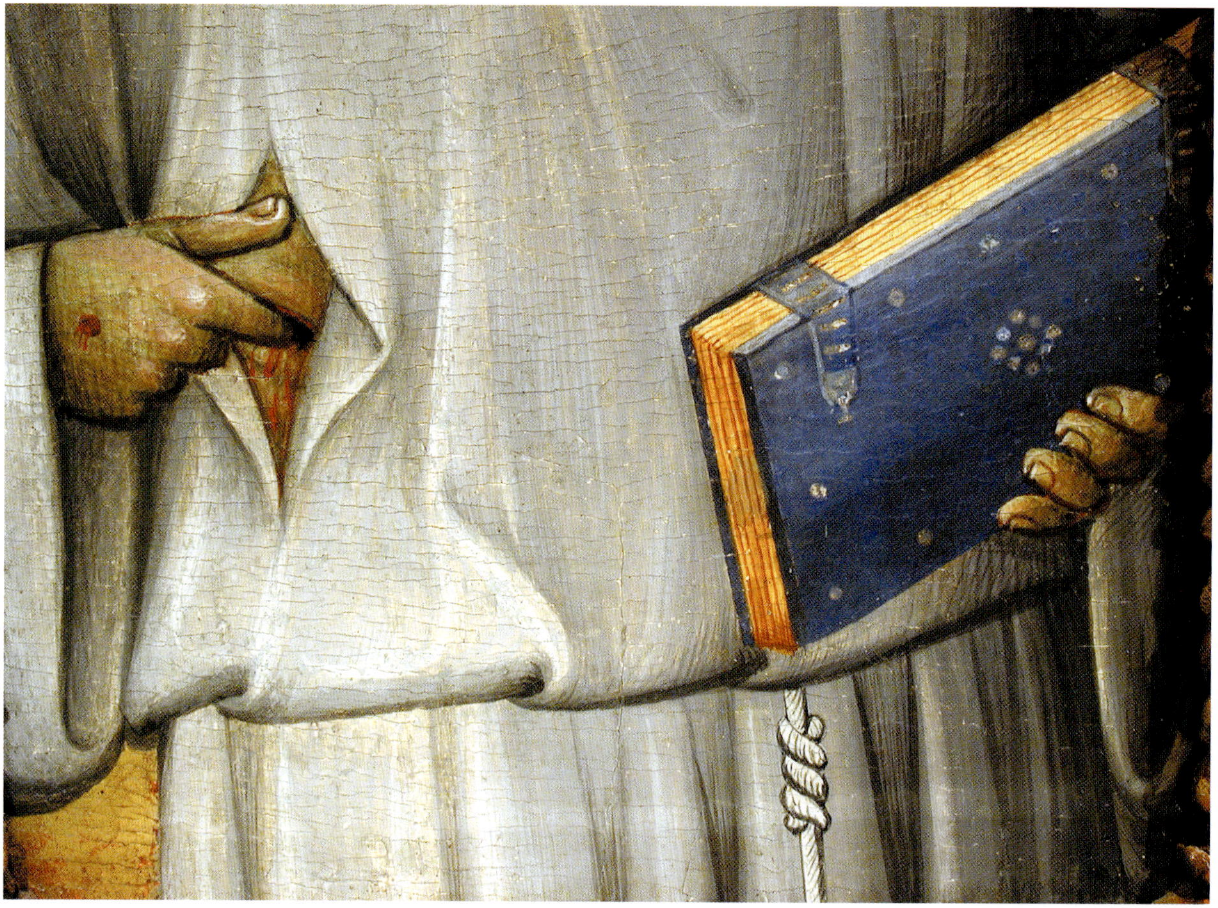

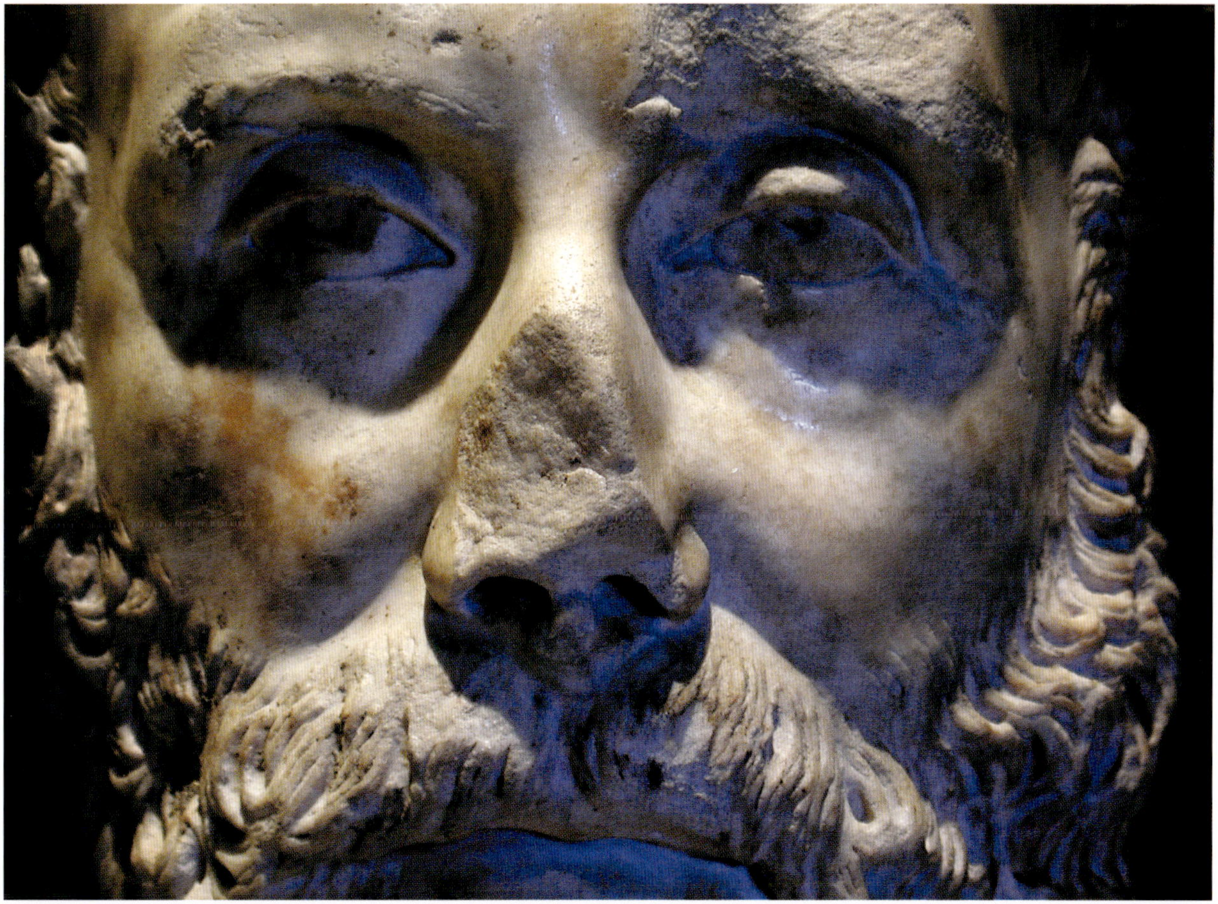

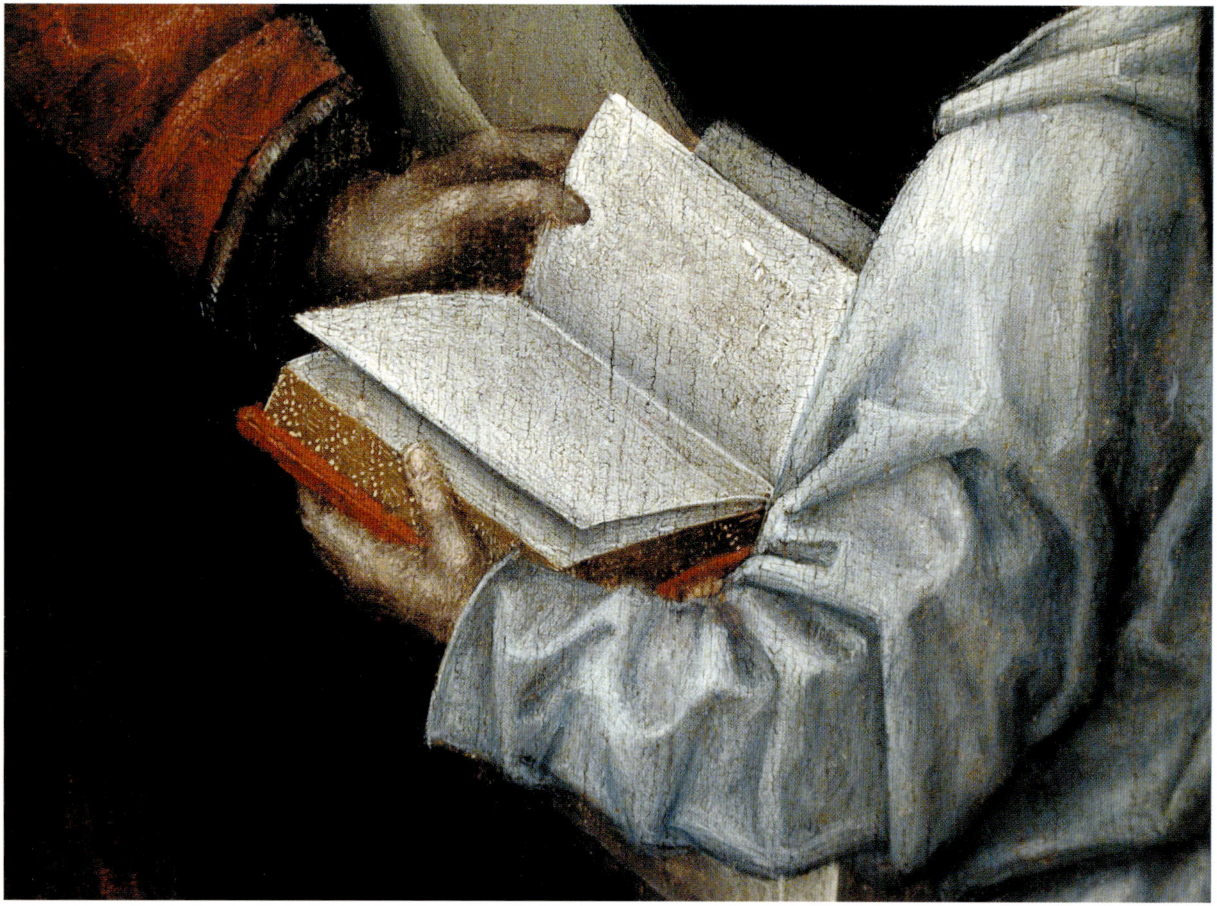

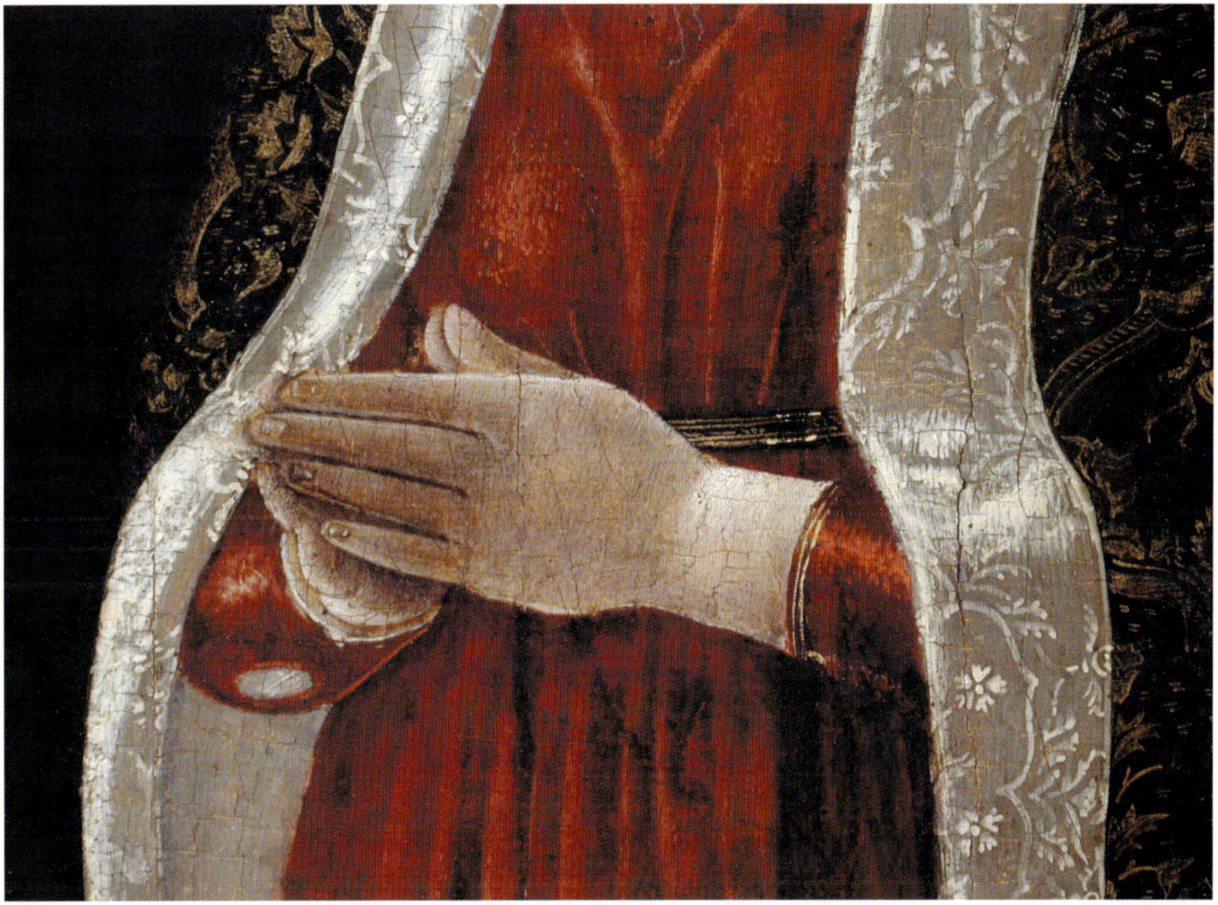

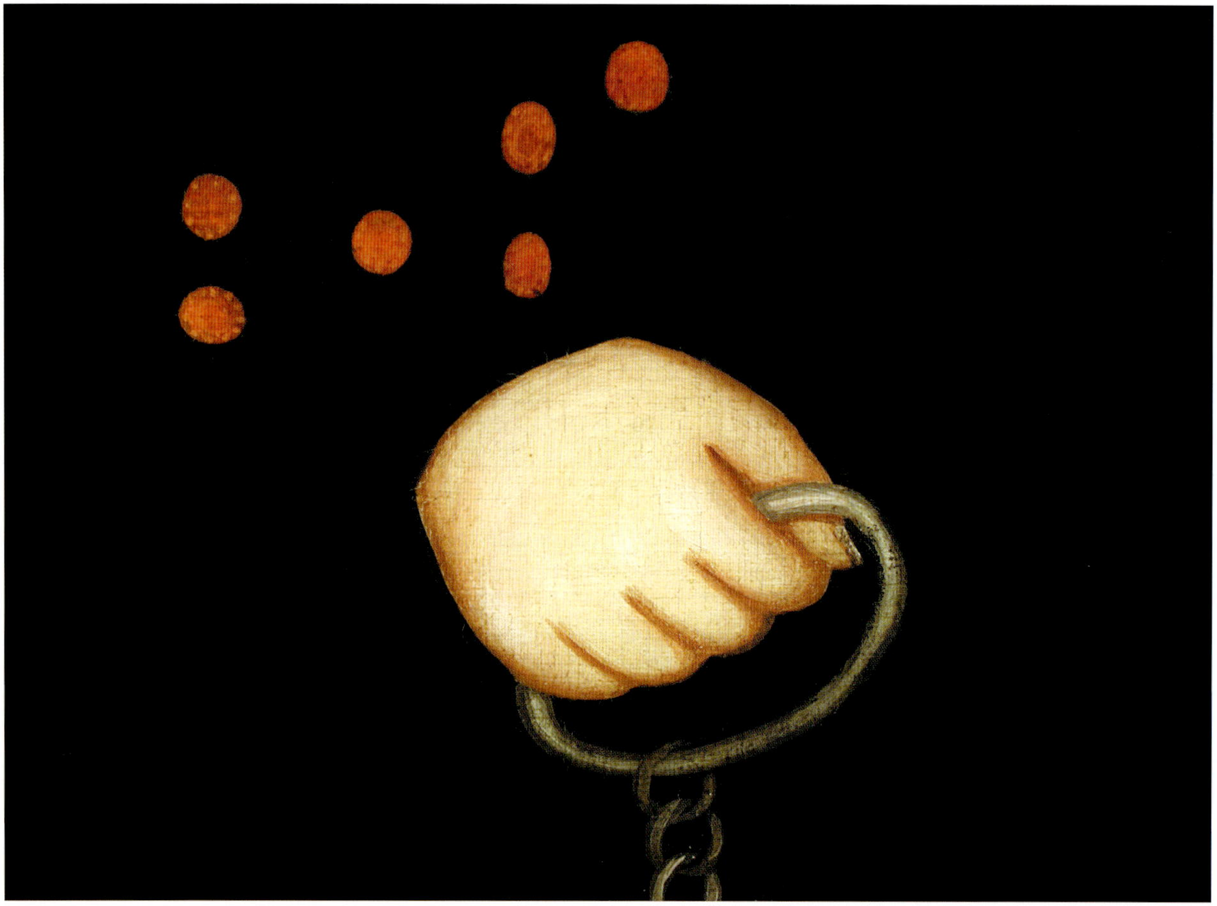

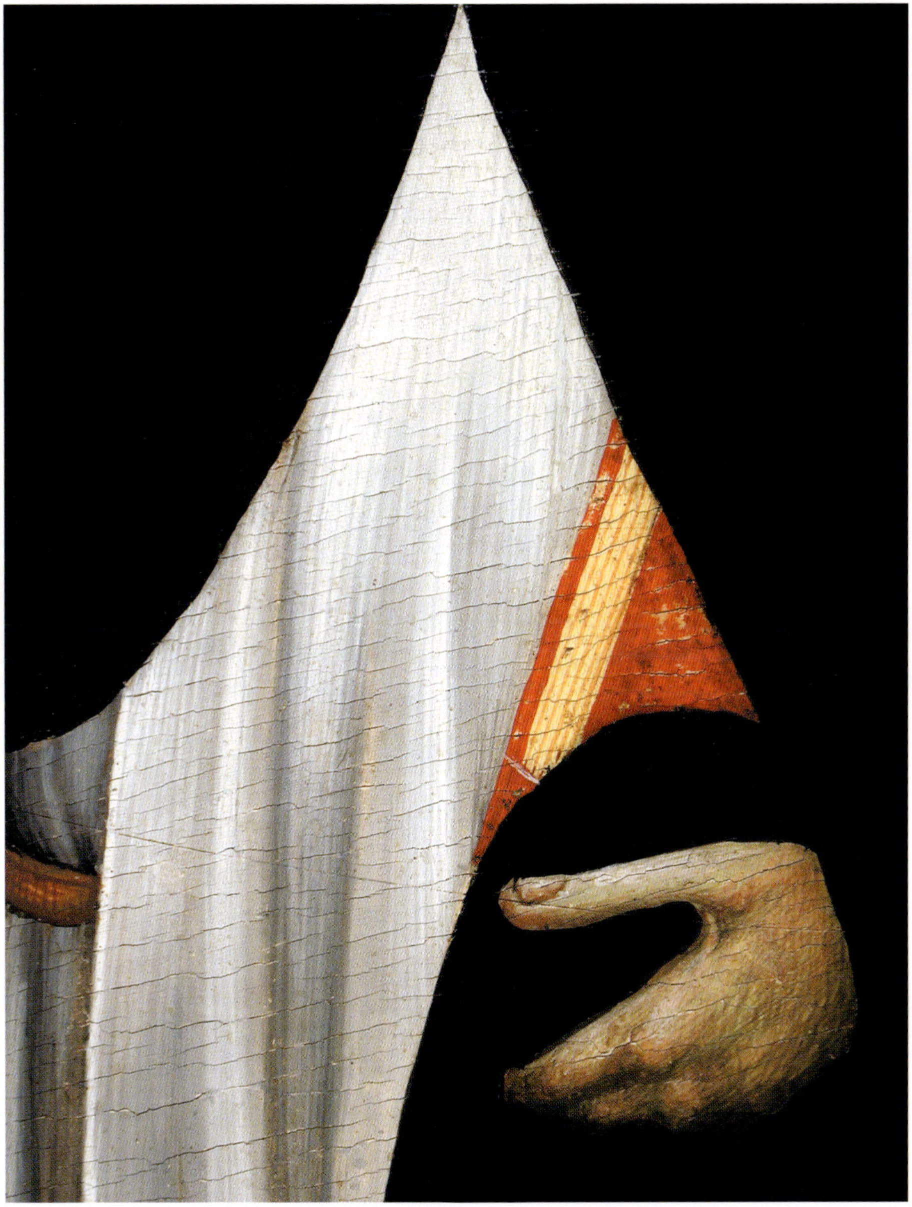

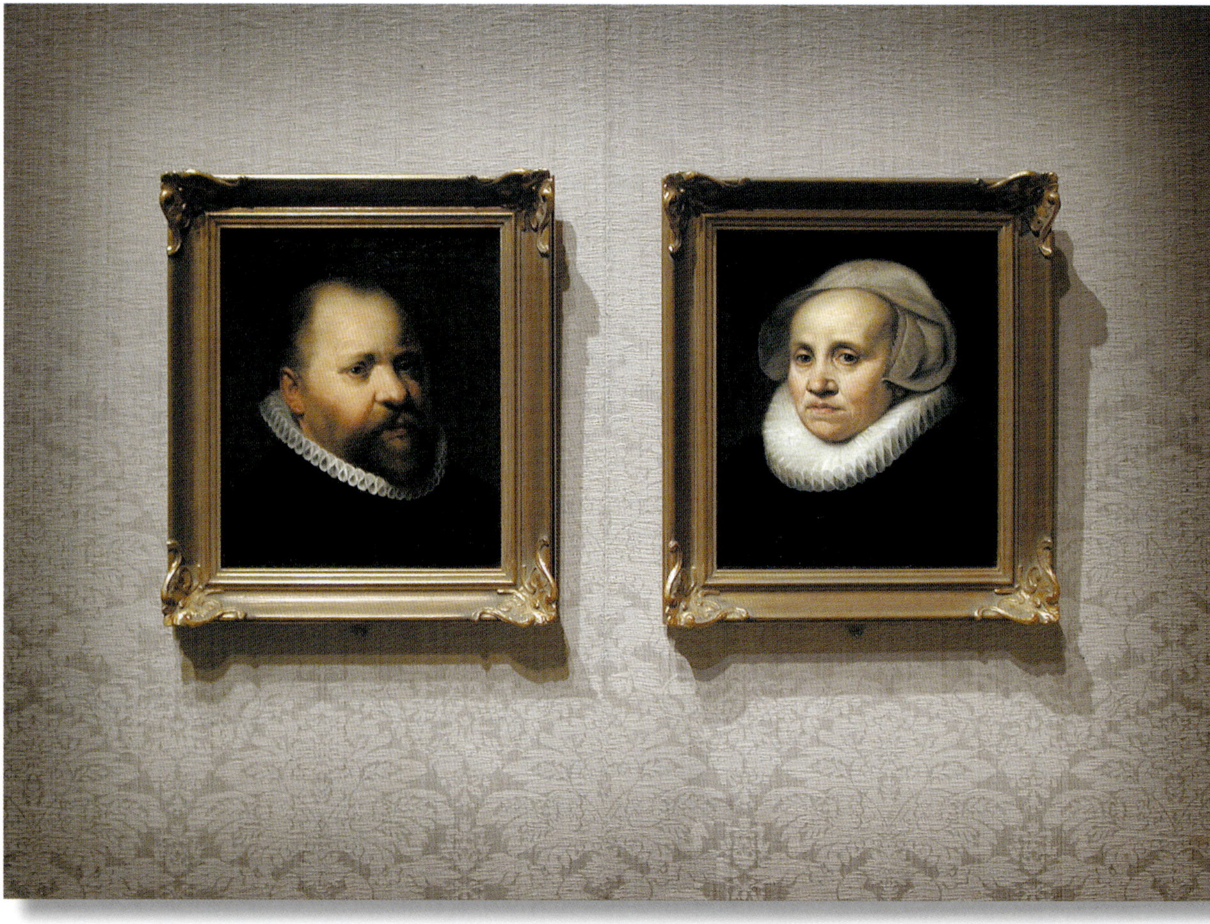

ON MEN AND WOMEN

ONE of the more important functions of a museum is to arrest time. This is necessary for a number of reasons, the most important perhaps being the preservation of the objects within the collection. The carefully controlled climate, the careful attention paid to lighting levels and the level of general security are all deployed in such a way as to minimize any deterioration of the artworks.

However, this preservation need, when combined with the practice of arranging of the artworks into periods of historical time, produces a strange effect. This dual concern with defeating the depredations of time while at the same time emphasizing the relevance of temporal progression as a categorical/curatorial tool, combines to create a palpable sense of time itself. The sensation created is as if the abstract and essentially invisible quality of time itself is somehow "there" on public display.

Once this sensation is recognized it is possible to look at the collection in an entirely new way. Rather than observe the differences between any two periods, instead we can now begin to appreciate the similarities and commonalities between them, and in turn compare these to our own contemporary experiences. By way of literary example and literal description of this phenomenon, Shakespeare in Sonnet 59 echoed centuries later Ecclesiastes' thoughts on this matter:[1]

If there be nothing new, but that which is
Hath been before, how are our brains beguiled,
Which, laboring for invention, bear amiss
The second burden of a further child!
O, that record could with a backward look,
Even of five hundred courses of the sun,
Show me your image in some antique book,
Since mind at first in character was done.

That I might see what the old world could say
To this composèd wonder of your frame,
Whether we are mended, or where better they,
Or whether revolution be the same.
O, sure I am, the wits of former days
To subjects worse have given admiring praise.

NOWHERE is this more evident than in the faces of men and women as they each experience the personal dramas that accompany the search for love, family and happiness. This enduring quest has been the subject of art for many centuries. However, as the following images show, many of the faces bear evidence of the strain of conflict, doubt, unfulfilled desire and overt disappointment. Their apparent sadness in the face of this search for happiness recalls the cautionary words of the I Ching, that ancient yet surprisingly (or not, in view of the above) modern text of divination:

> *Here the source of a man's strength lies not in himself but in his relation to other people. No matter how close to them he may be, if his center of gravity depends on them, he is inevitably tossed to and fro between joy and sorrow. Rejoicing to high heaven, then sad unto death—this is the fate of those who depend upon an inner accord with other persons they love. Here we have only a statement of the law that this is so. Whether this condition is felt to be an affliction or the supreme happiness of love, is left to the subjective verdict of the person concerned.* [2]

[1] Chapter 1, verse 9: "The thing that hath been, it is that which shall be; and that which is done is that which shall be done: and there is no new thing under the sun."
[2] From the hexagram 61: Inner Truth, six in the third place.

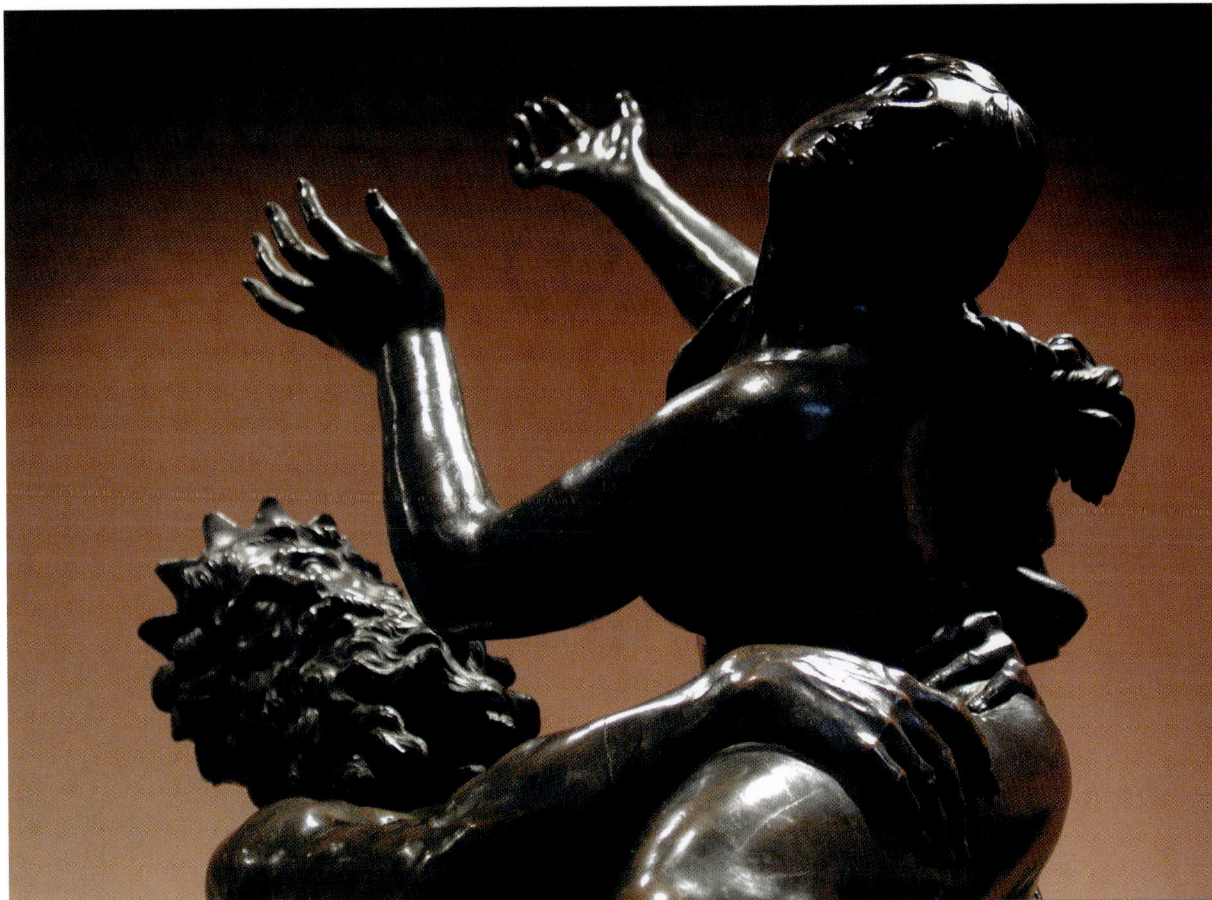

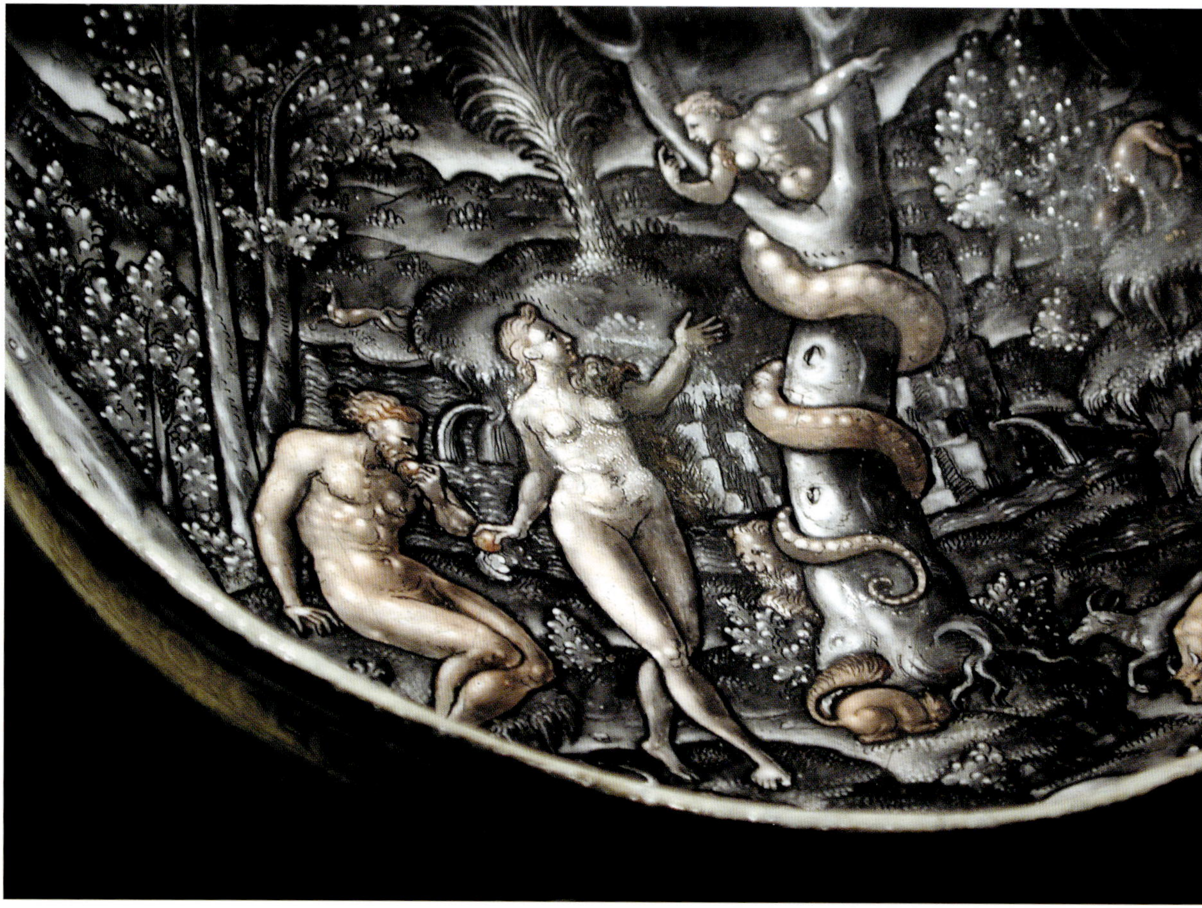

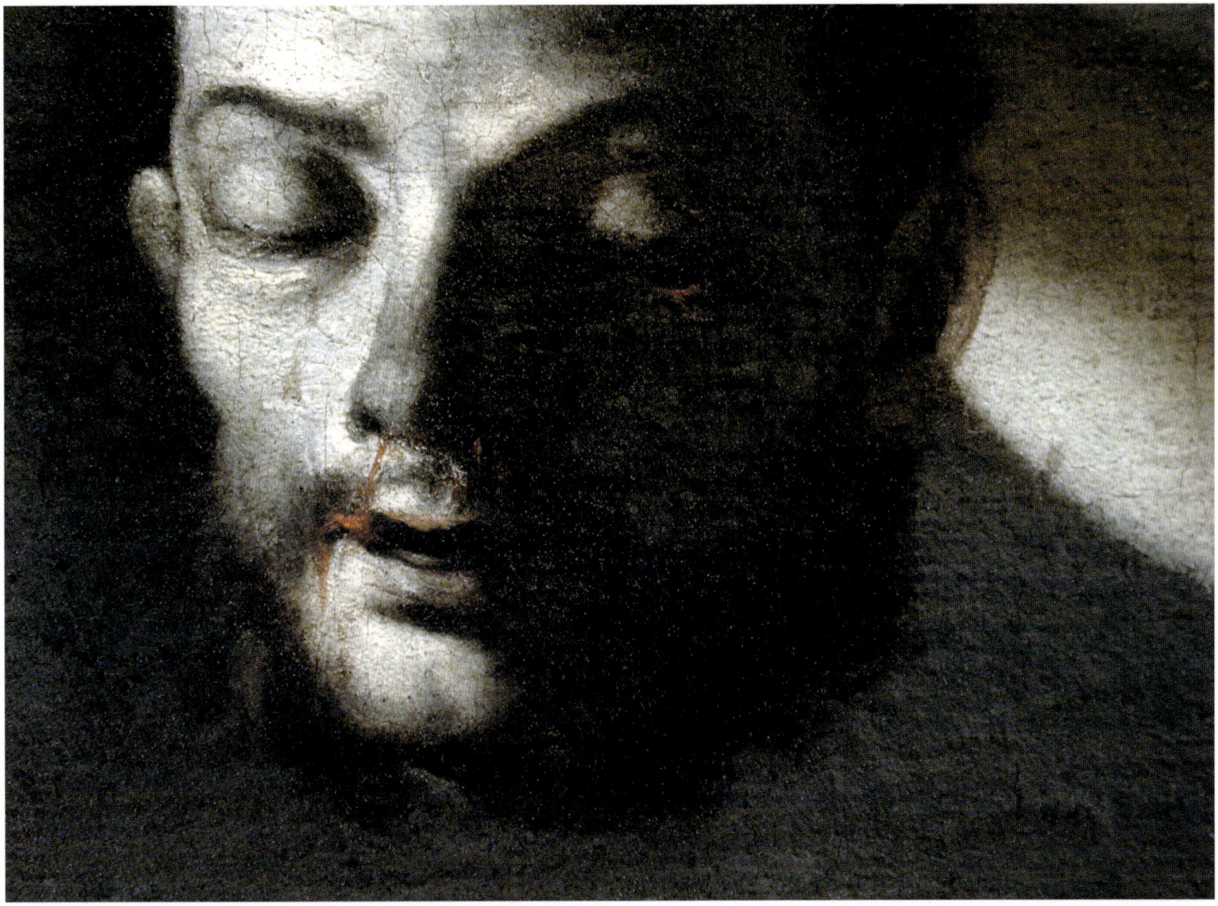

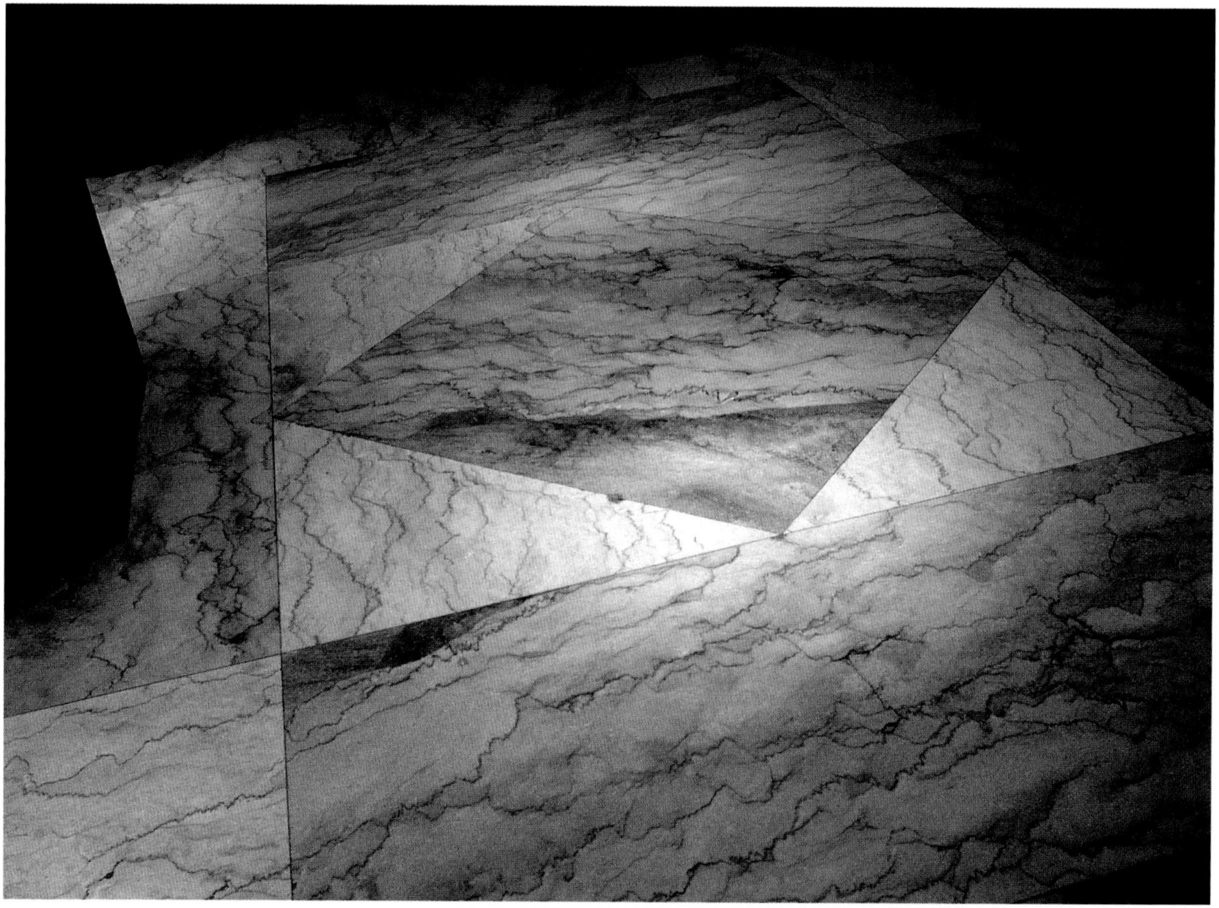

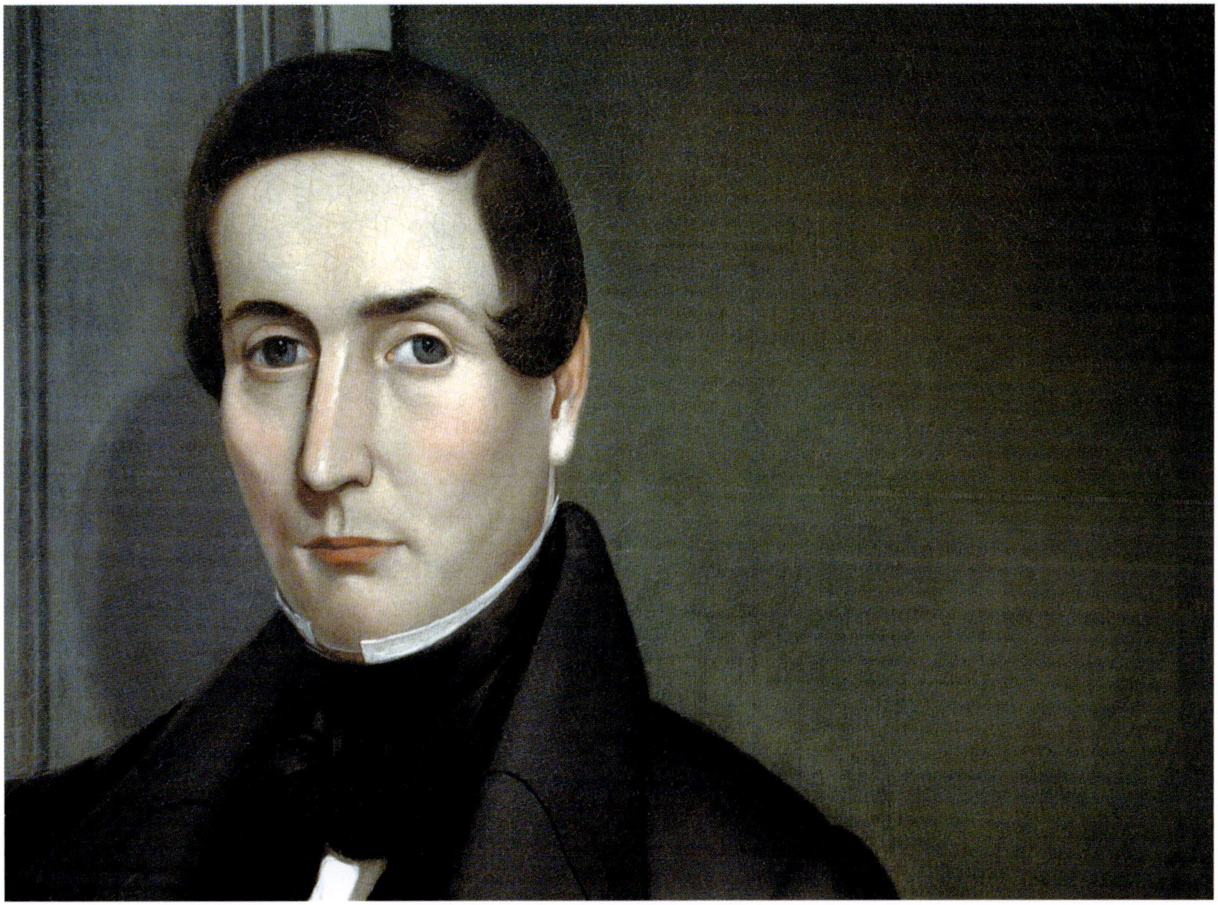

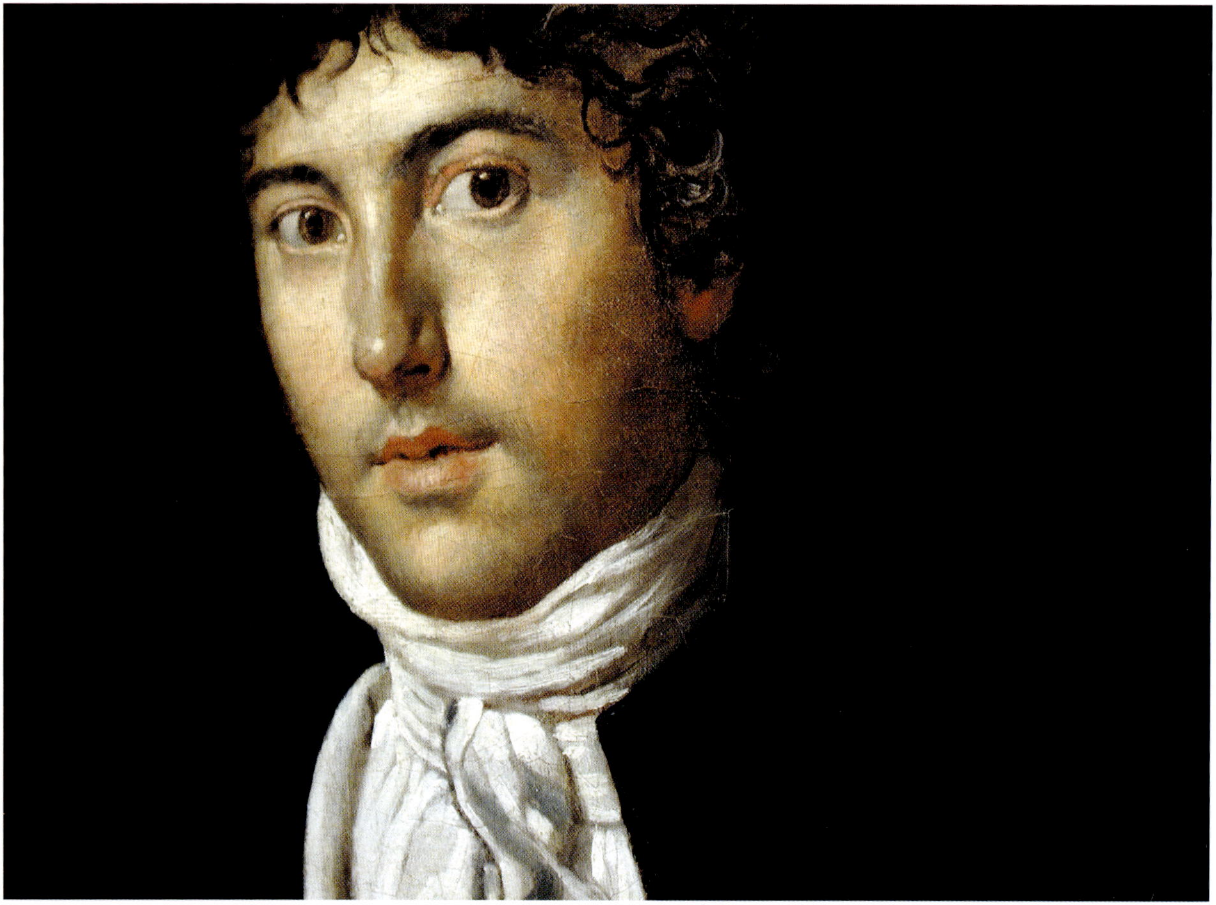

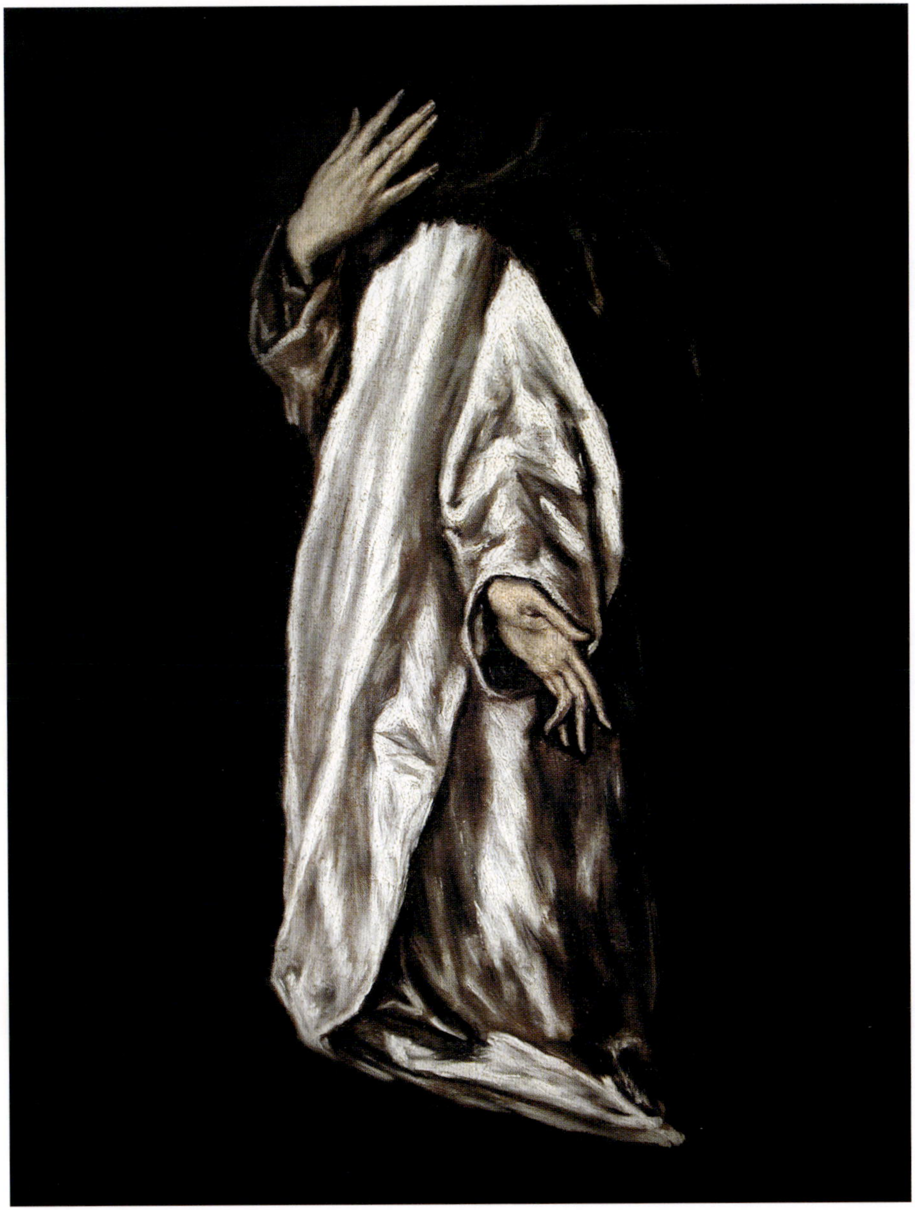

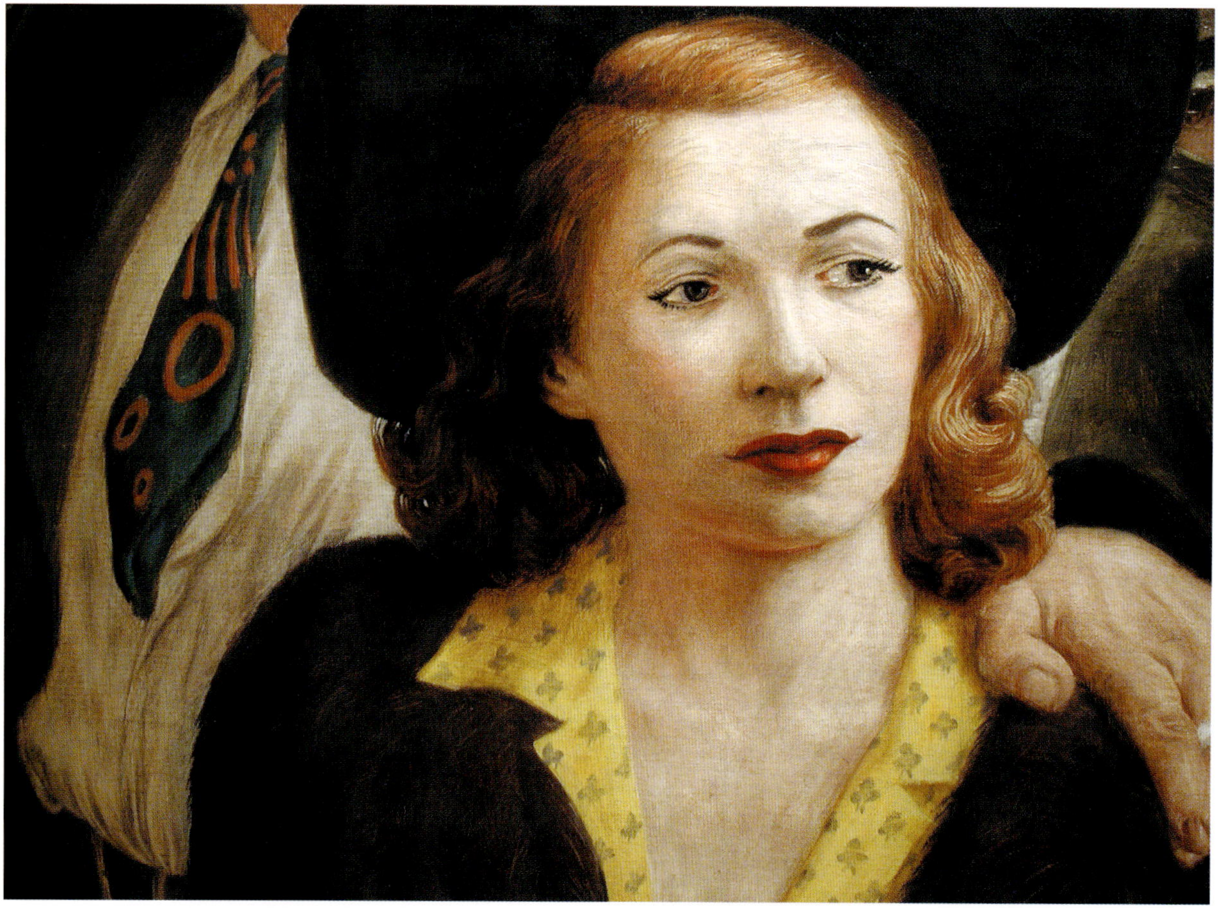

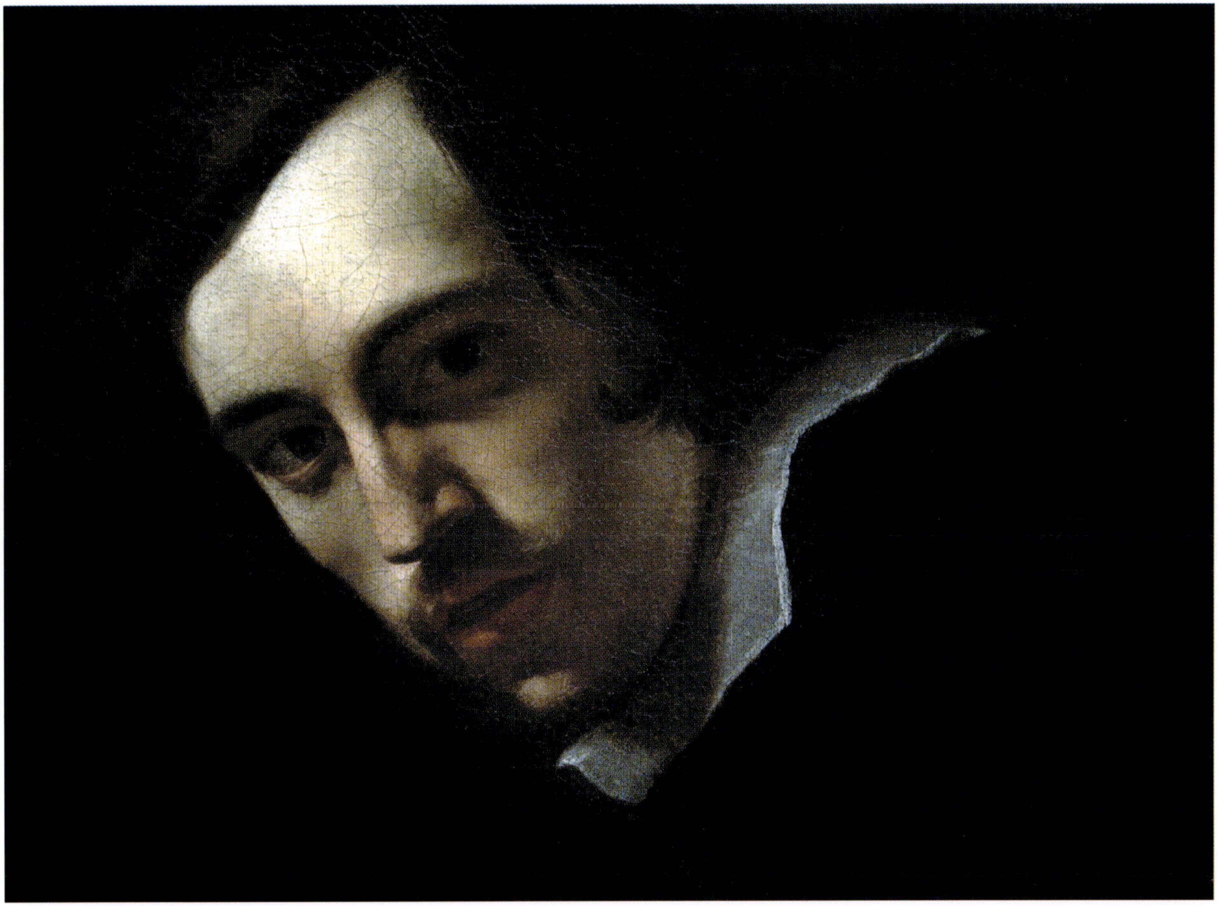

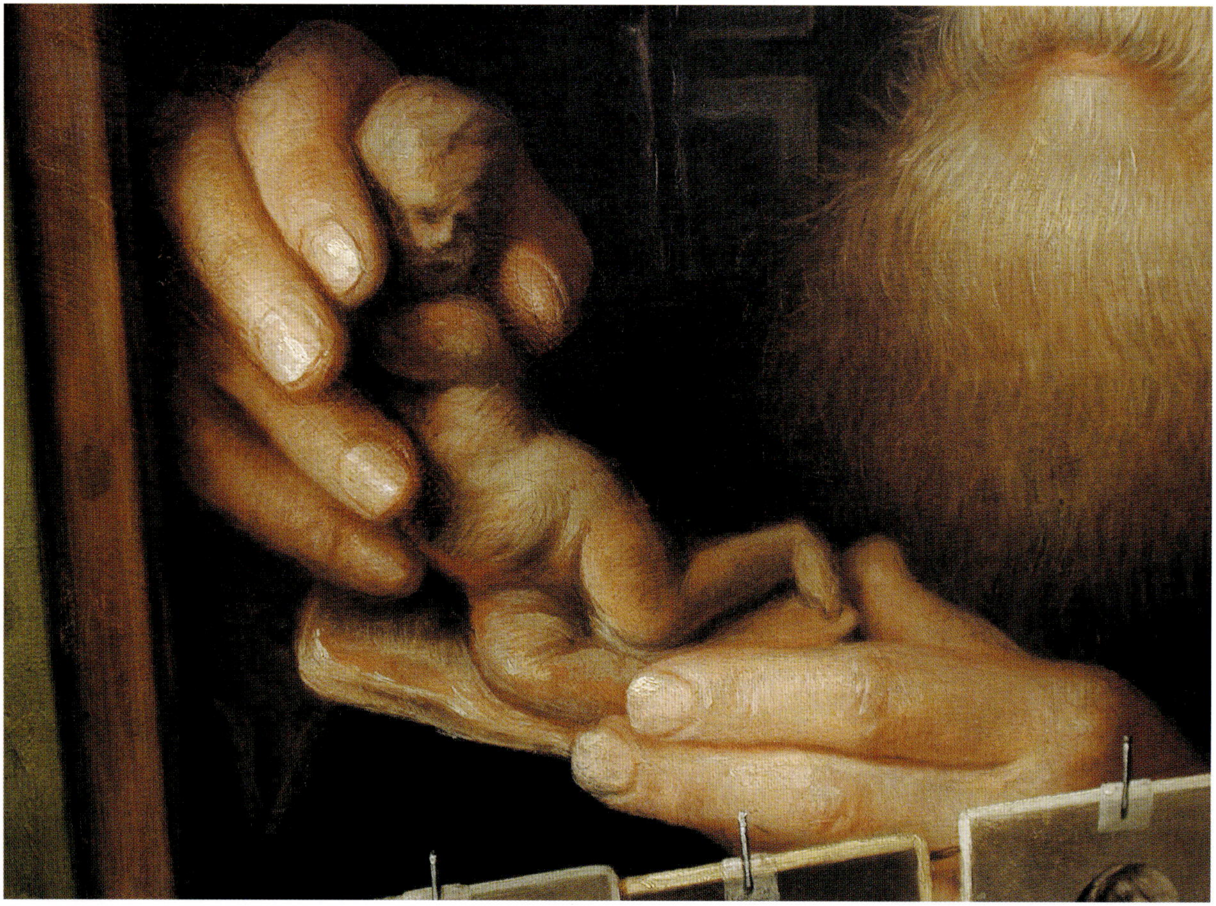

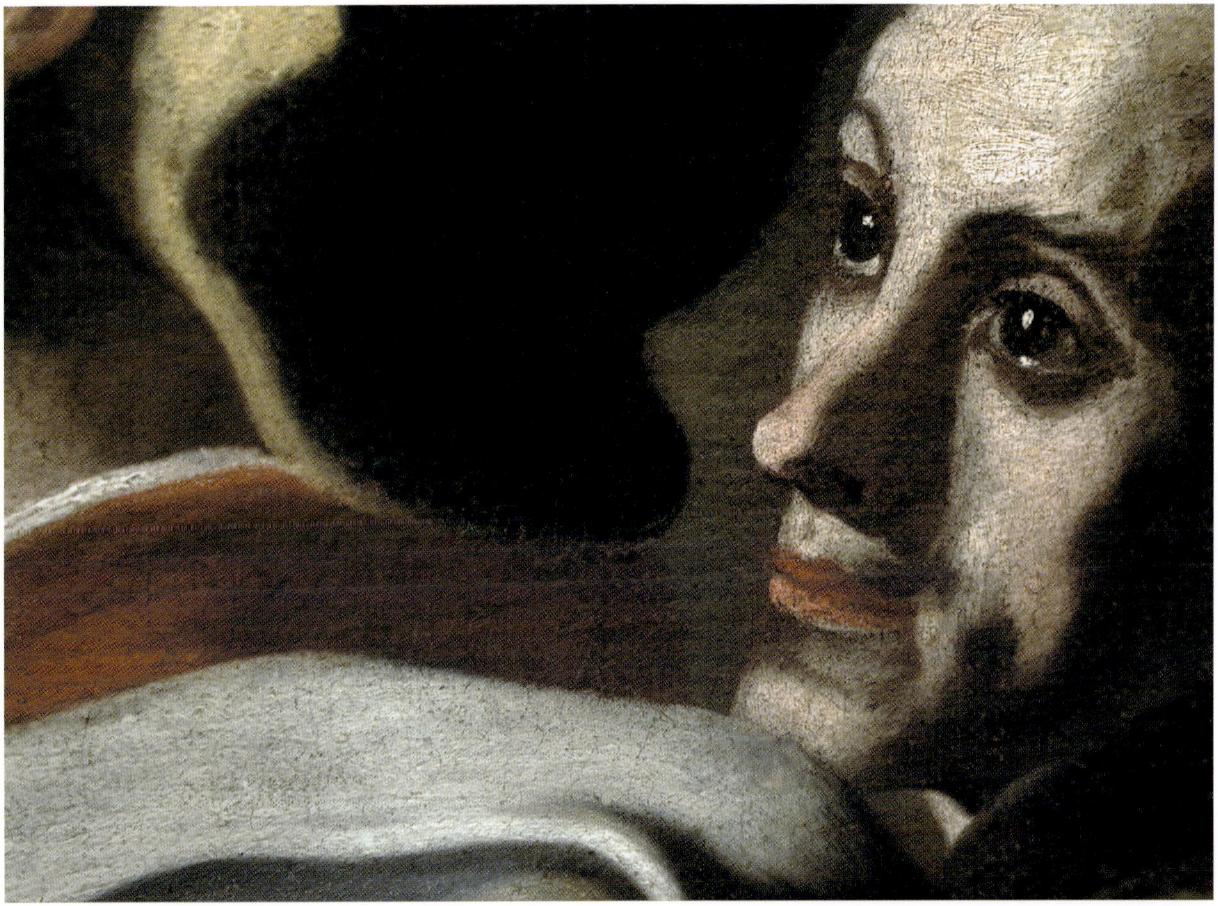

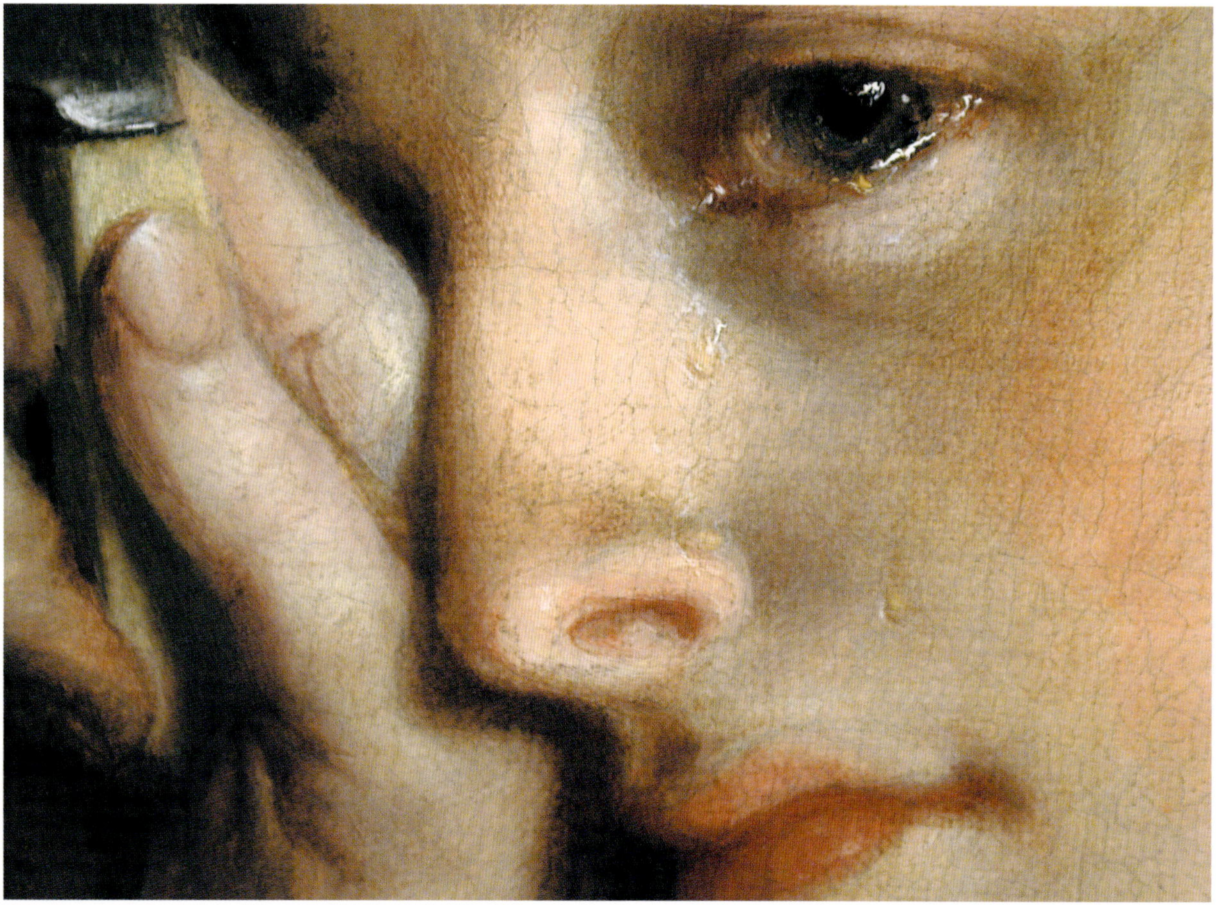

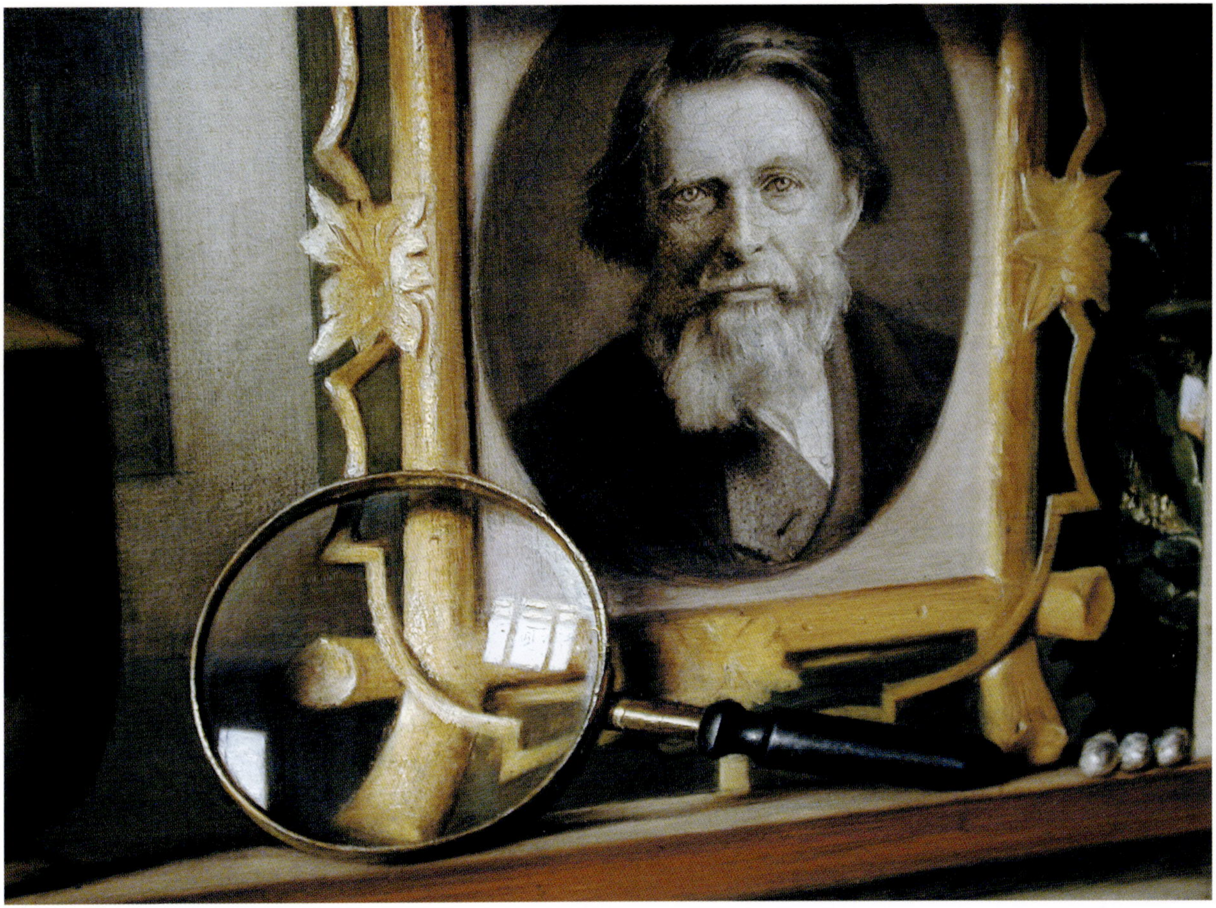

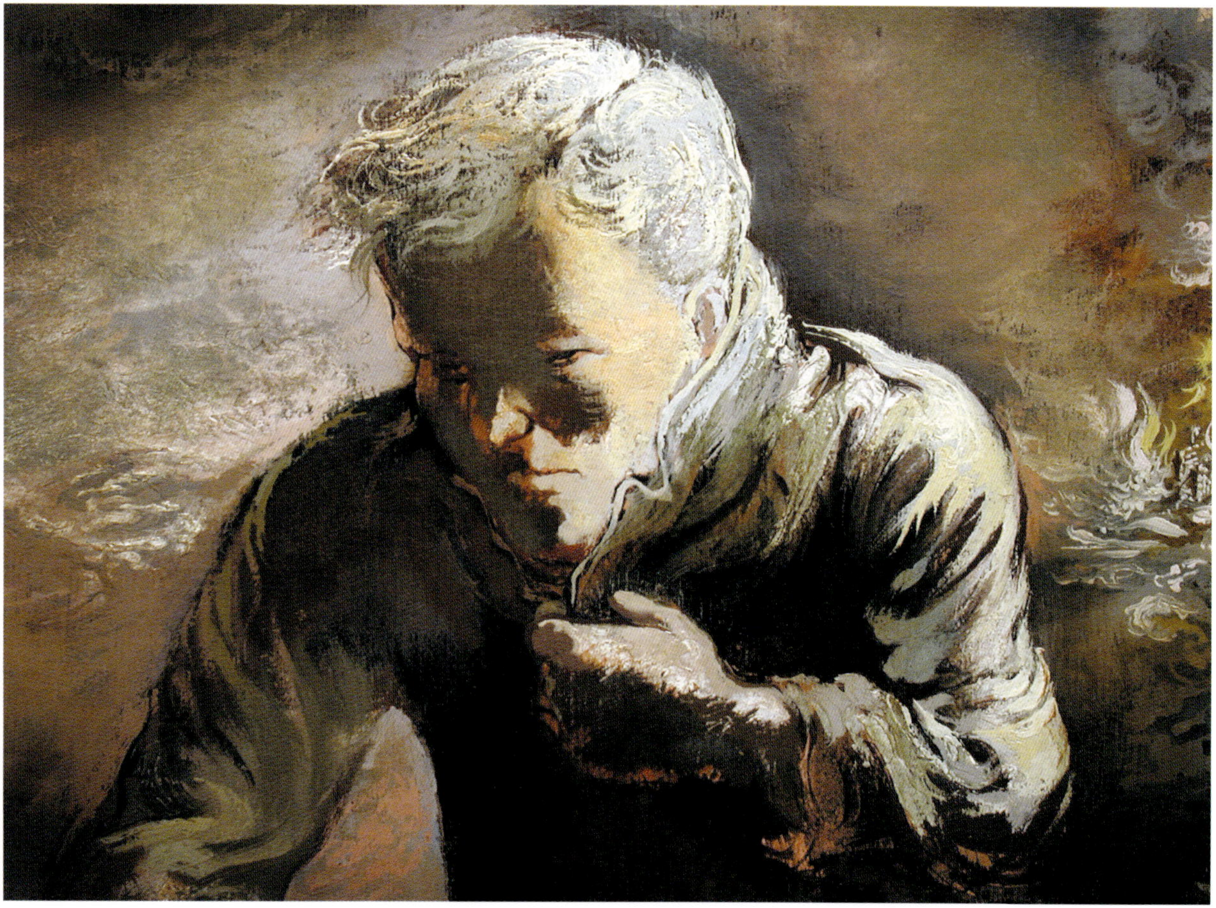

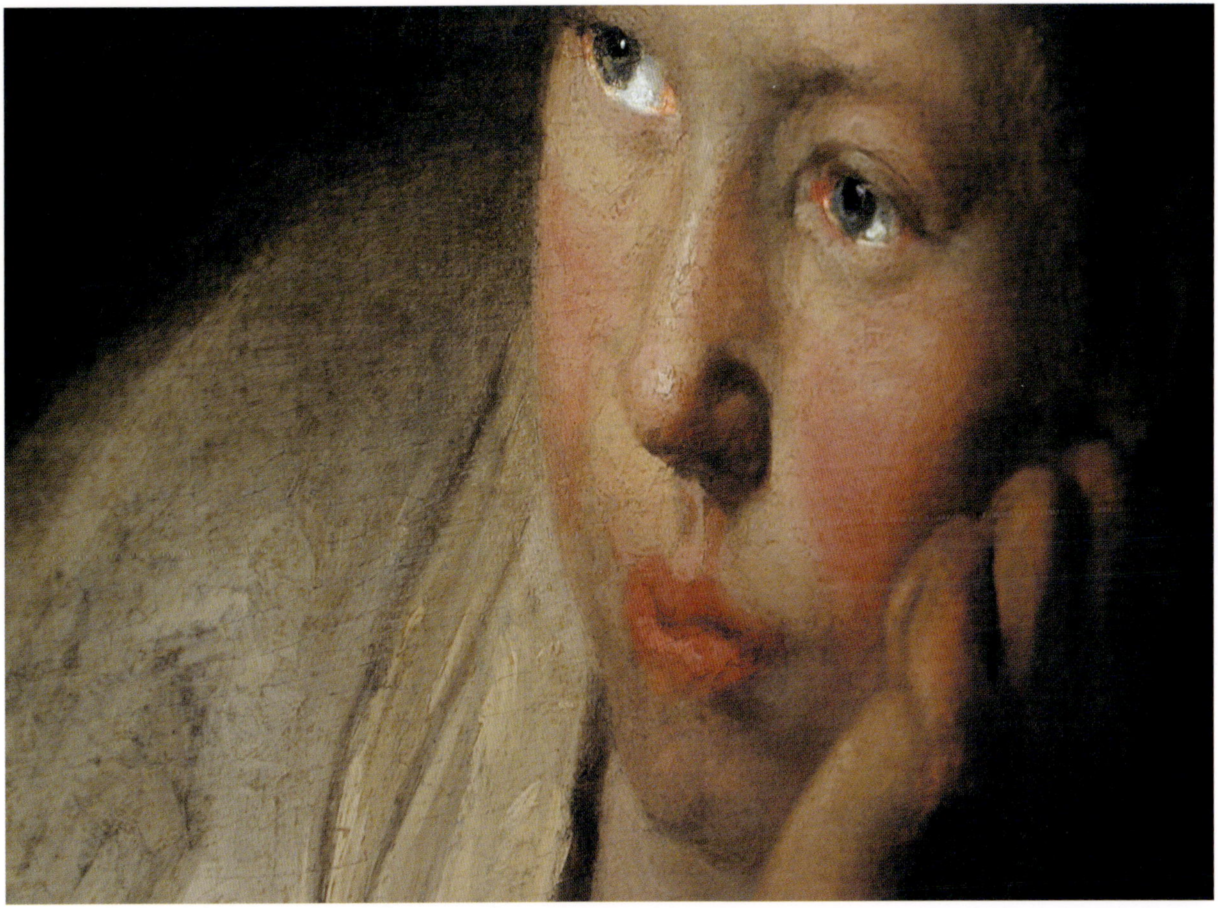

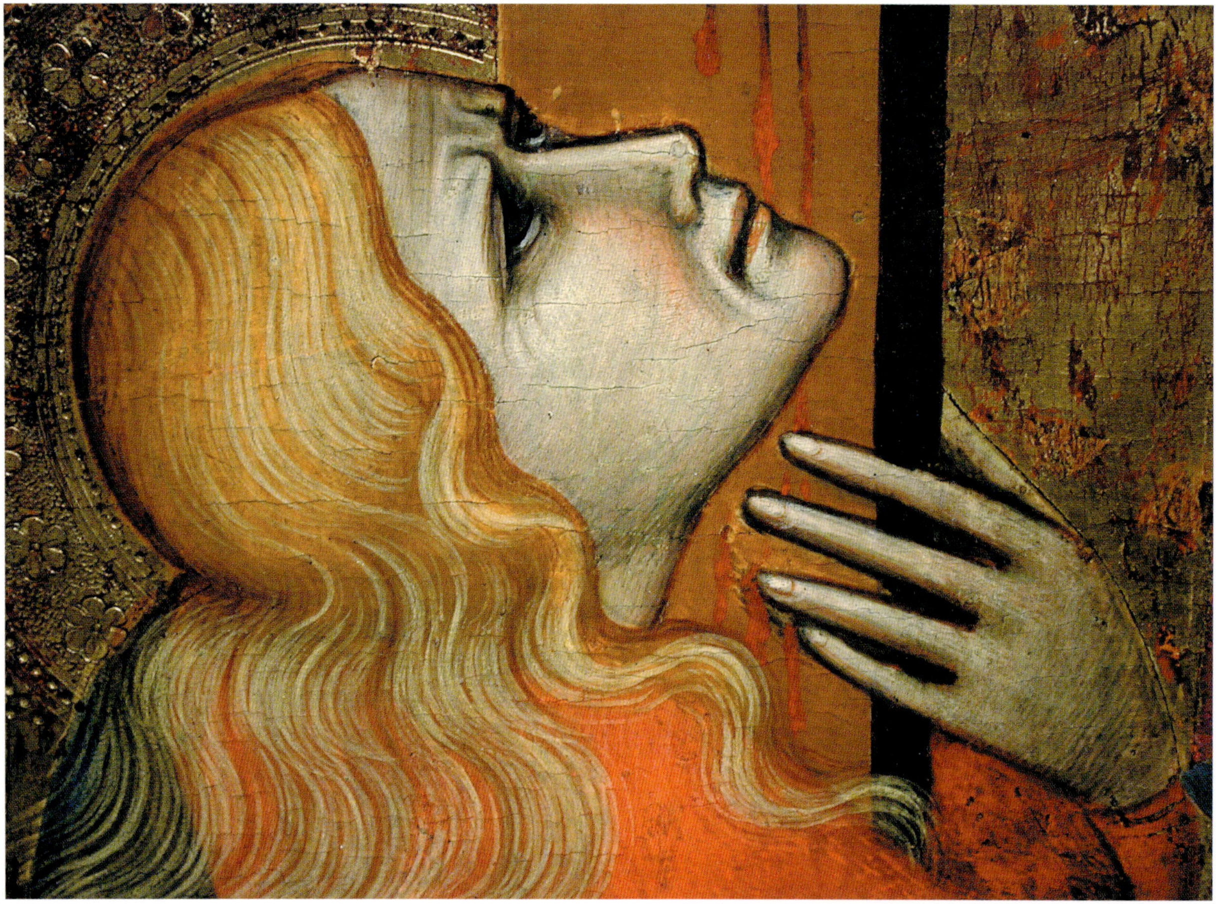

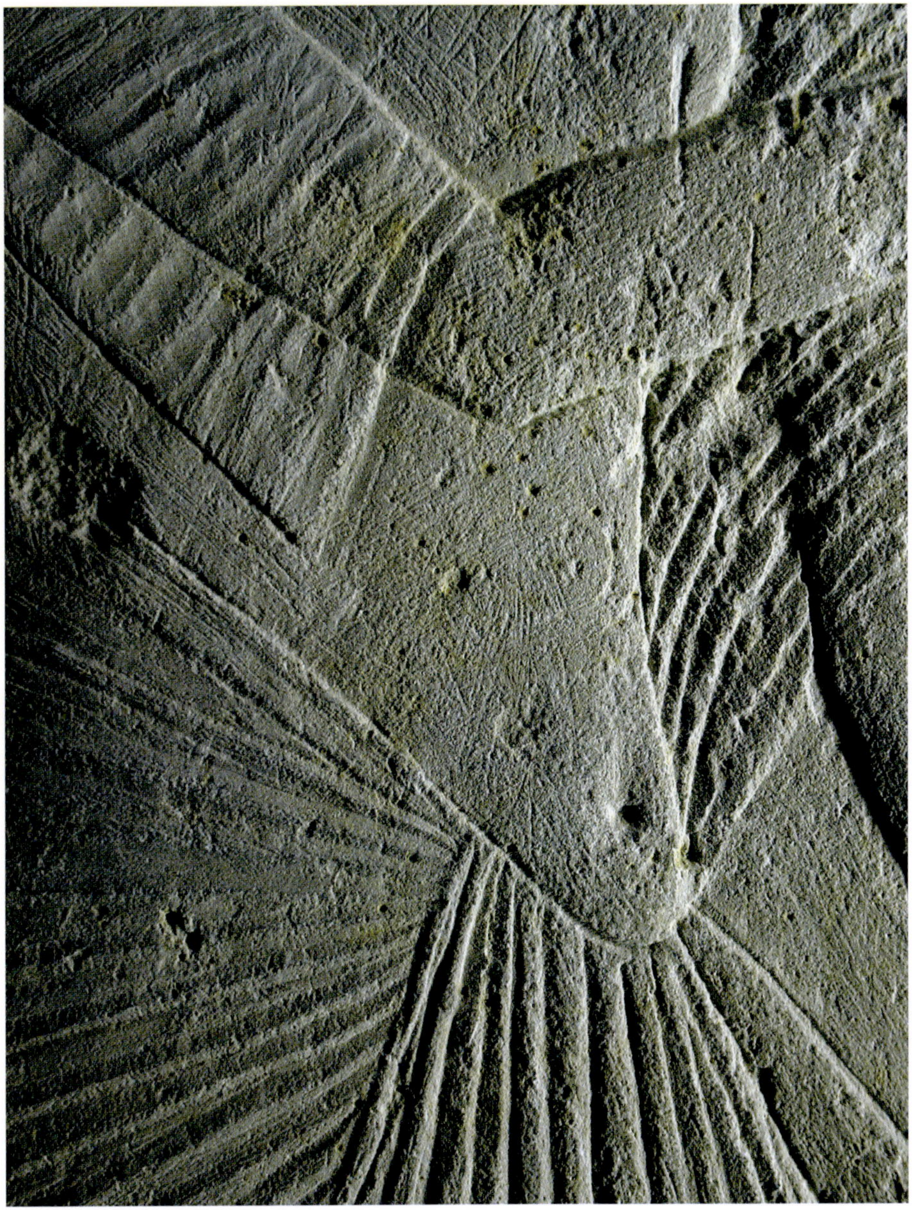

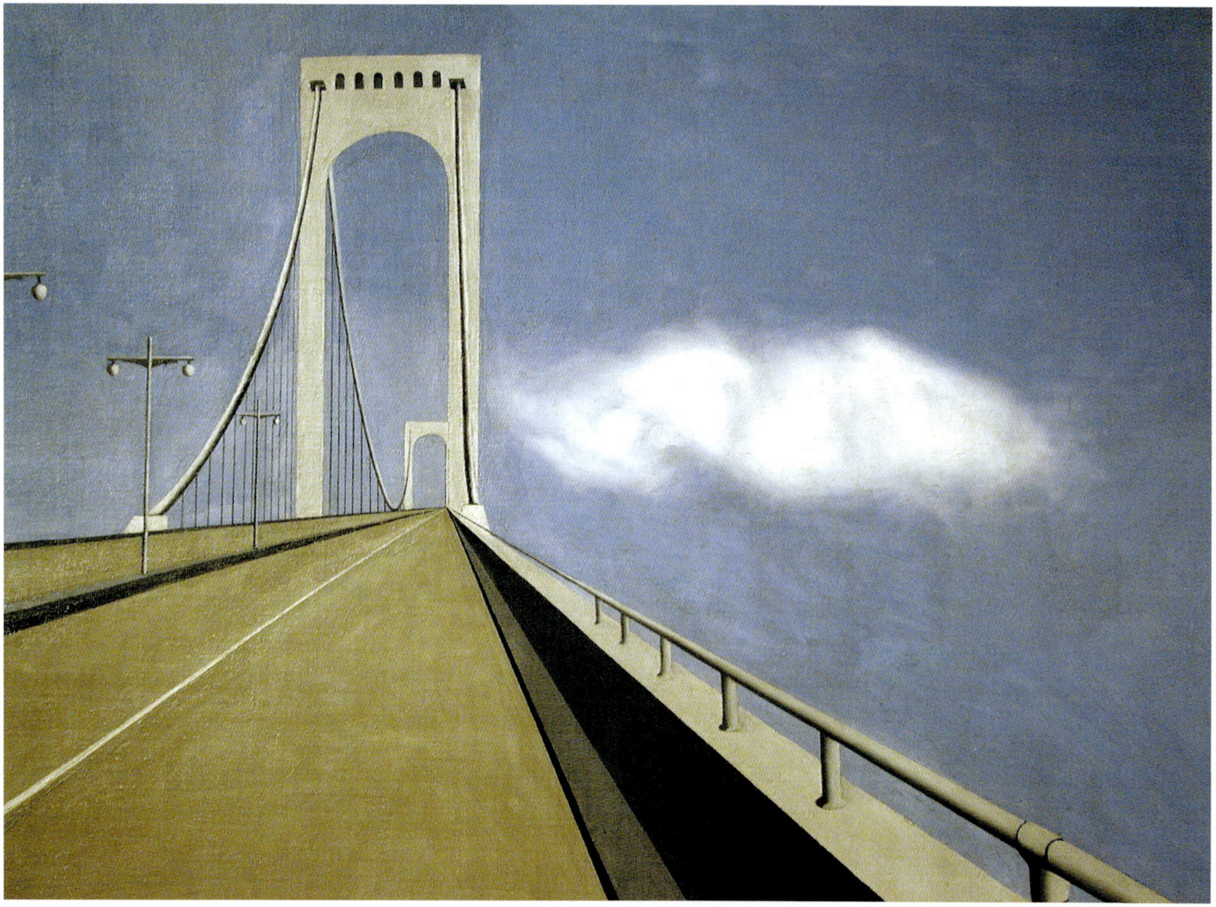

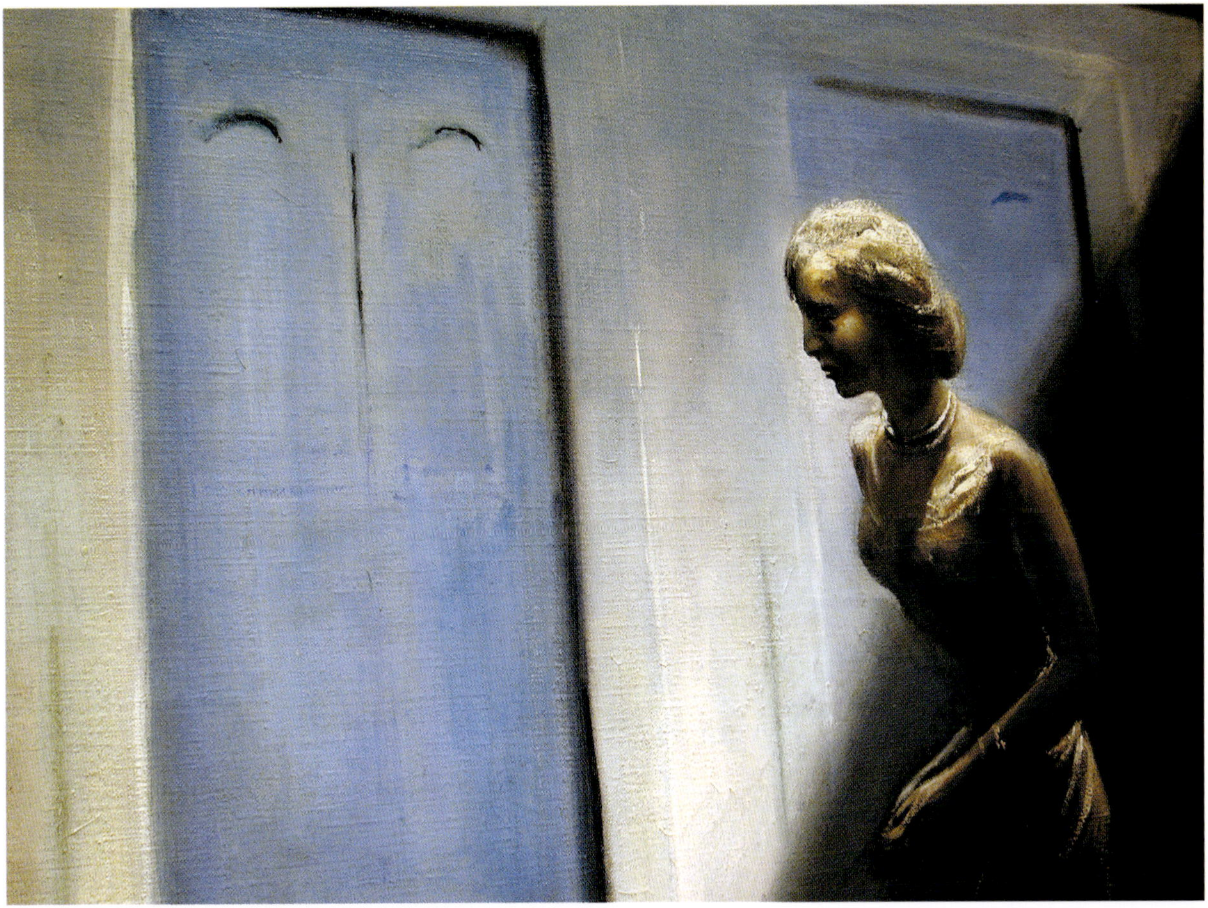

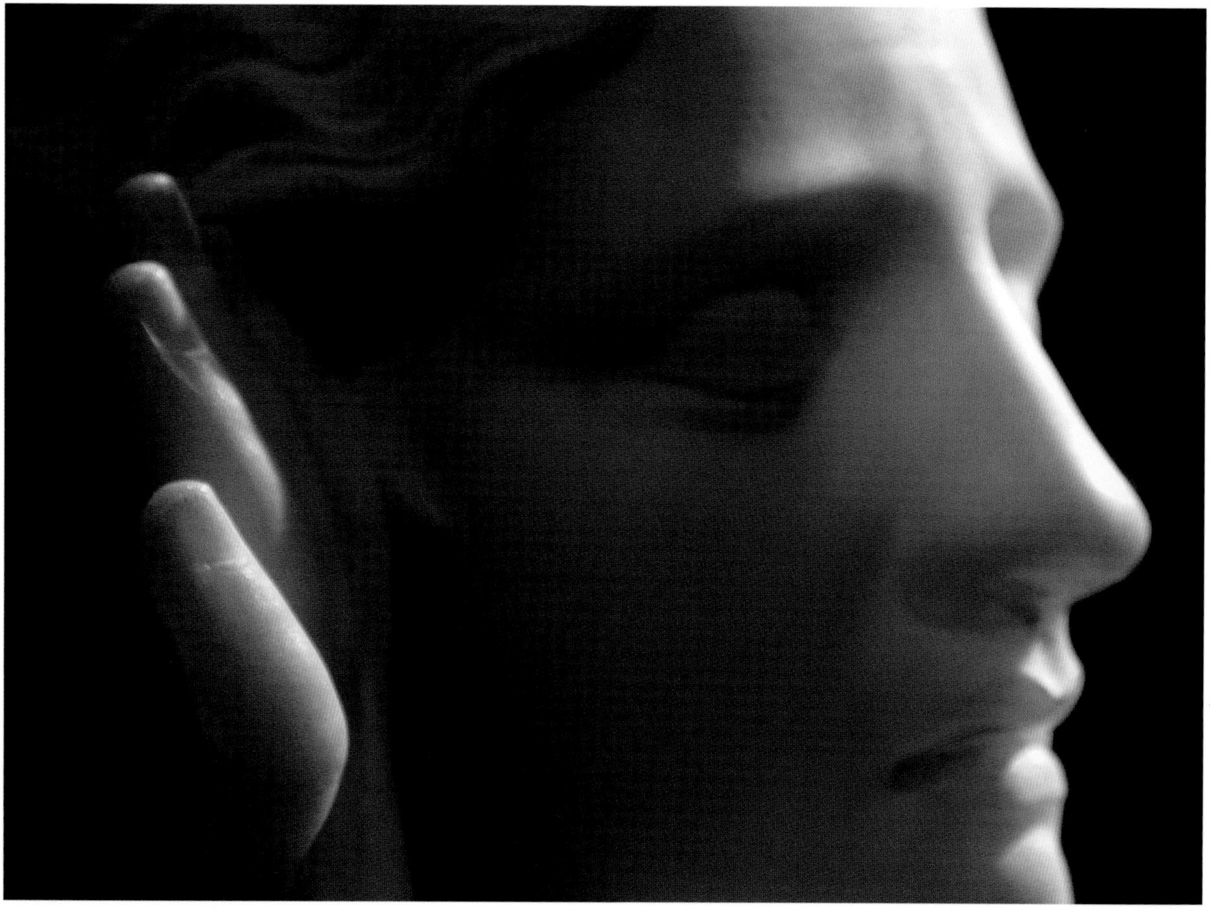

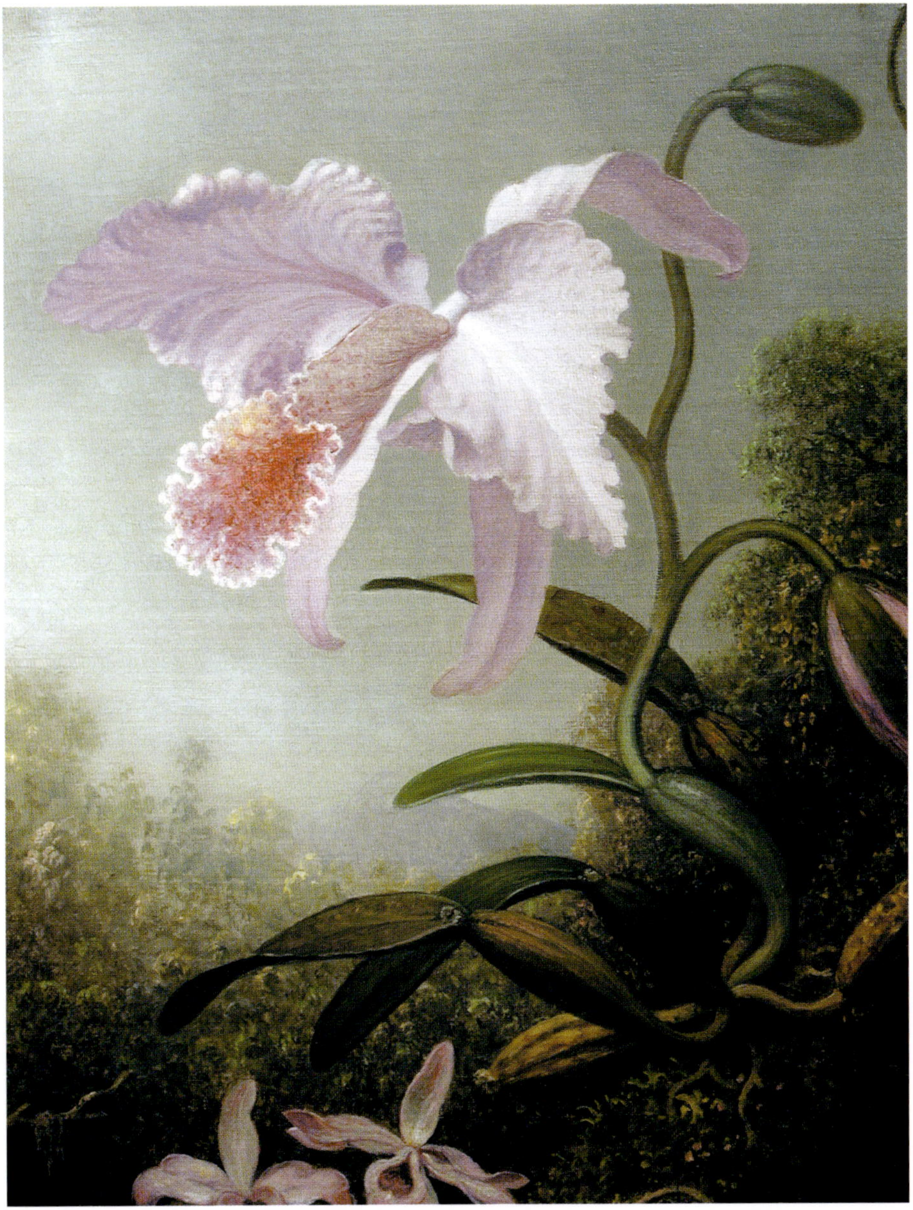

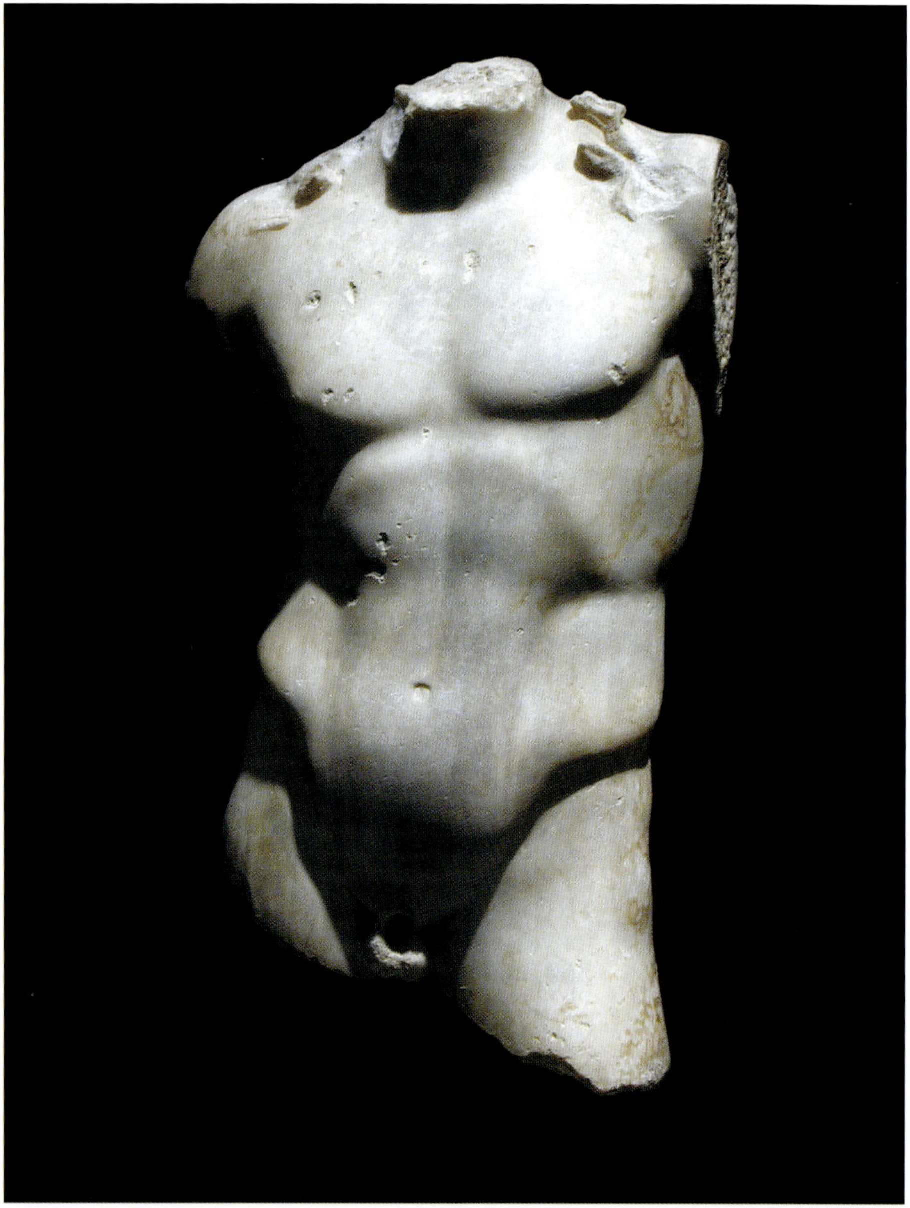

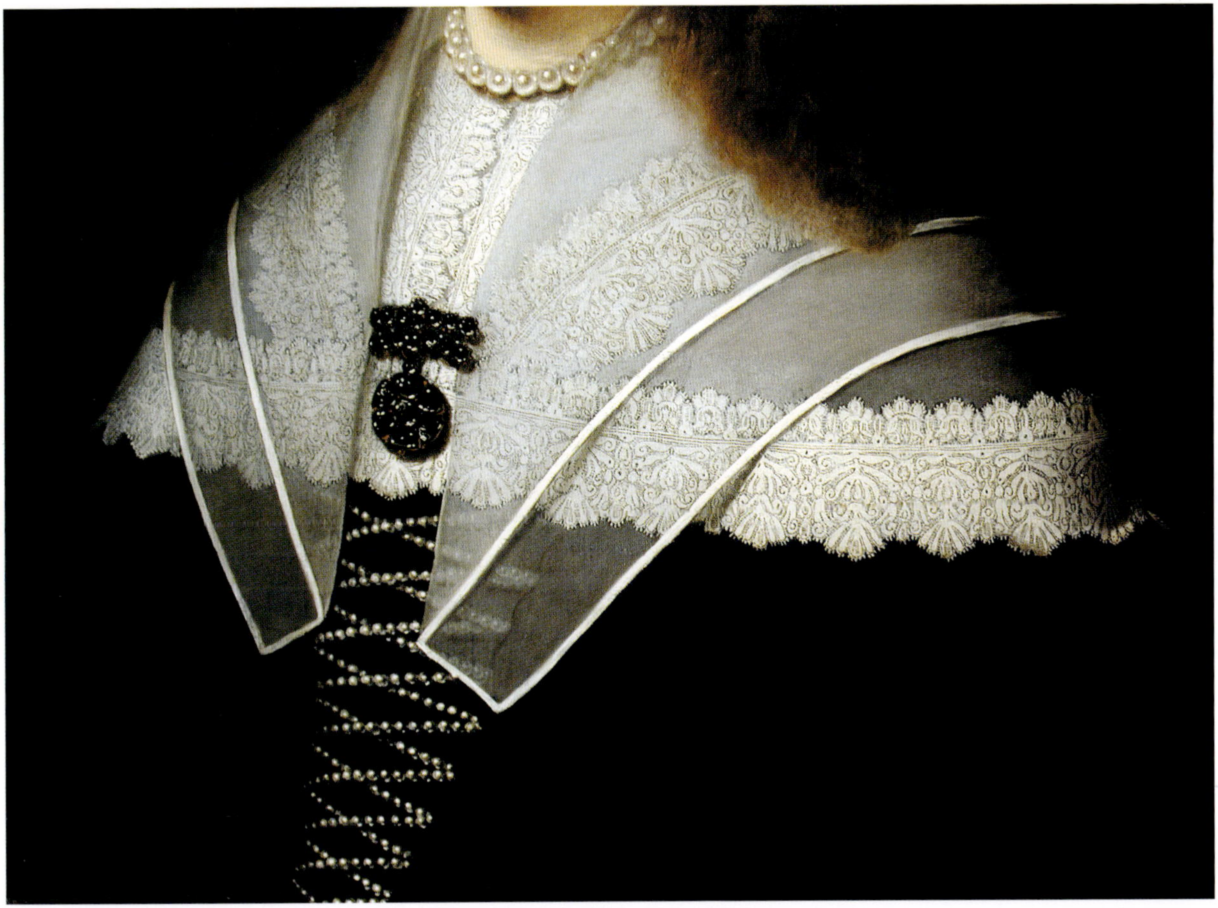

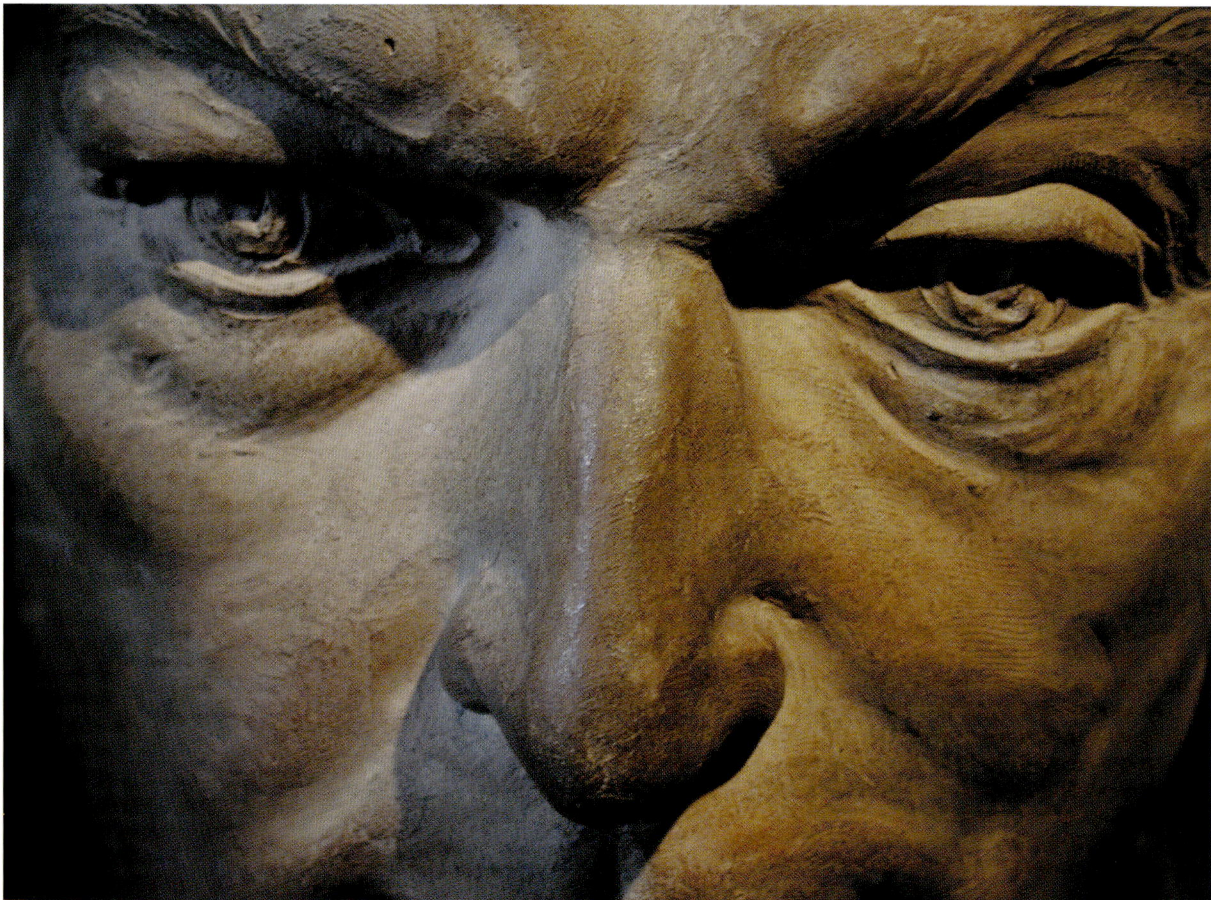

ON THE LAND

WITHIN the collection there are many examples of landscape paintings. Surprisingly I chose to photograph very few, probably because they stubbornly tend to look much the same when (re)photographed. This resistance to change means their potential for revealing alternative meanings is less than the portraits, or the still life (nature mort) images. Although direct depictions of the natural world are conspicuous by their absence, nevertheless the following group of images coalesced around the theme of the land and some of the insensitive things we have done to it.

Only two images in this chapter actually show anything like what is commonly called a "landscape." The first of these is a detail of a bird hunt. This painting was transformed into a poster for the Colt firearms company during the nineteenth century. It shows one of its products, a shotgun, blasting away at a flock of flamingos. Here the graceful geometry of their flight path and the almost calligraphic quality of their communal sign writing in the sky is interrupted by falling and shattered bodies which hover mockingly in the air like randomly-disconnected, punctuation marks.

The second at first glance looks like a primal sylvan glade. A glorious light illuminates a small valley and lake and the initial impression created is one of a paradise created by God, placed on earth for the pleasure of the human race. Closer inspection, however, reveals that this apparent paradise is far removed from what we might think of as the natural world. A train rumbles on the distant shore; a strangely minute steam boat sits uncomfortably on, rather than in, the water; and in the foreground, in pride of place, yet slightly overlooked by the light, is a chopped down tree, its truncated stump proclaiming victory in the war to tame this environment.

As I write I notice how often I have concentrated on sad things. Why this is so I have no idea. It has been said that there is always a melancholy side to beauty. Perhaps this is reason enough. However, it seems difficult to ignore the fact that western society's proprietorial attitude to God's gifts has done much damage to the world—damage that inevitably will be revisited upon us if we do not change our ways.

It is for this reason the chapter concludes with a strange meal, and an even stranger guest at the table. The claw-like hand resting on the empty plate is a solemn reminder that famine is not simply a historical artifact bordering on Biblical metaphor, but a very real, and very frightening possibility should we continue to make the same mistakes we have made in the past.

The trouble is of course, as the previous essay suggested, that the past is also the future. To again quote Ecclesiastes, Chapter 1, verse 11:

> *There is no remembrance of former things; neither shall there be any remembrance of things that are to come with those that shall come after.*

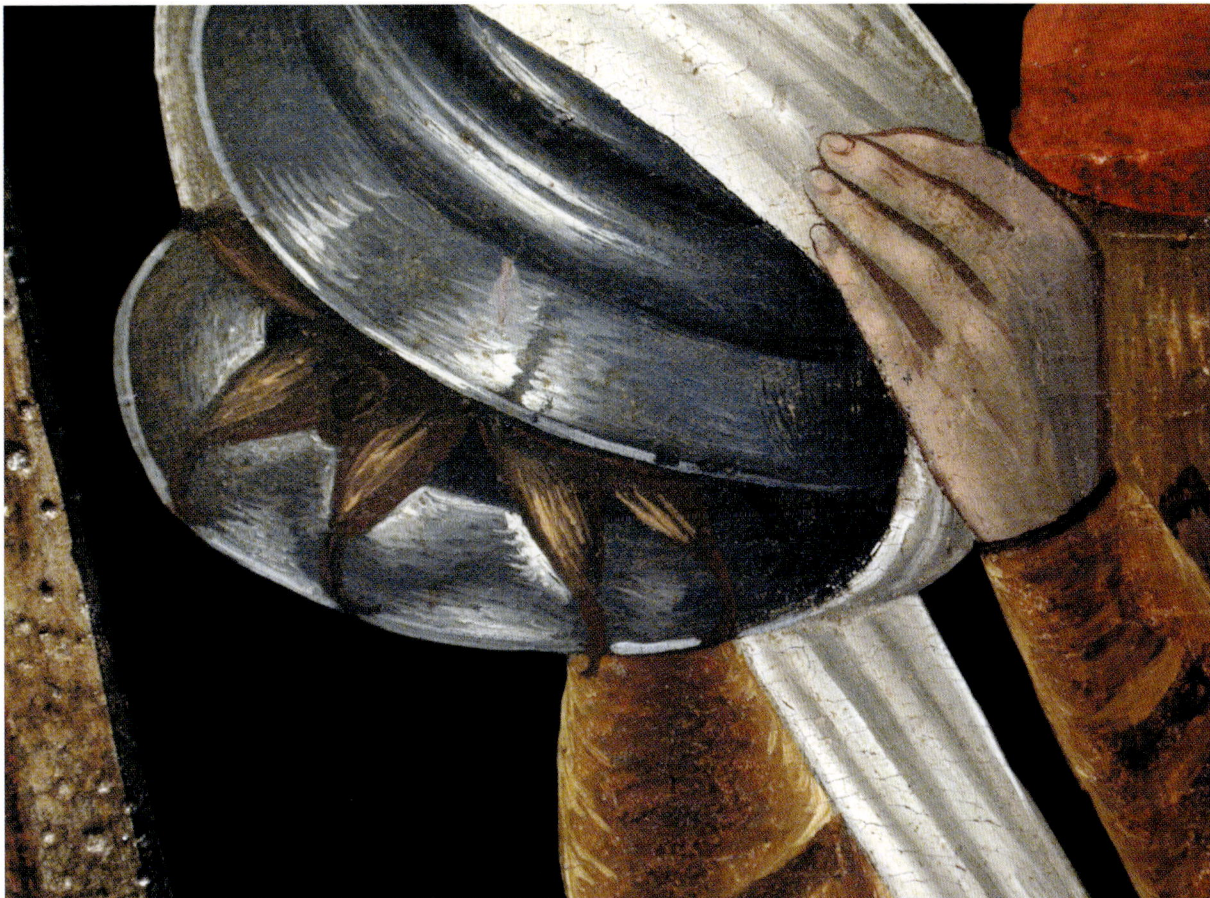

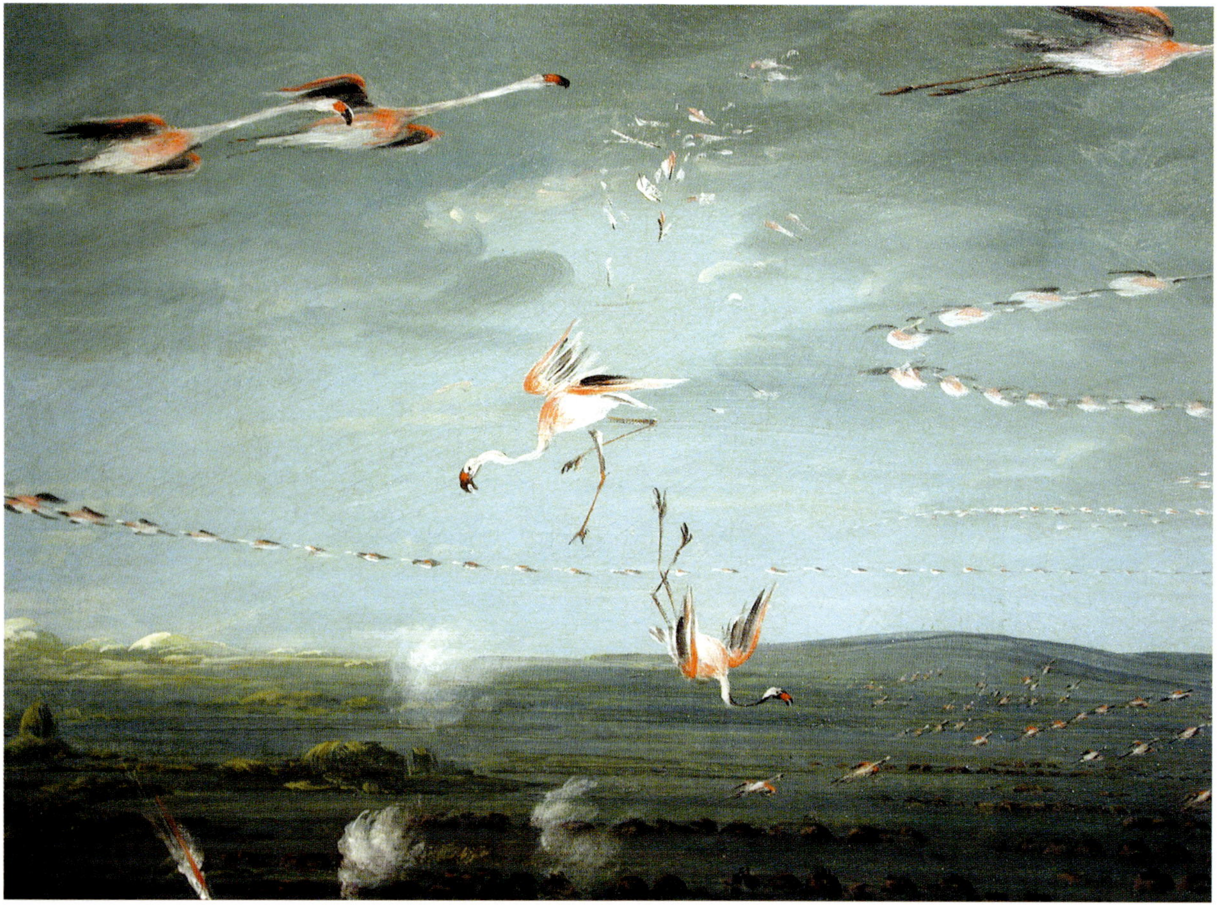

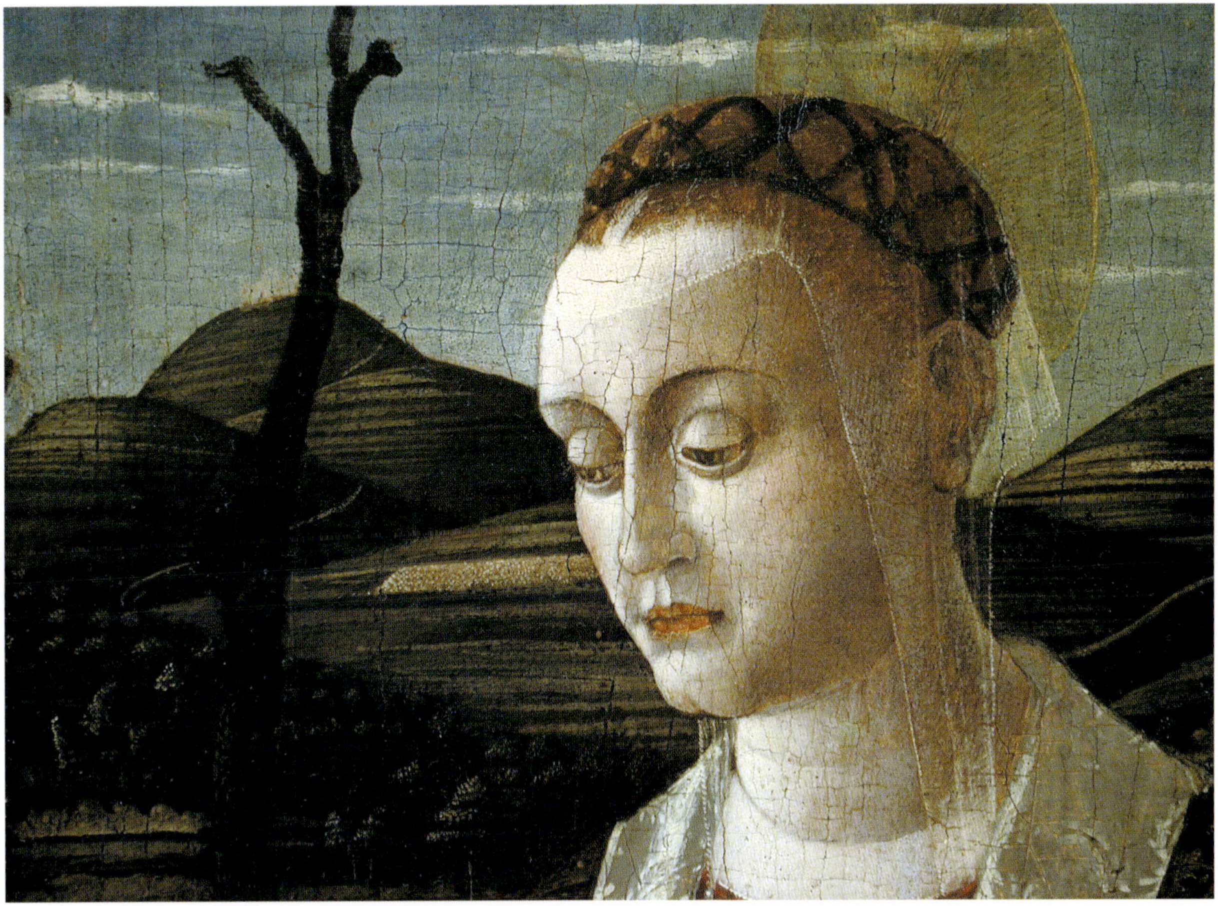

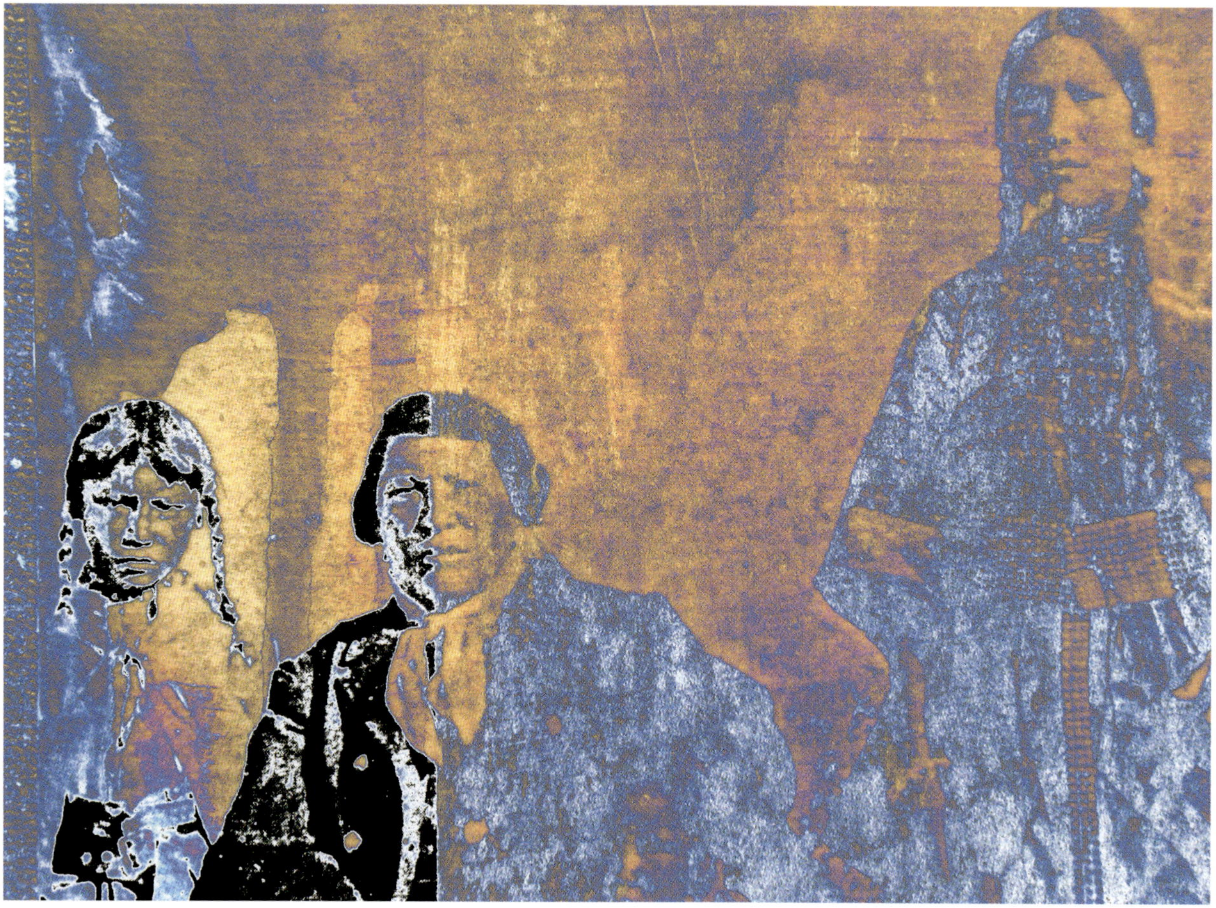

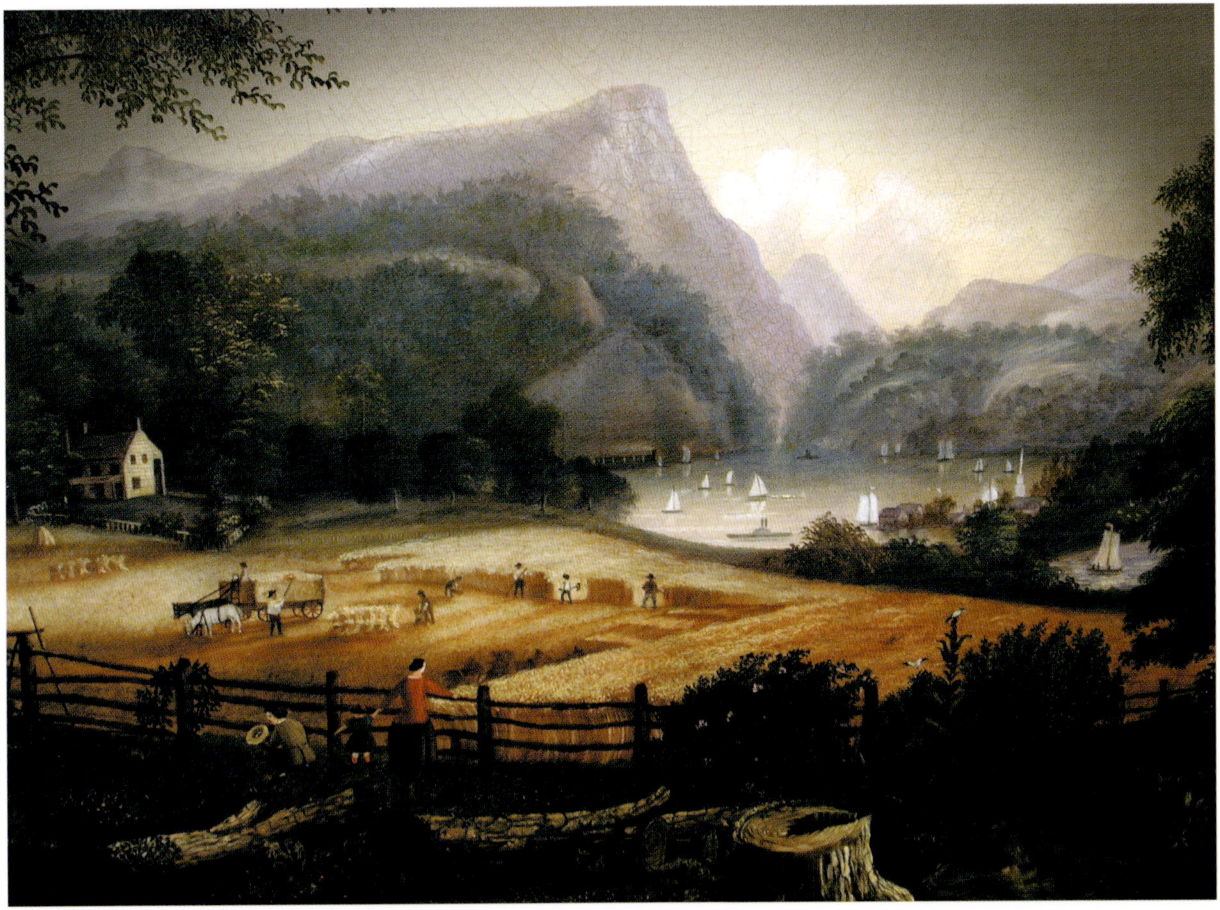

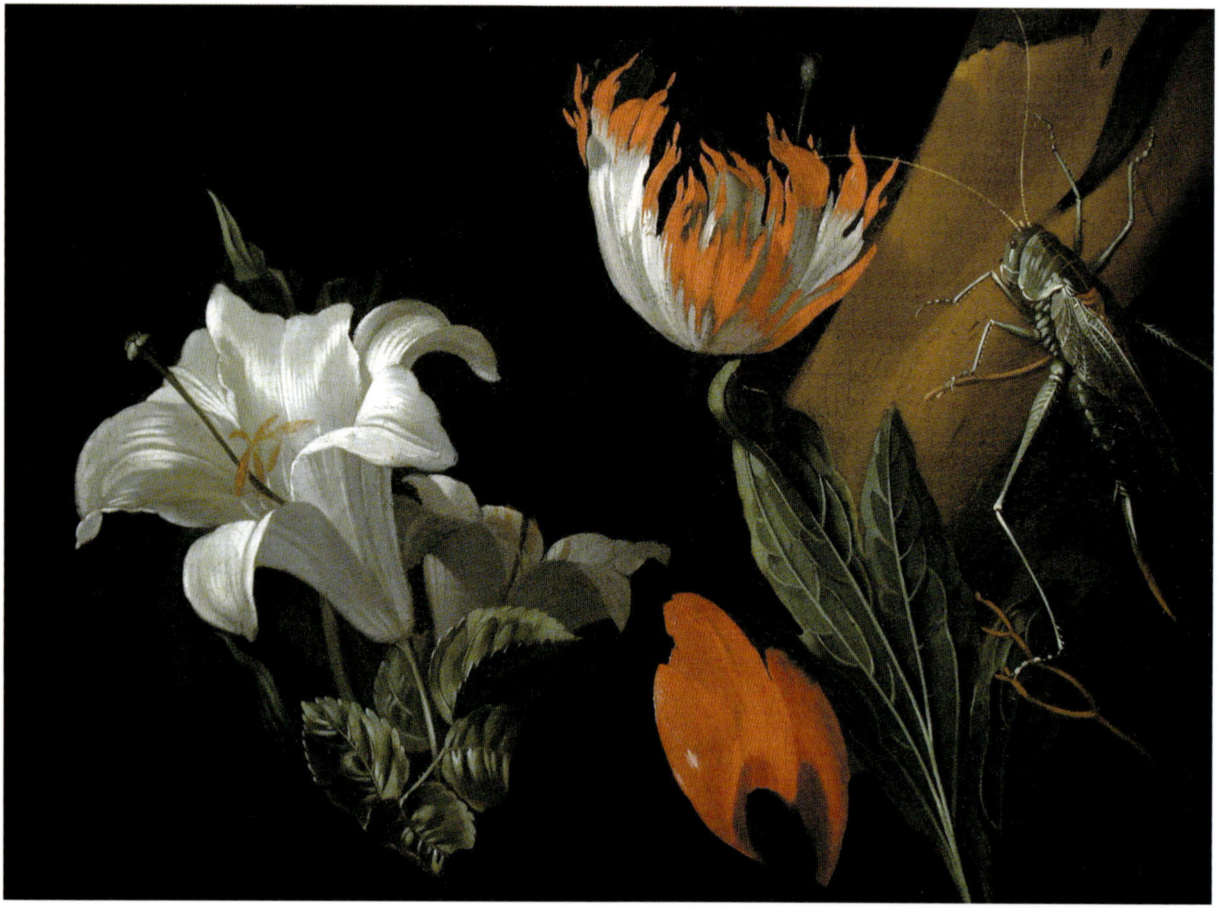

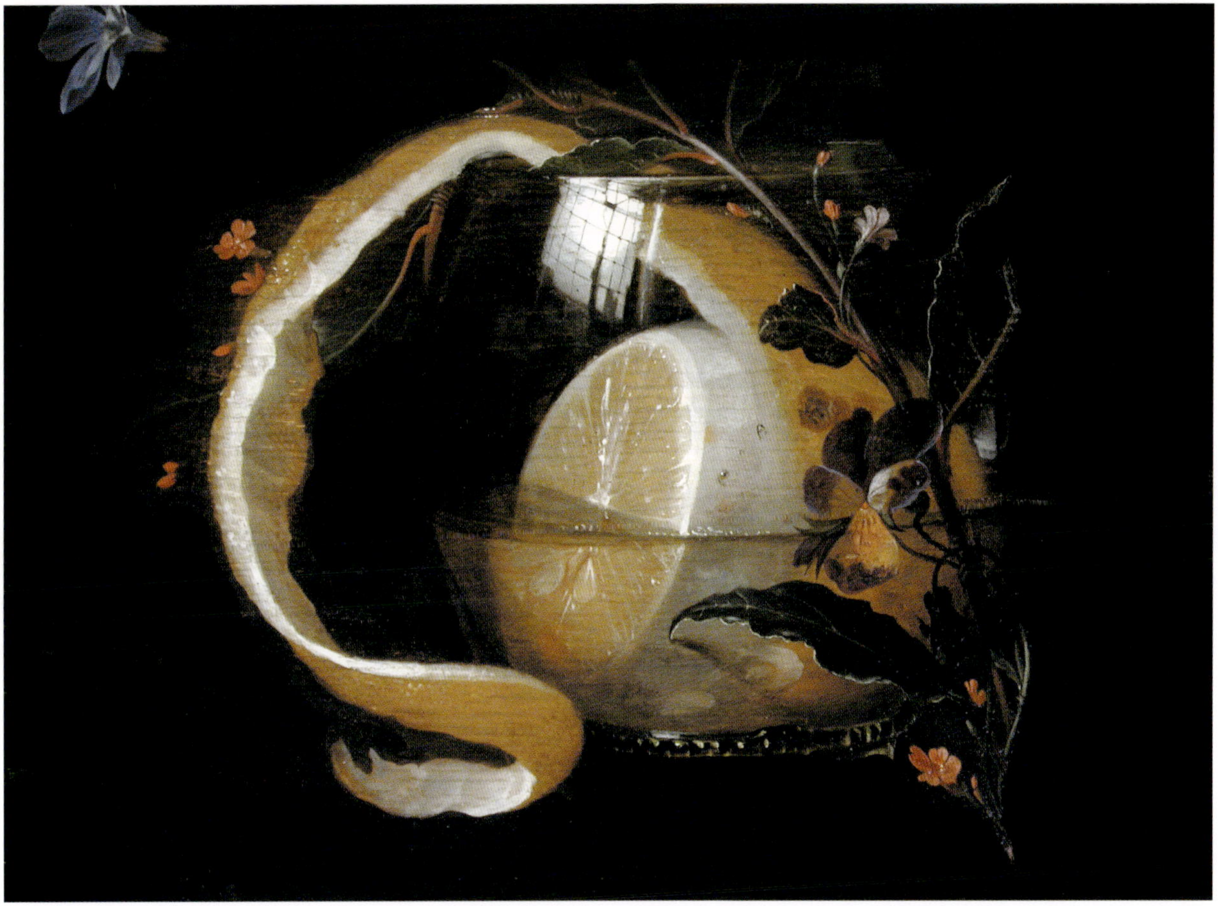

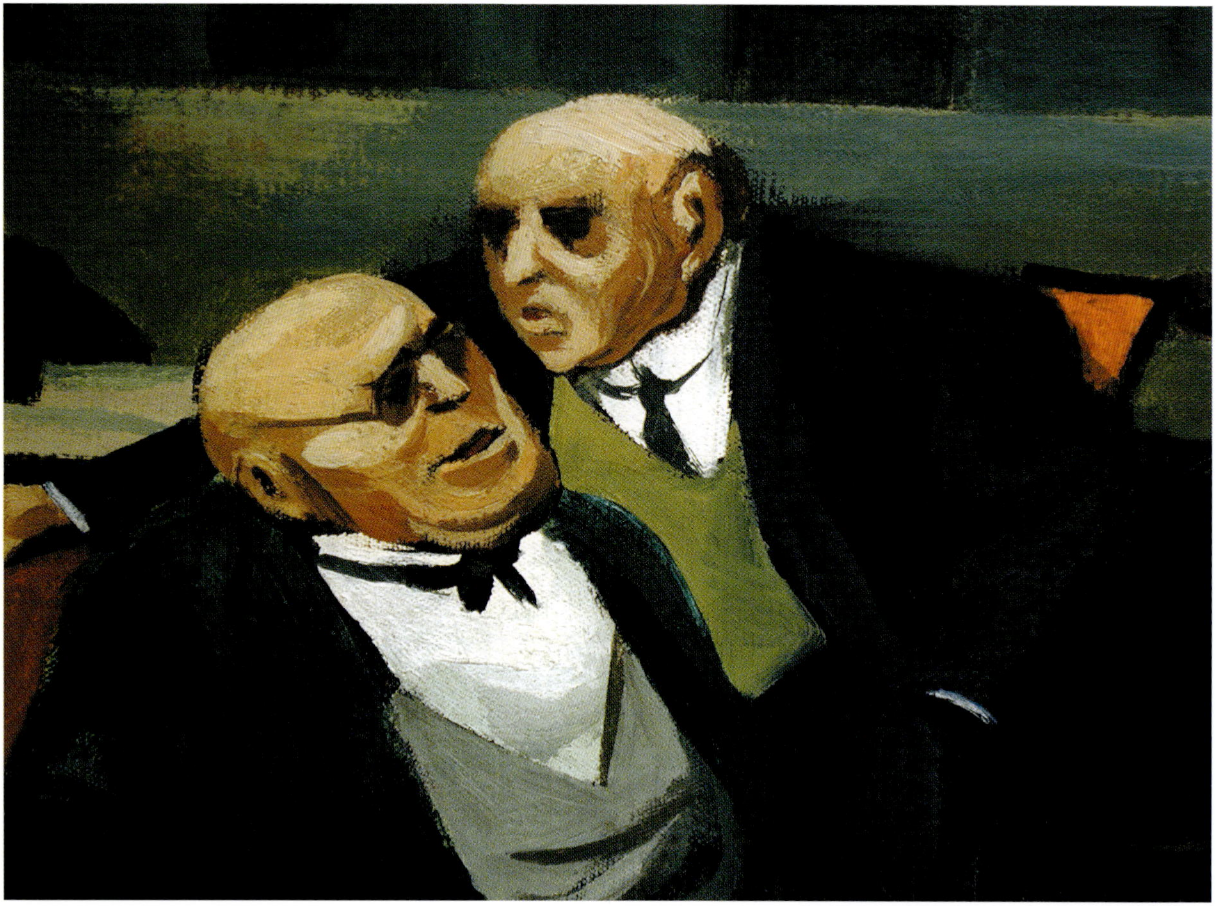

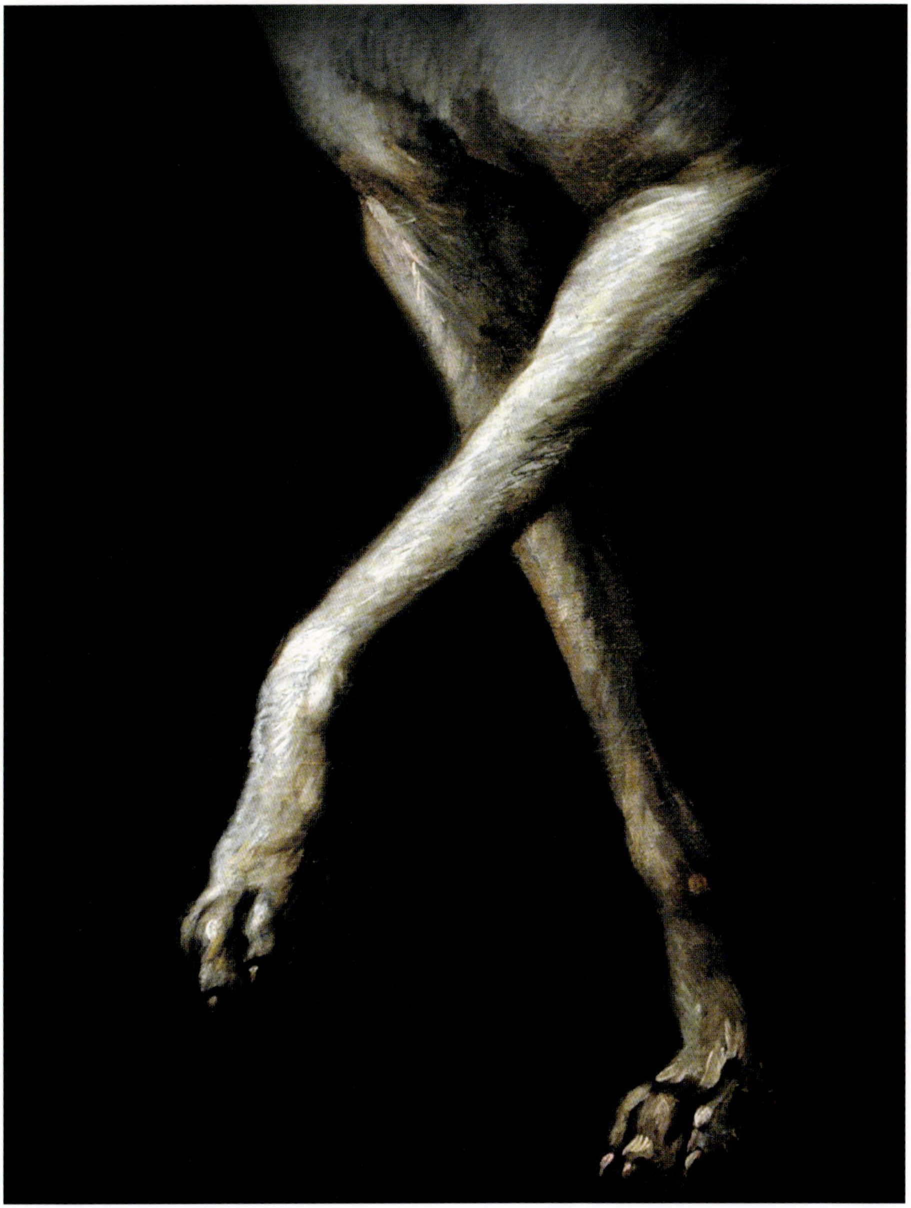

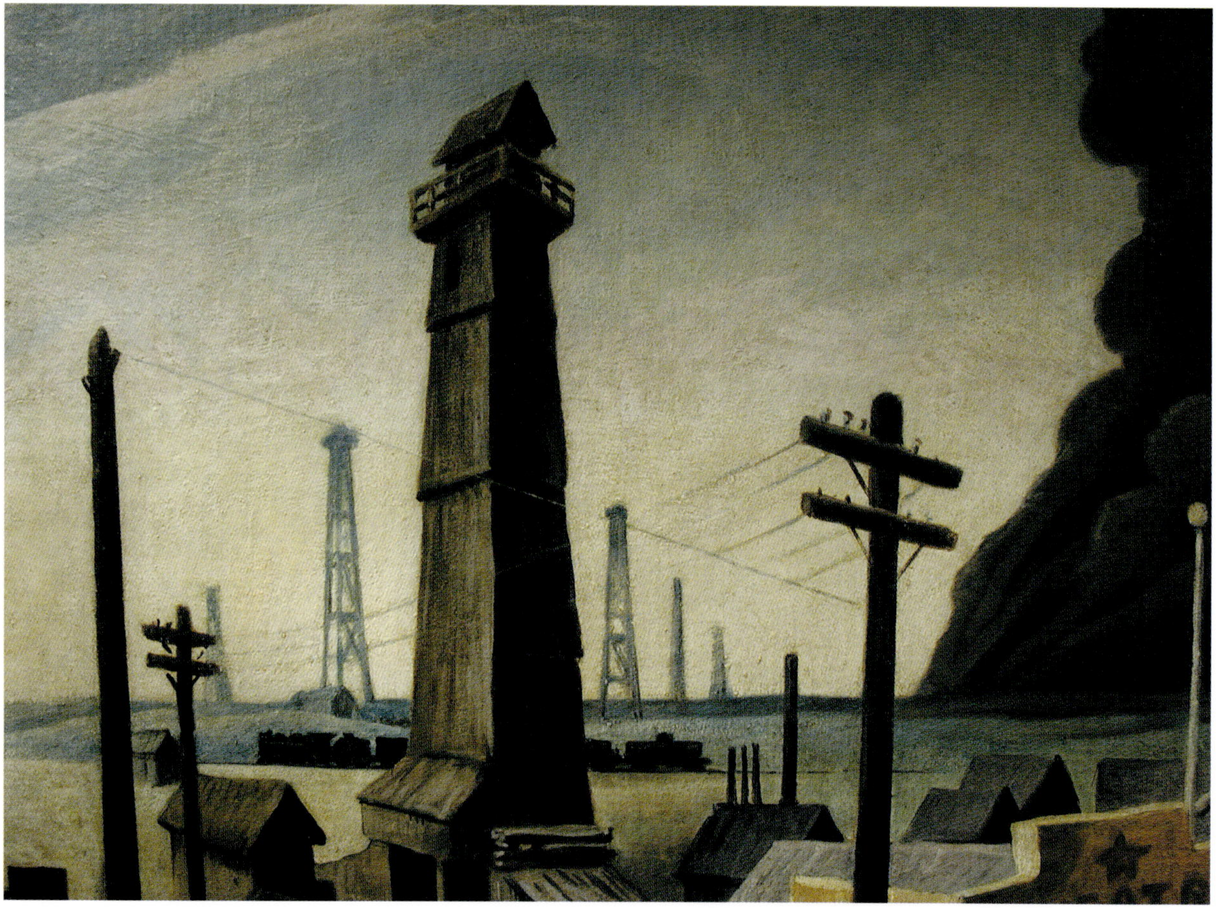

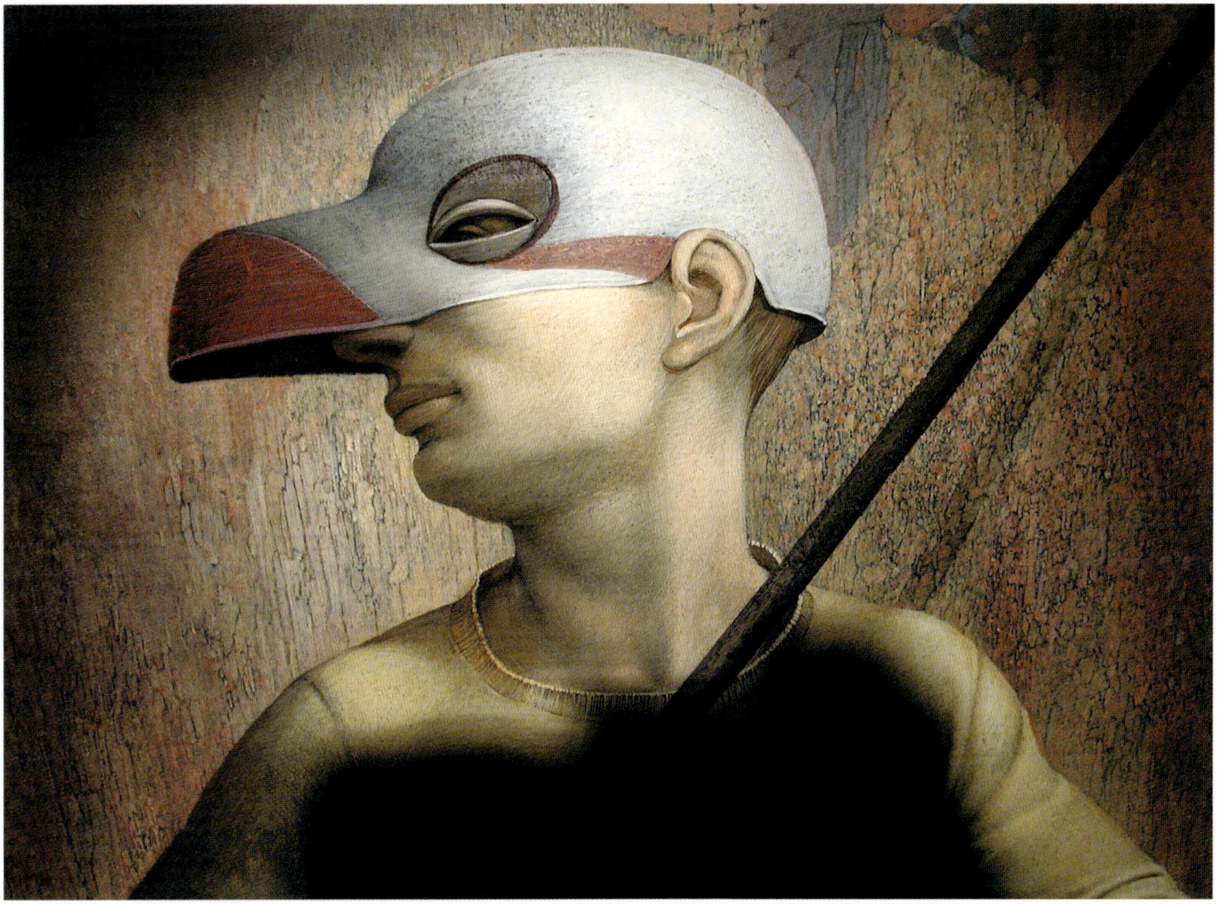

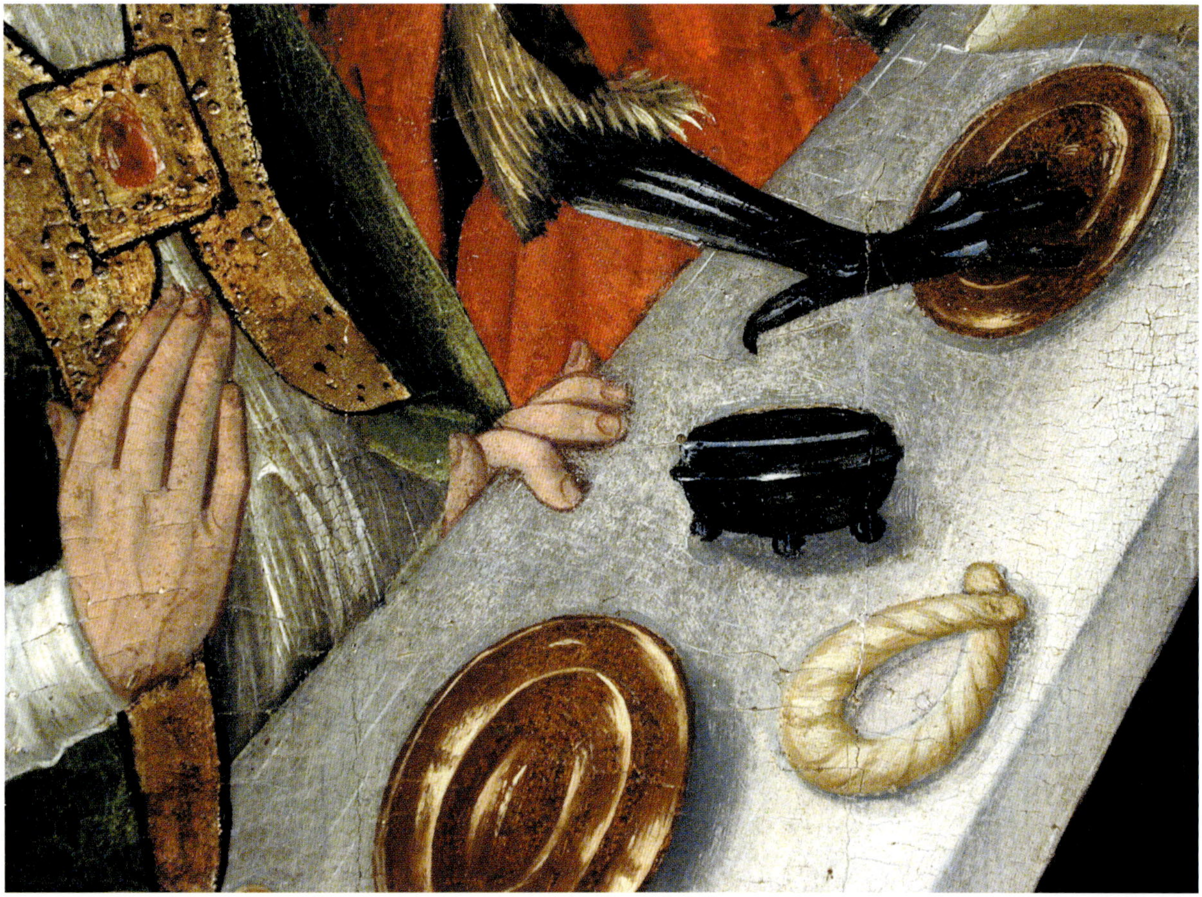

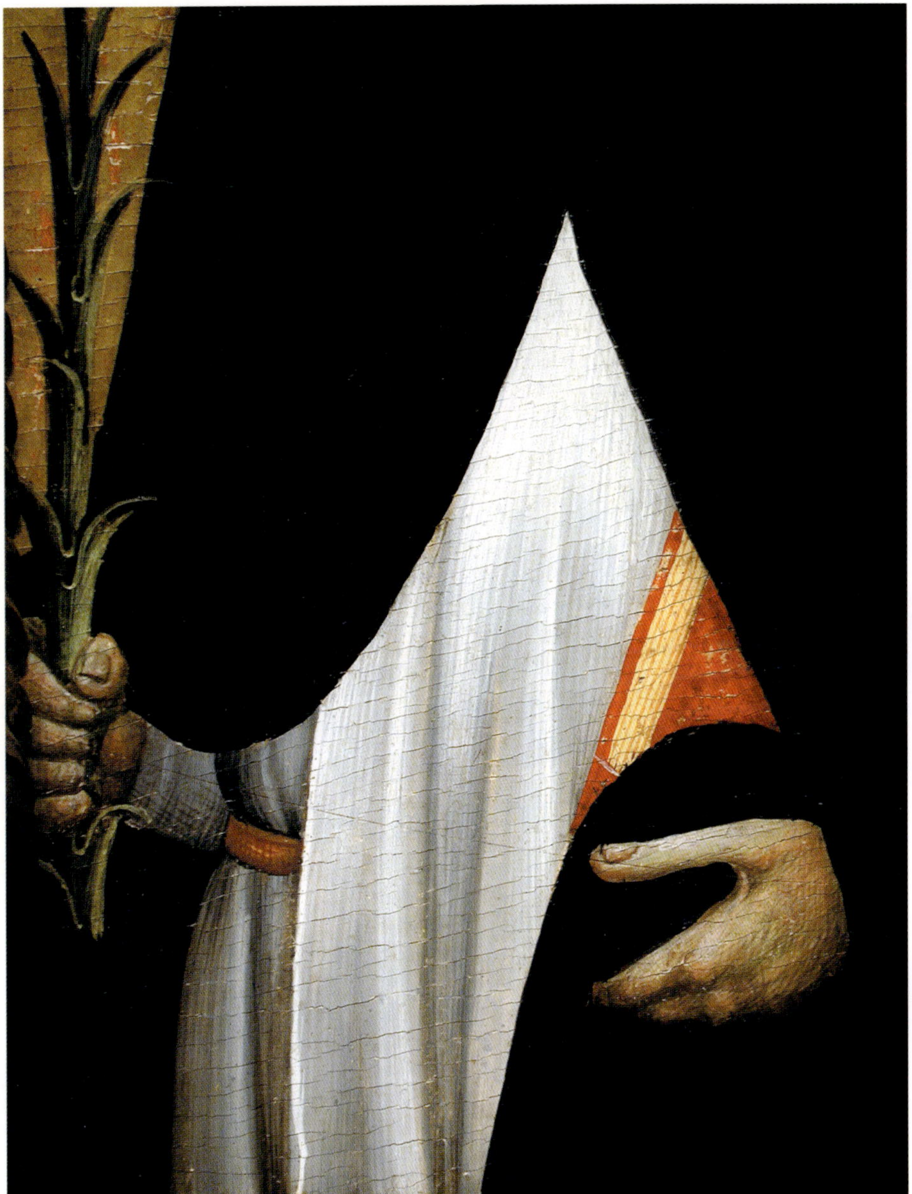

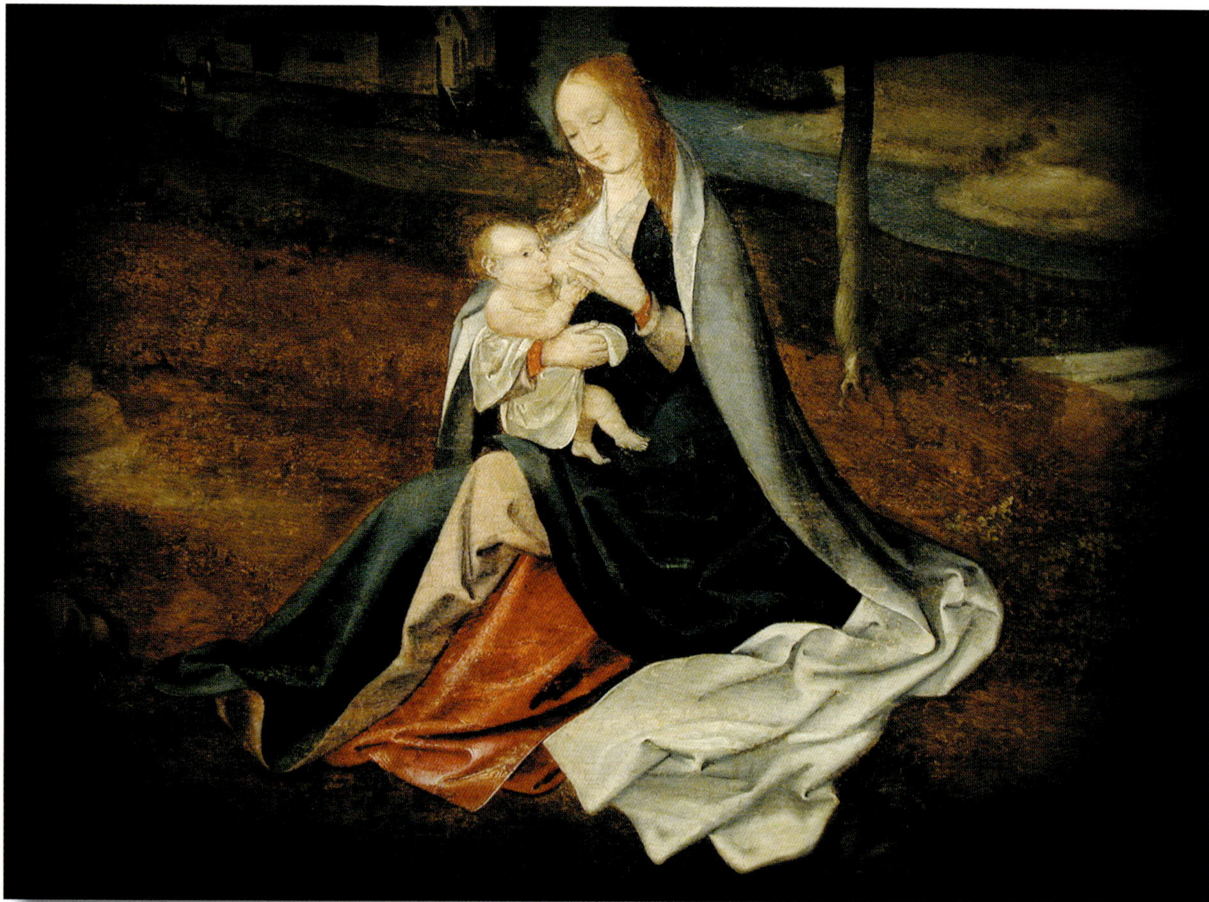

MELIORA

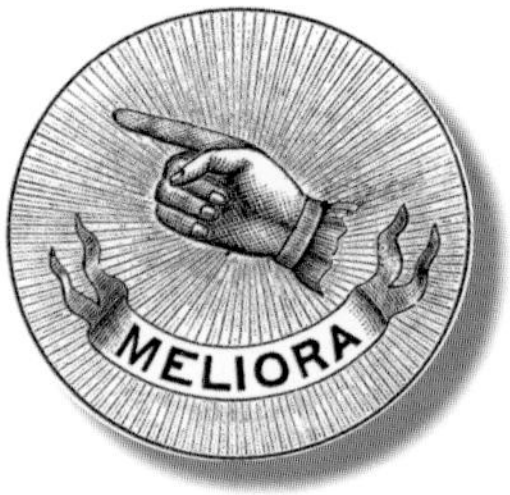

The motto also appears on the University's seal. This seal has undergone three major changes. Initially the seal adopted in 1850 as an interim measure was a half dollar coin. On March 8, 1851, the Board of Trustees made the following resolution:

"Resolved that we adopt as Corporate Seal of the University till permanent seal is procured the American half dollar and that the same be fixed to the Bond and Mortgage to be executed against the University buildings and land recently purchased."

Shortly after, on July 22, 1851, the permanent seal was adopted as shown above. The seal was engraved by John E. Gavit of Albany and used until 1928 when the image of the hand was replaced with the shields of the (then) three colleges, Arts and Science, Music and Medicine.

THIS most graceful of words is the motto of the University of Rochester and as such is shared by the Memorial Art Gallery. The motto is believed to have been suggested by Dr. Asahel Clark Kendrick, first professor of Greek, who served in that capacity from 1850 to 1888.

On May 30, 1990, Professor Alfred Geier of the Department of Religion and Classics made the observation that "Meliora is an adjective and may also serve as a noun meaning 'better things.' Melior is the masculine, melius the neutral—the neutral plural of melius is meliora. My guess is that the original quote comes from Ovid's Metamorphoses, book 7, lines 20–21, 'video meliora proboque' or 'I see and appreciate better things.'"

This entire body of work, and this final chapter in particular, is dedicated to this view of the world. Here the sense of grace and optimism that this word embodies finds its form in depictions of women and children. Many of these images render the women in a highly idealized, even sensual manner. However, the risk of them being simply seen as objects of desire is tempered by the inclusion of symbols that suggest more fundamental generative forces.

The image of Fiaschi's "Standing Woman" juxtaposed with the Chihuly glass is one of the more lyrical examples. The woman's gently swelling body implies the promise of new life. This sensation is further amplified by the accompanying image. At a simple level the photograph reminds us of the shell on which Botticelli's Venus stands. However, more importantly, the photograph's visual structure as a whole, created by light modulating through Chihuly's transluscent creation, suggests the rhythm of the sea. In doing so it encourages us to recall that primal, amniotic ocean of grace from which we all emerged—hopefully to seek and embrace better things.

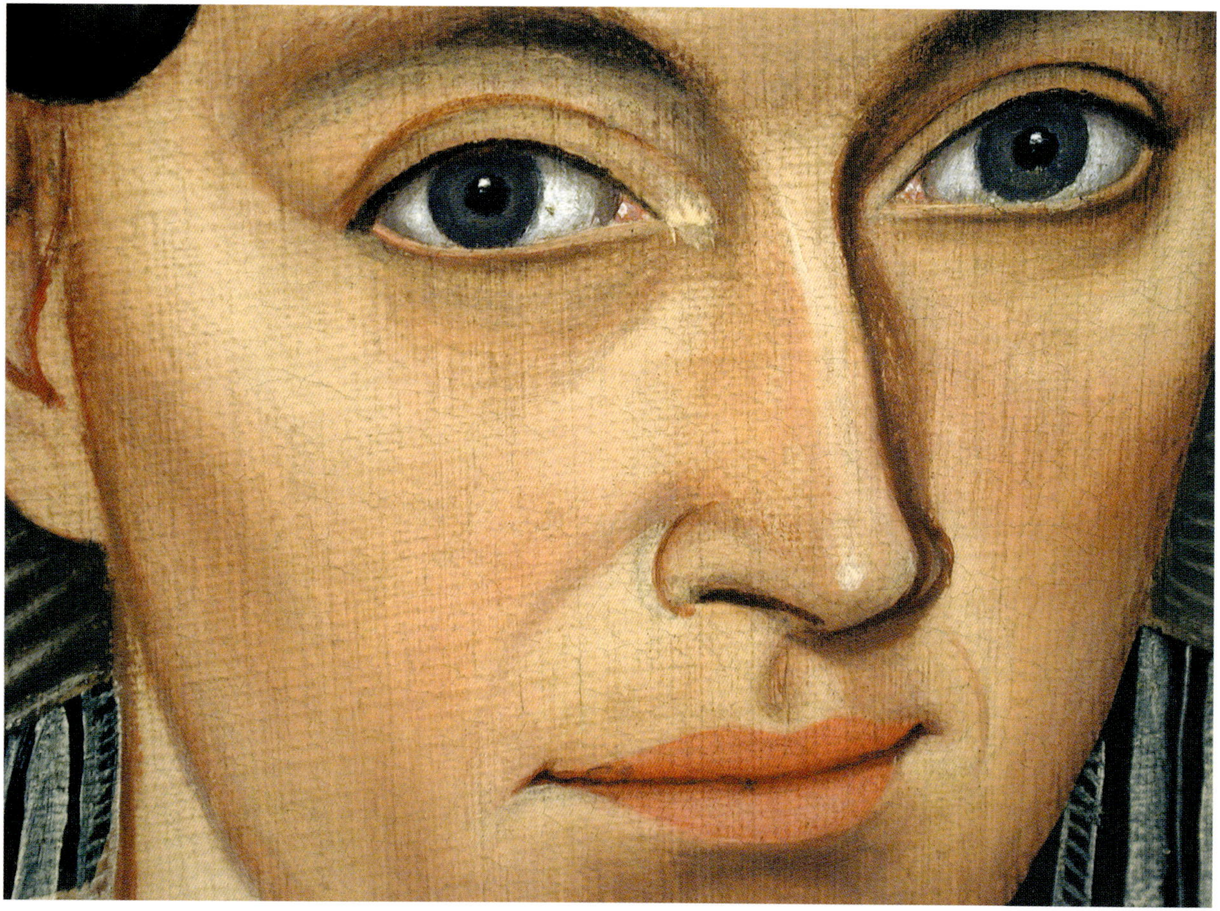

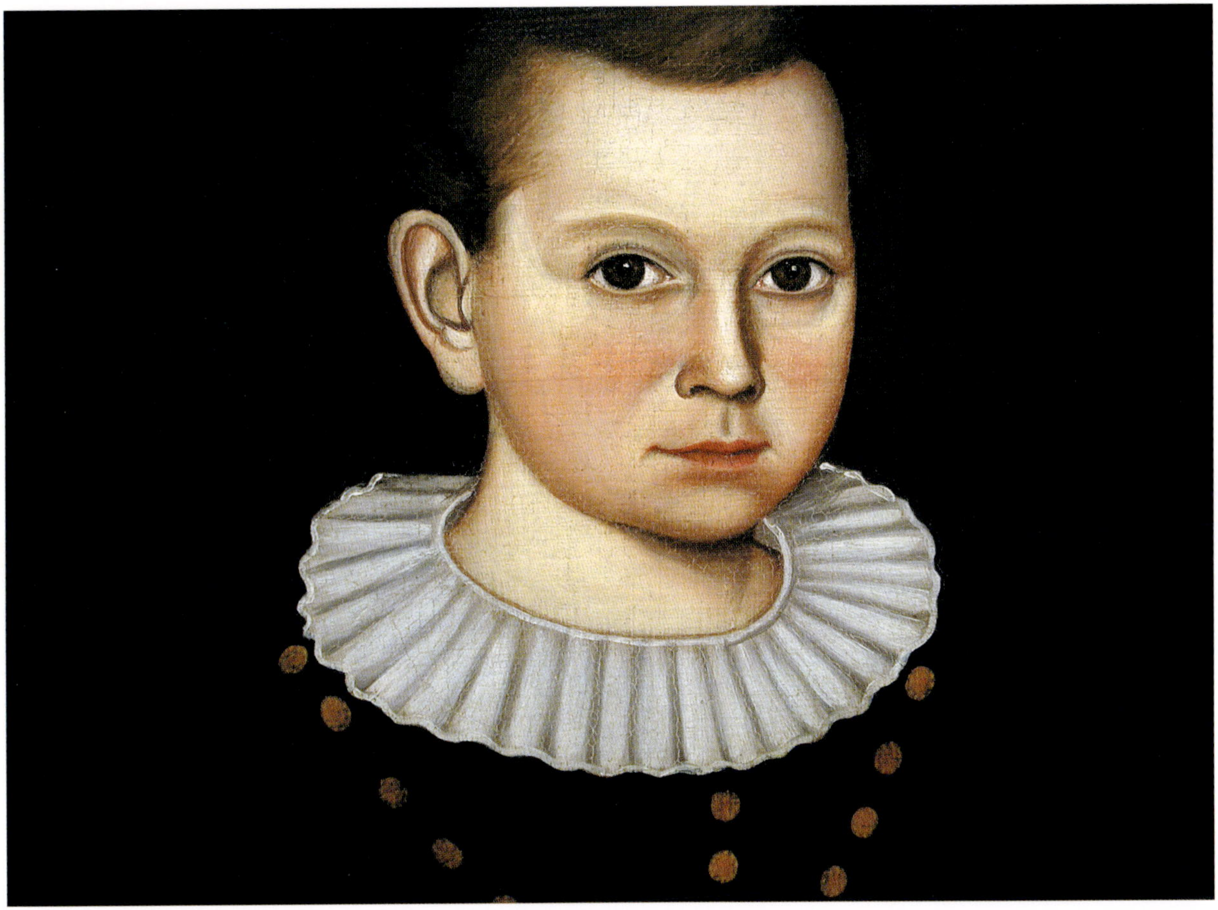

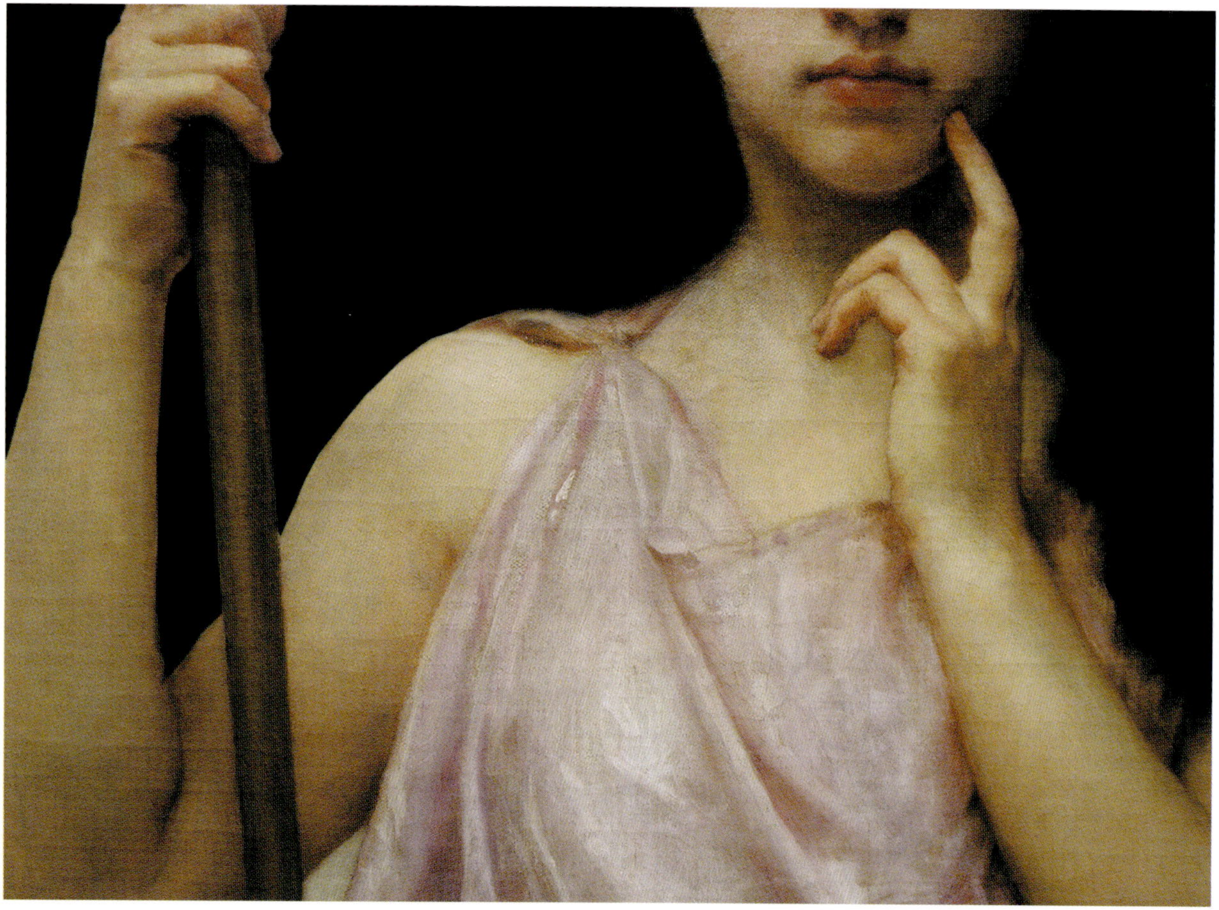

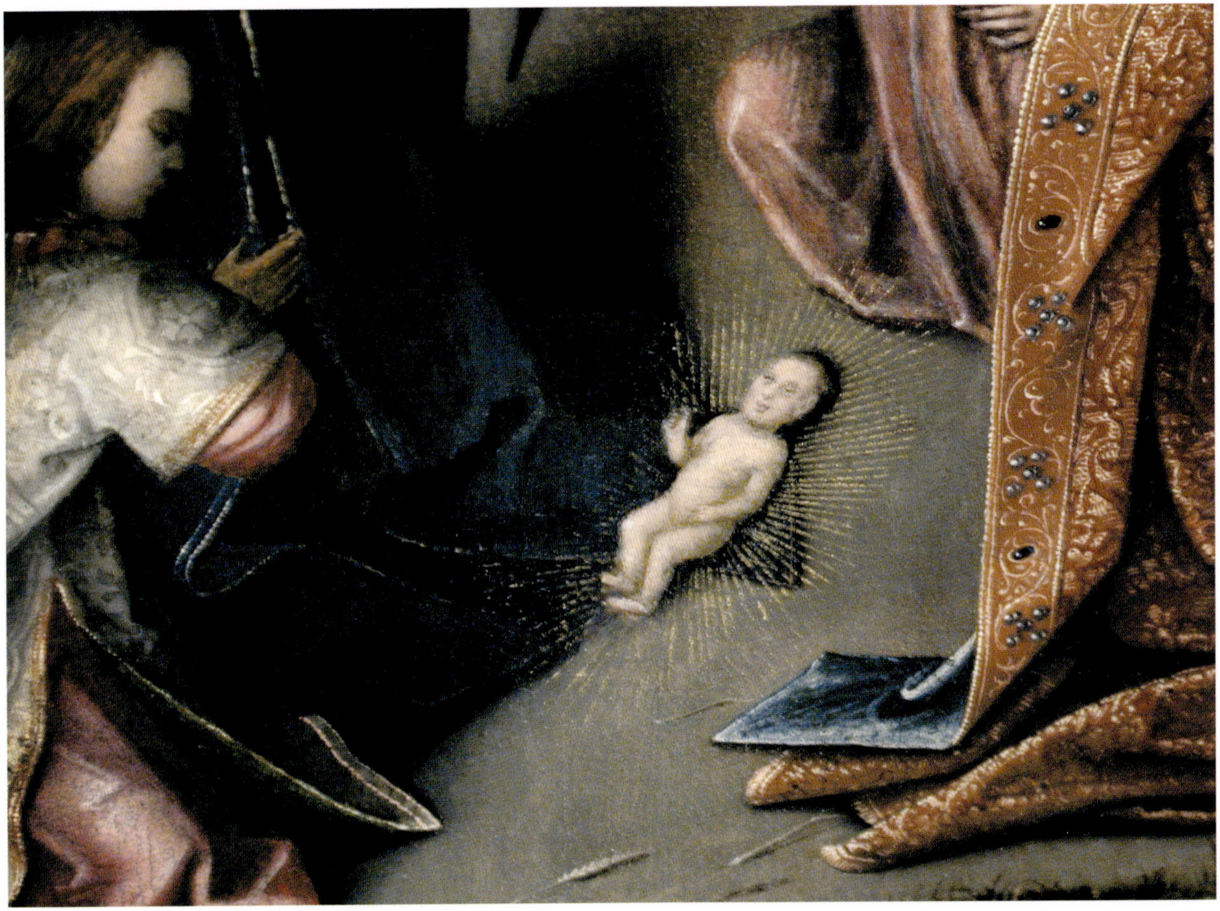

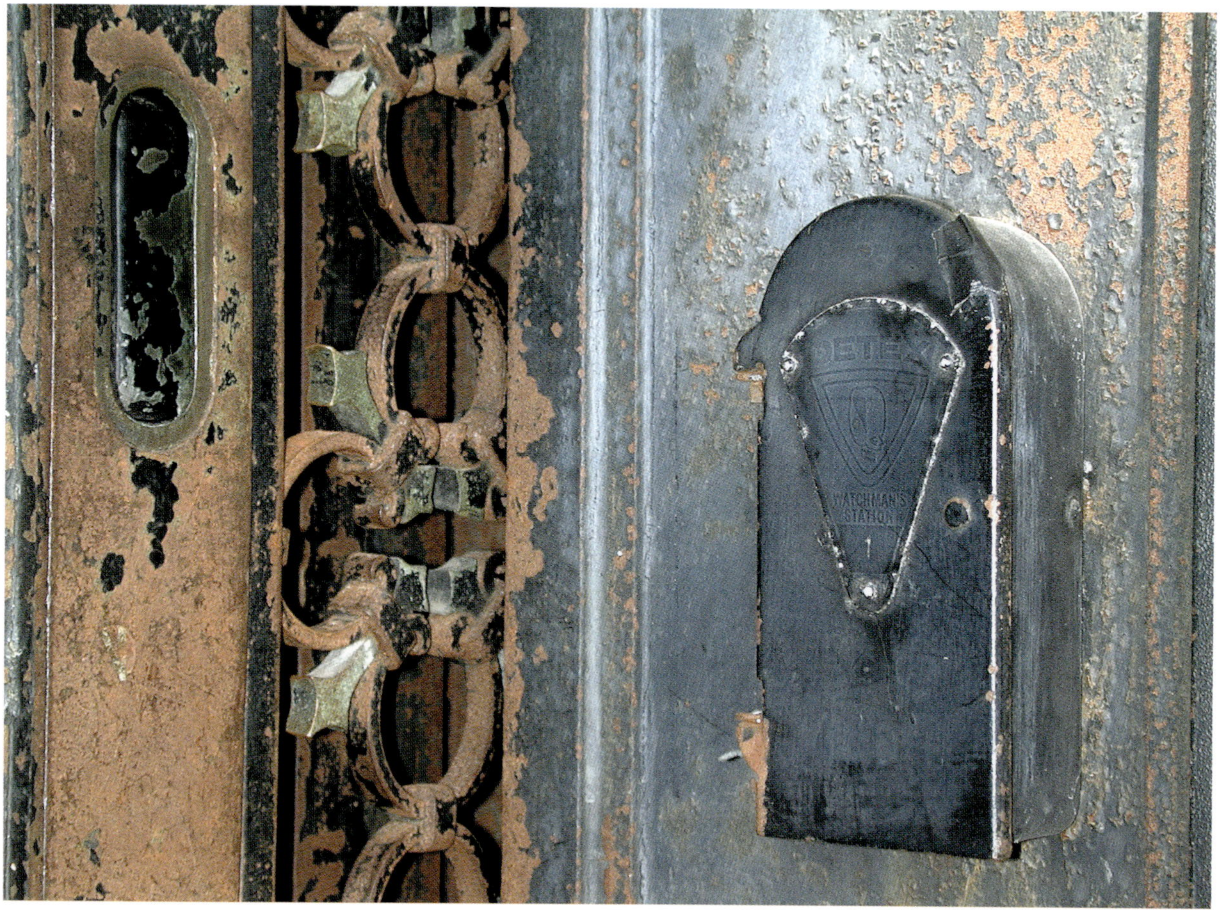
WATCHMAN'S
STATION
1

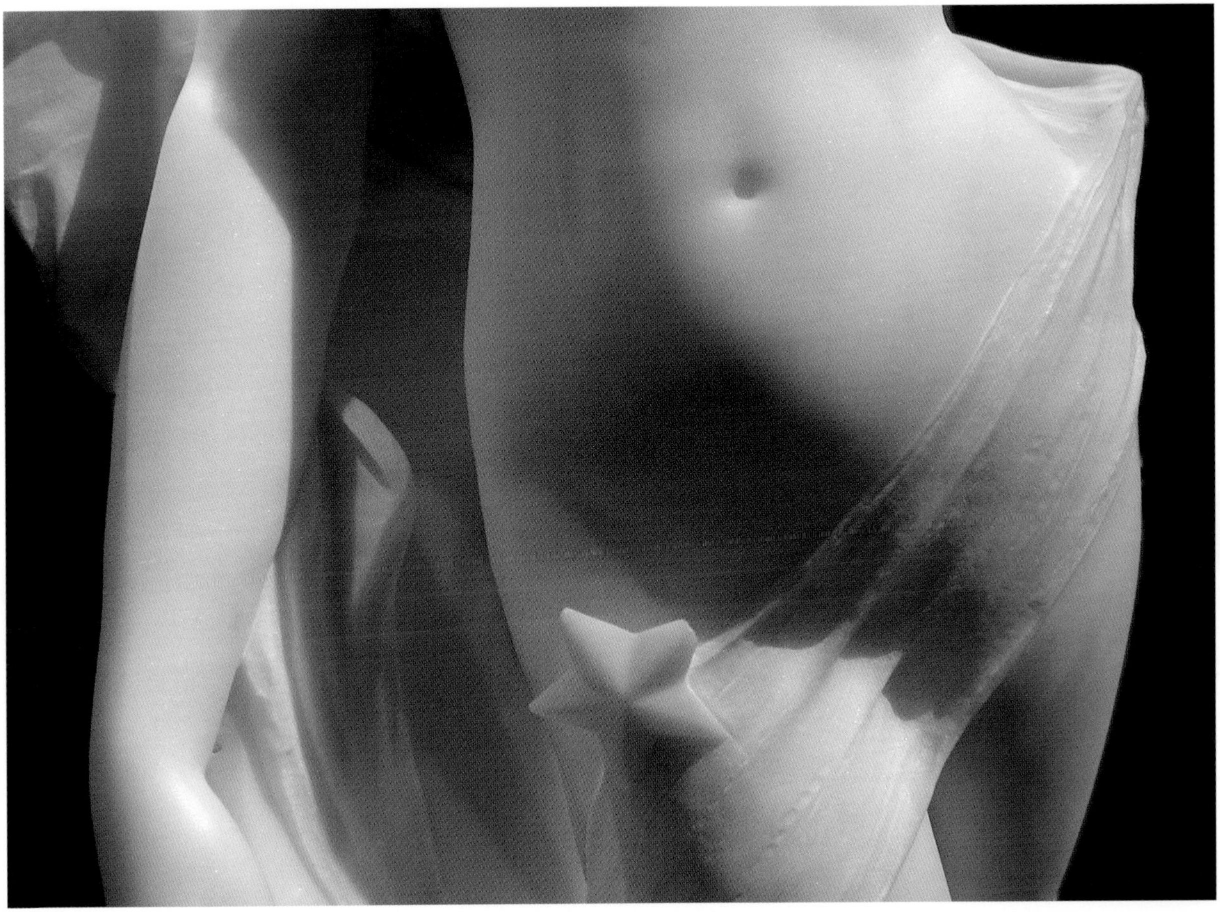

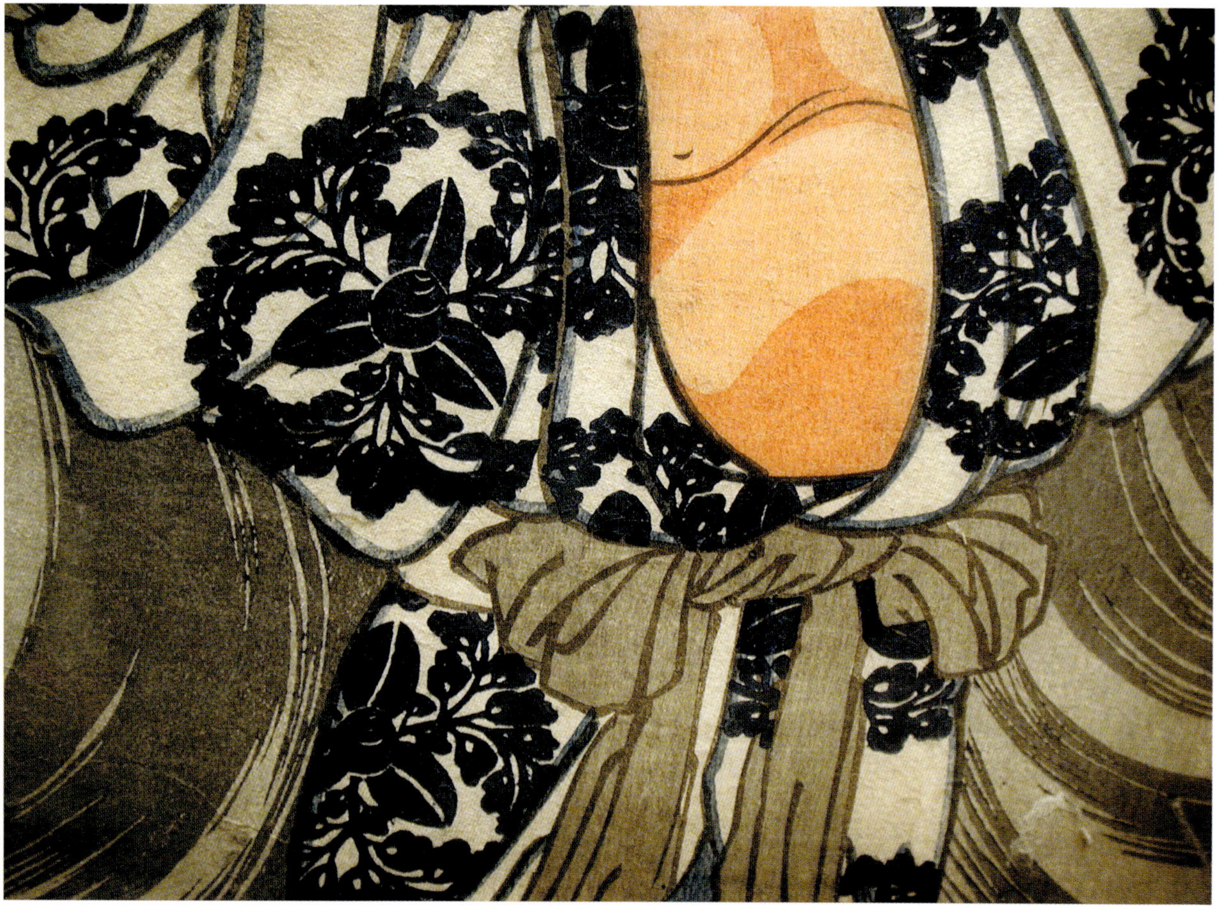

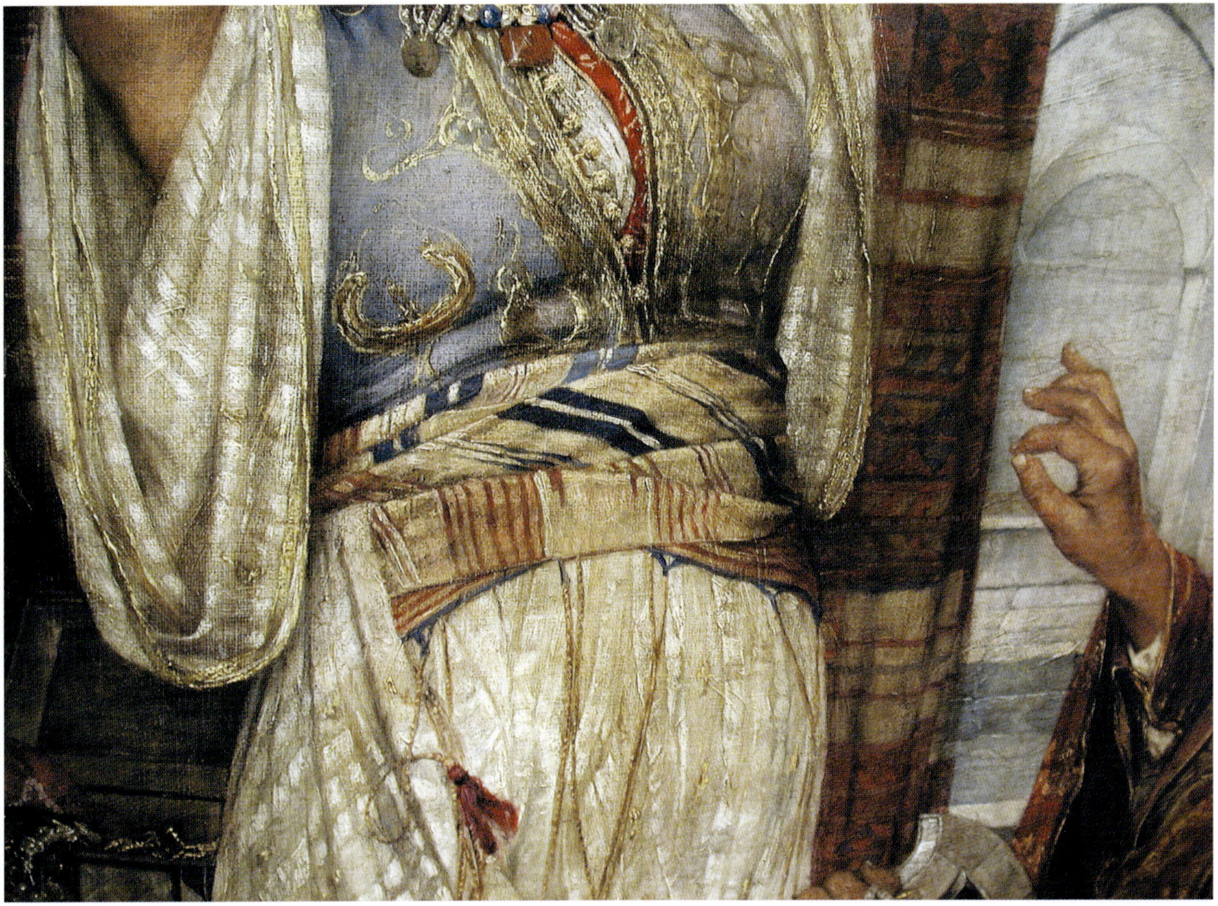

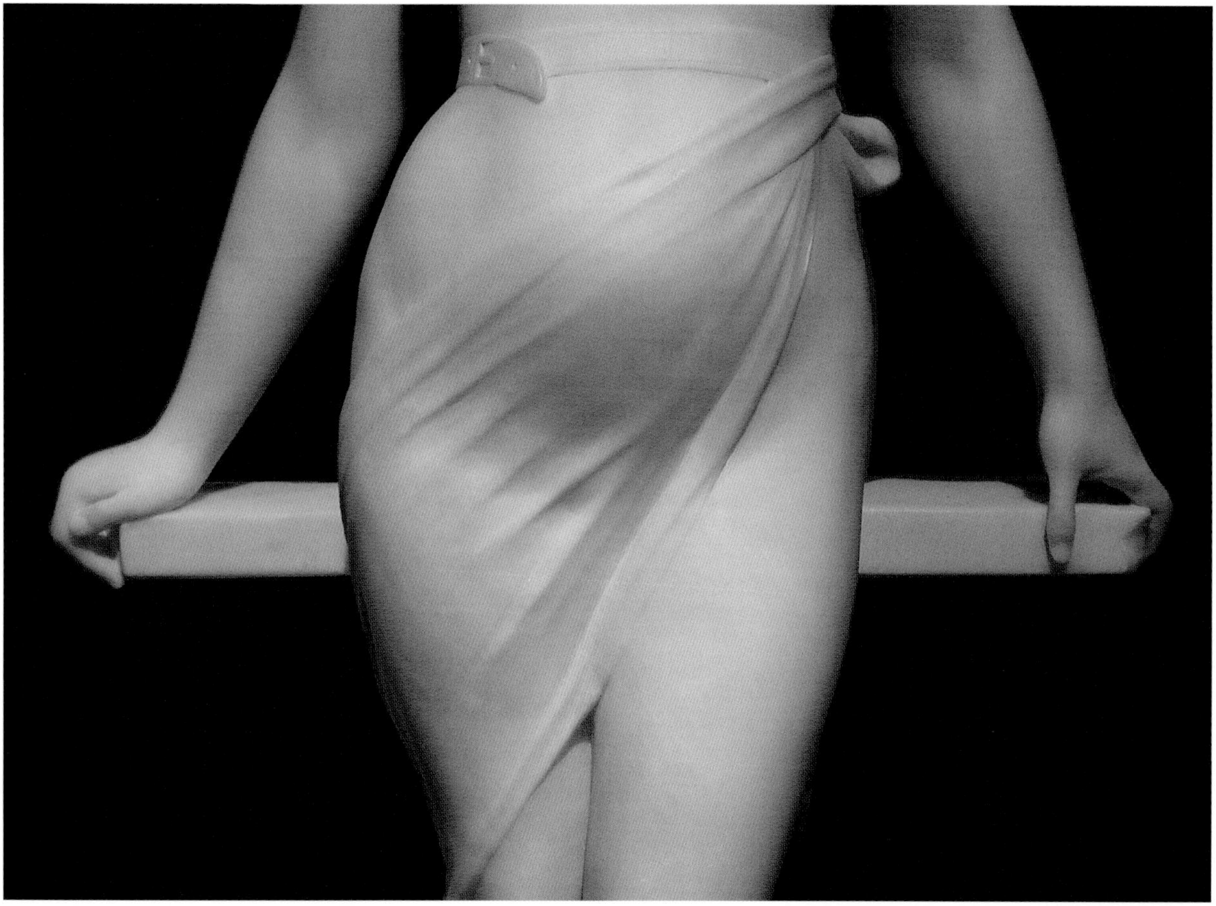

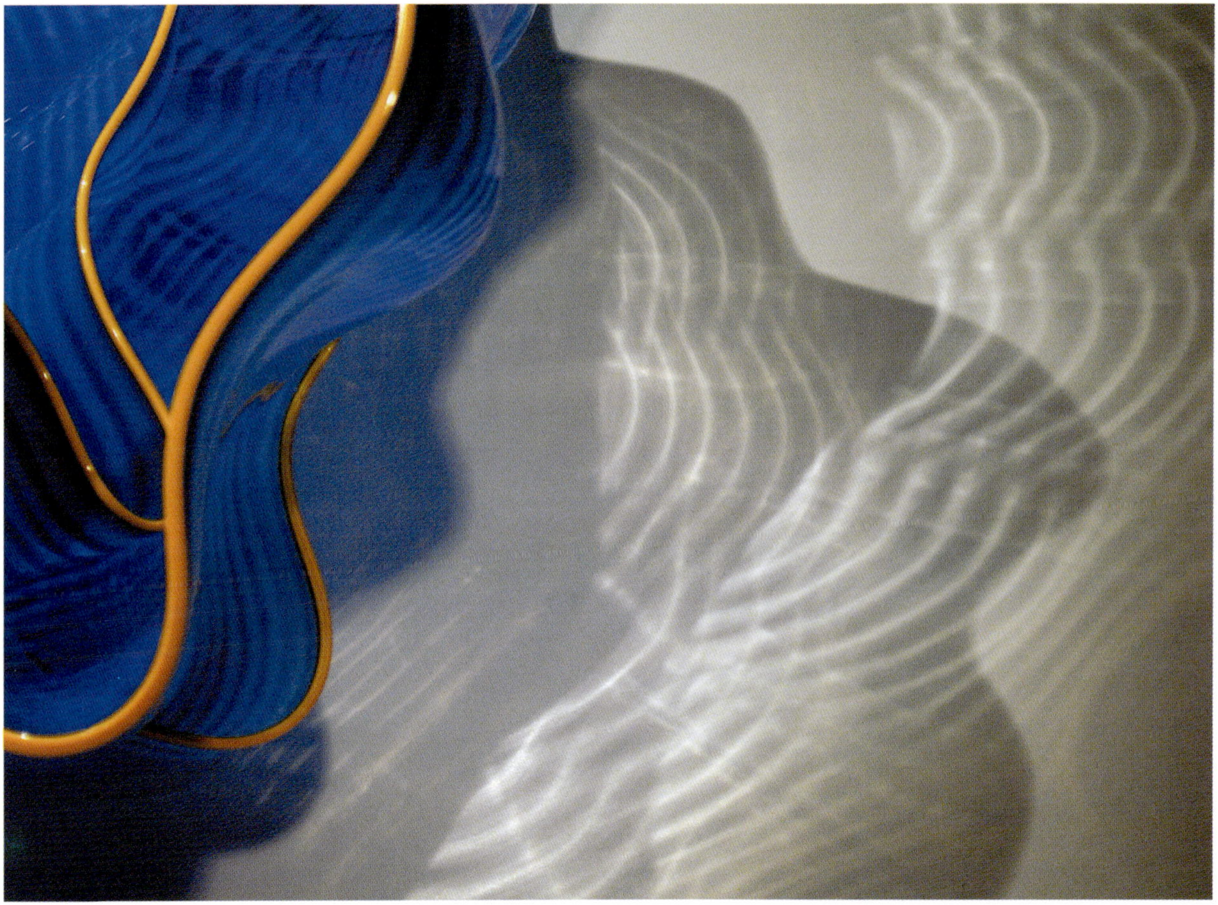

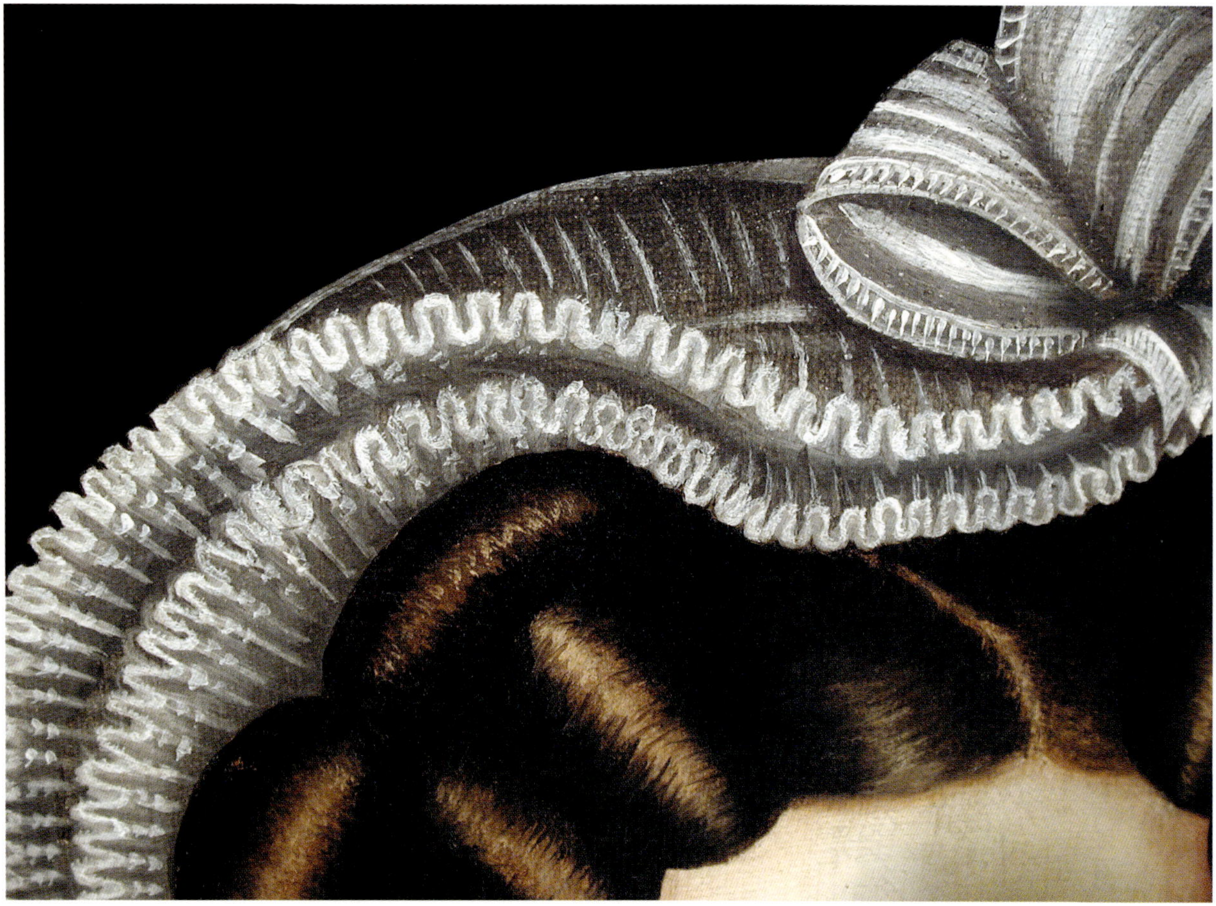

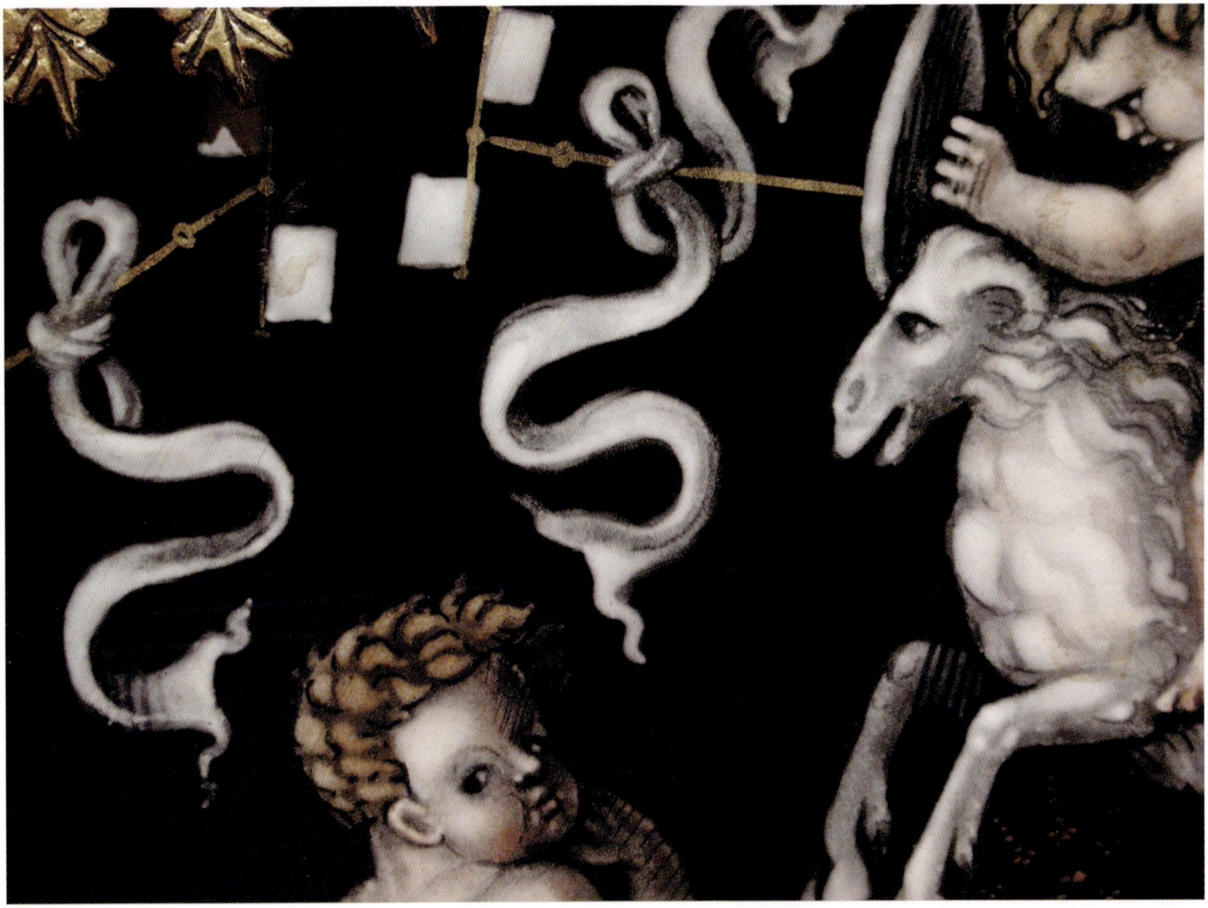

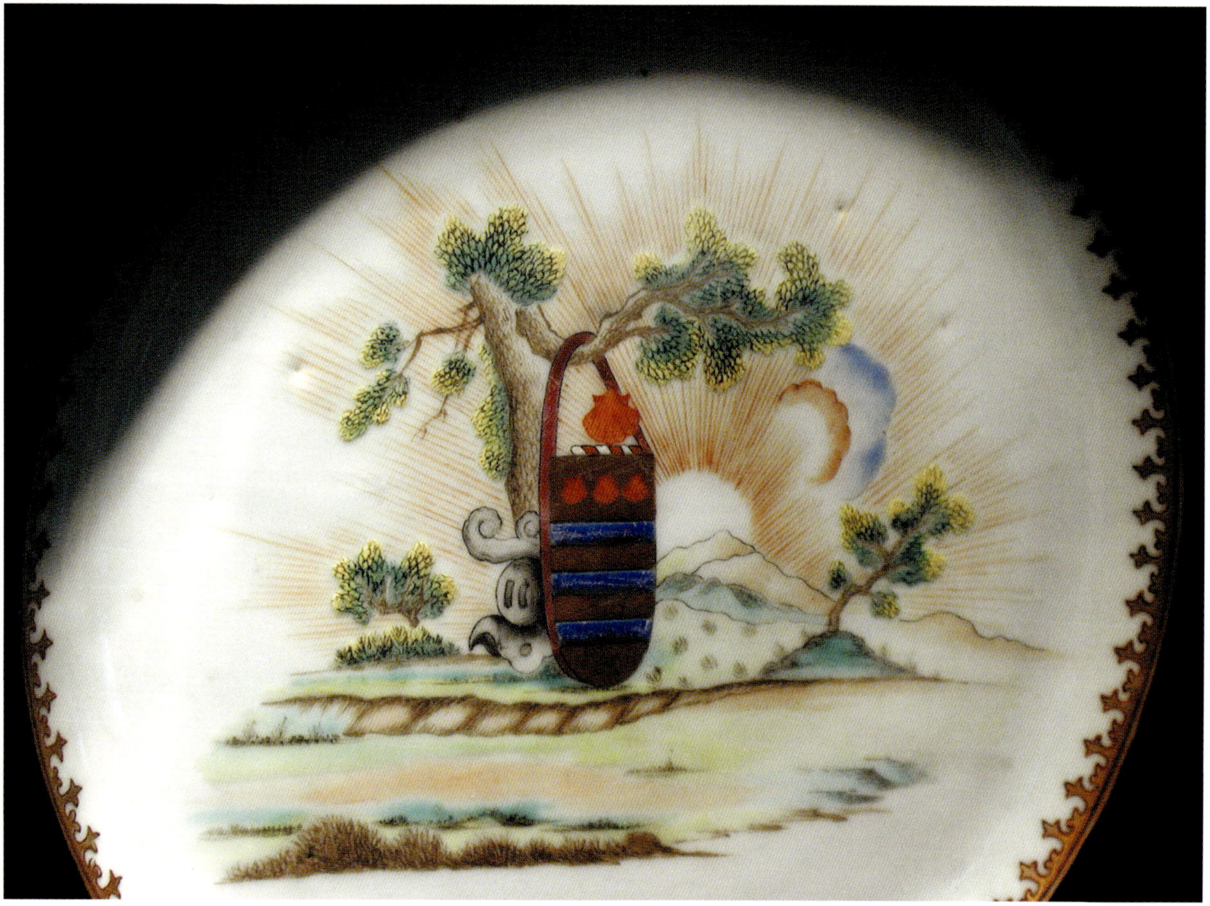

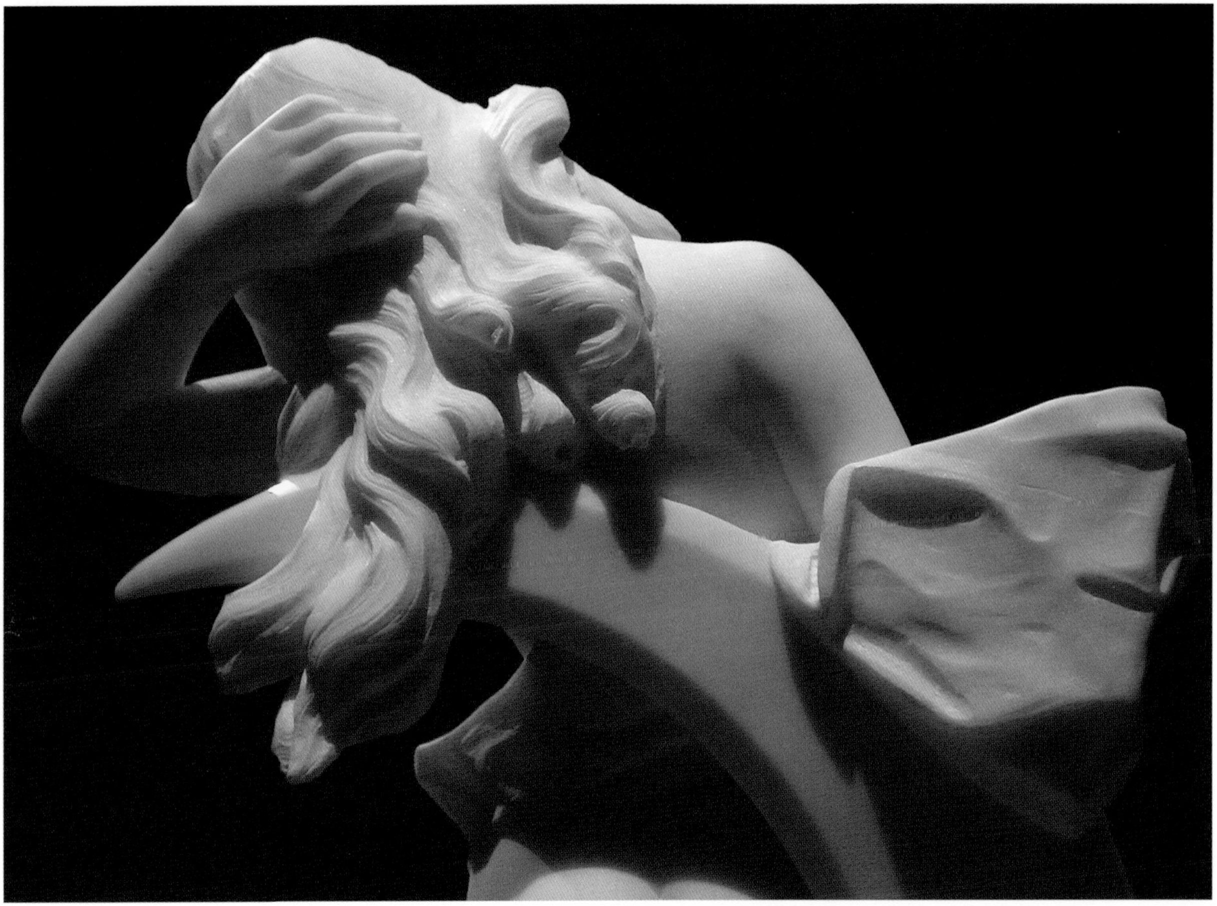

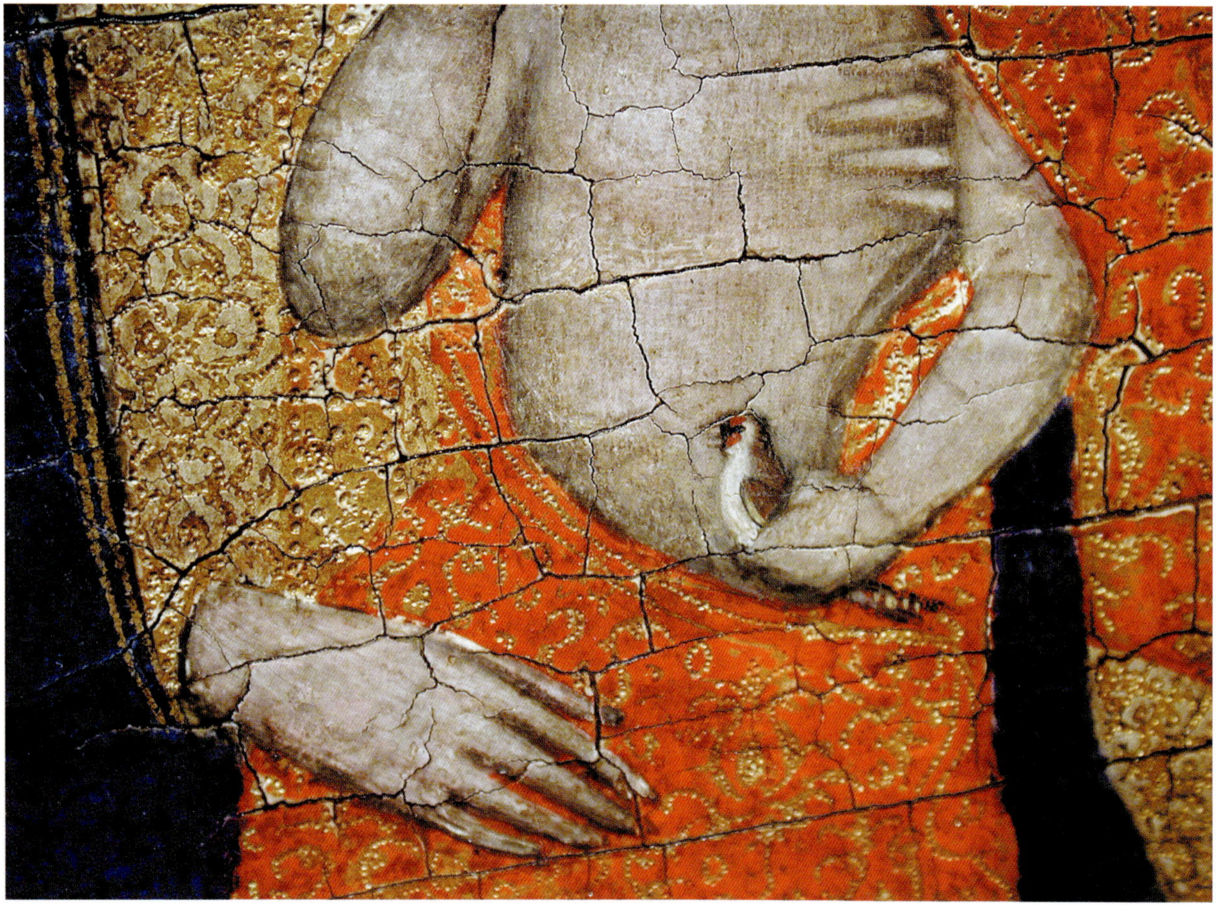

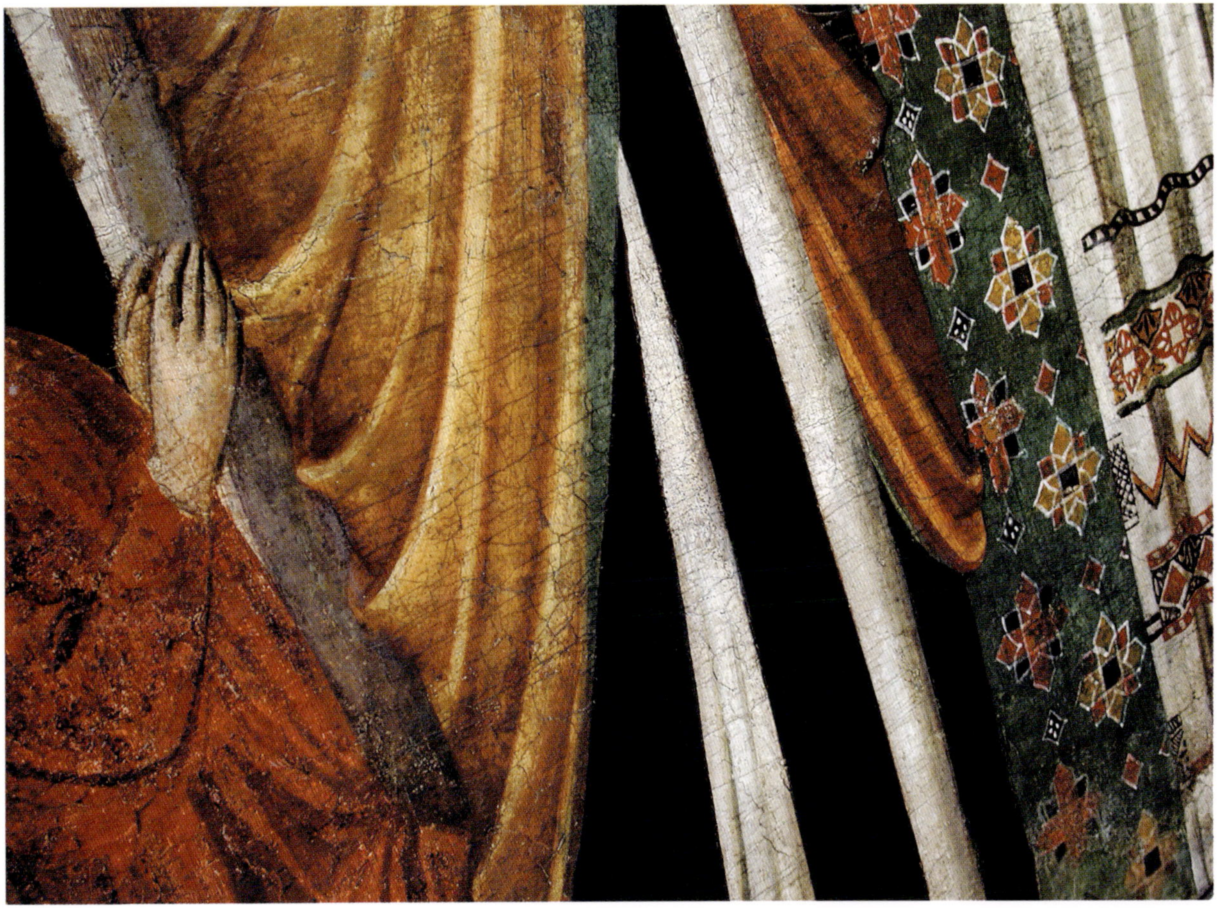

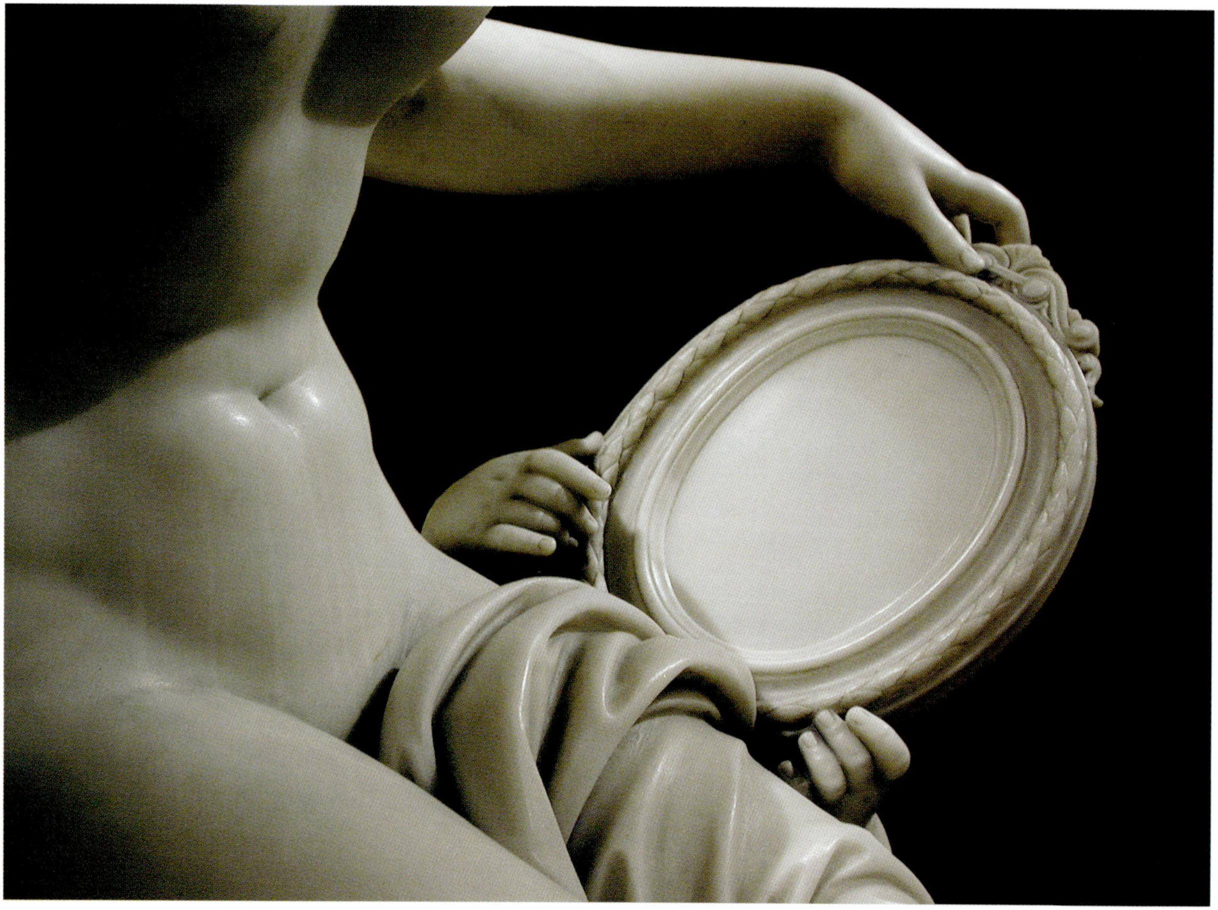

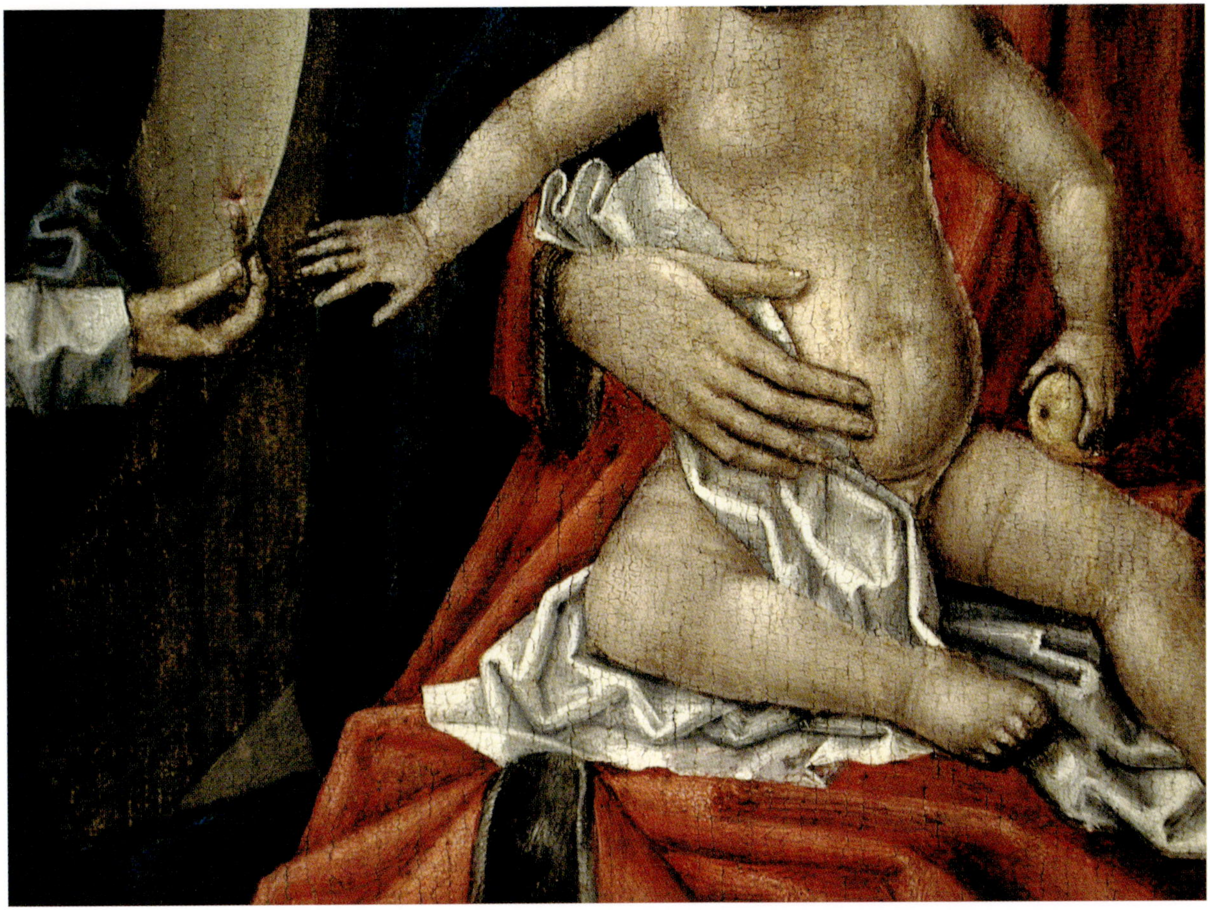

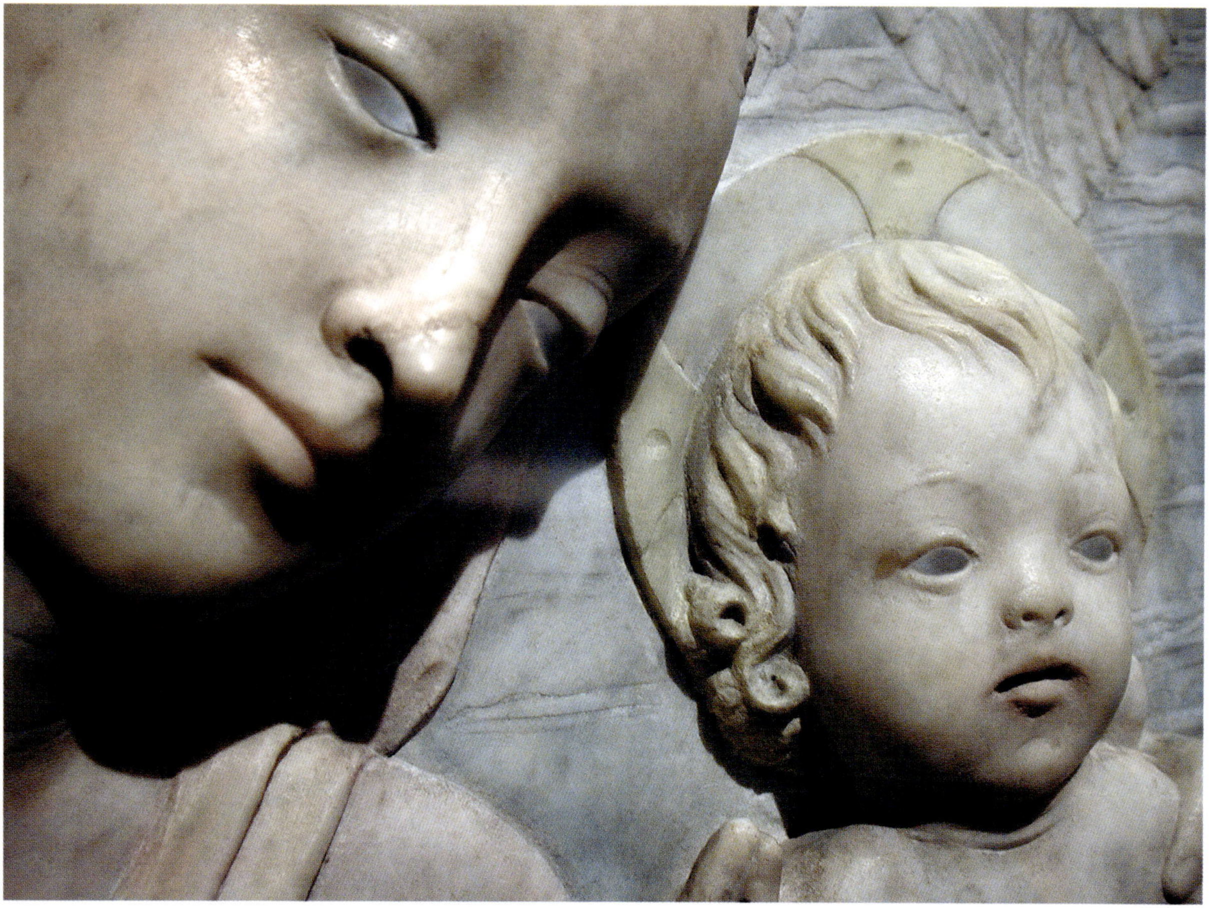

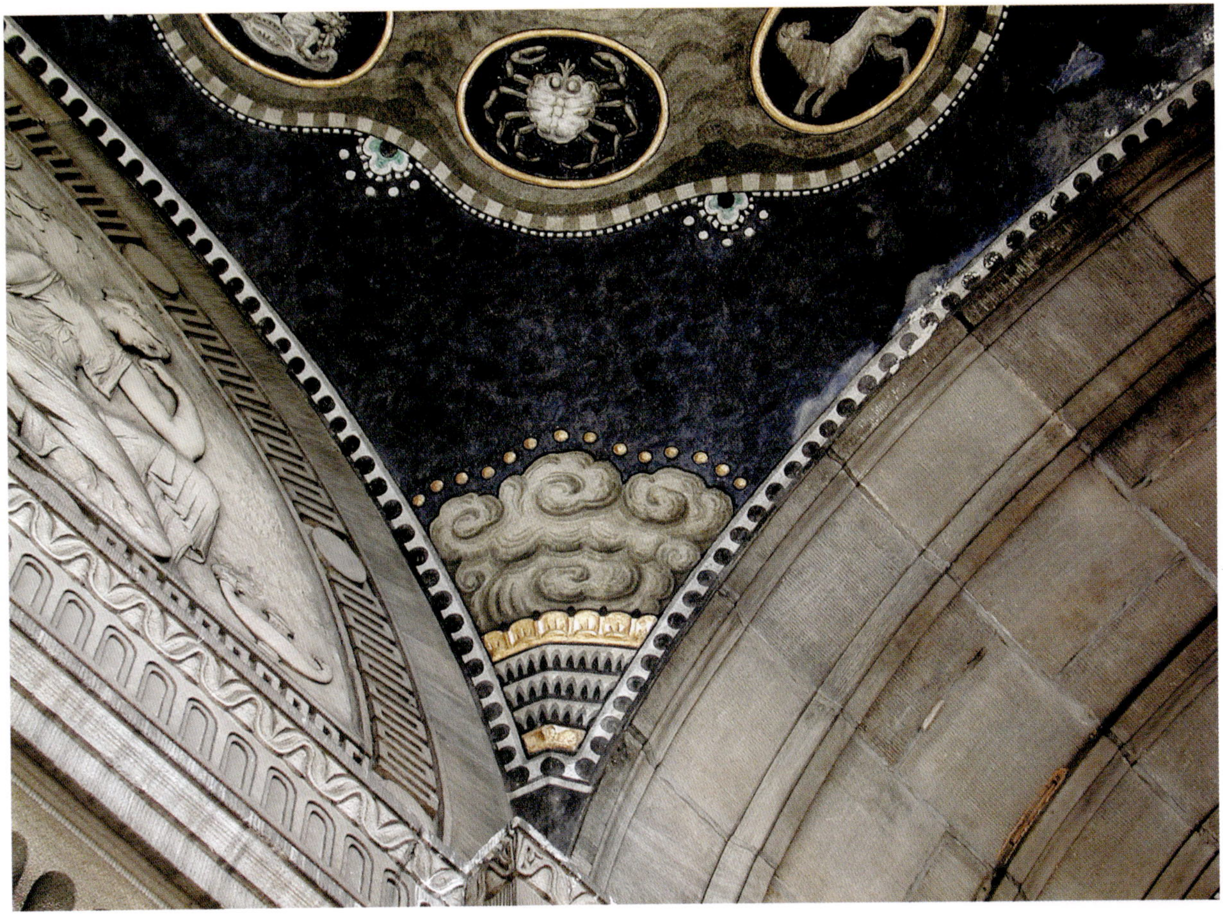

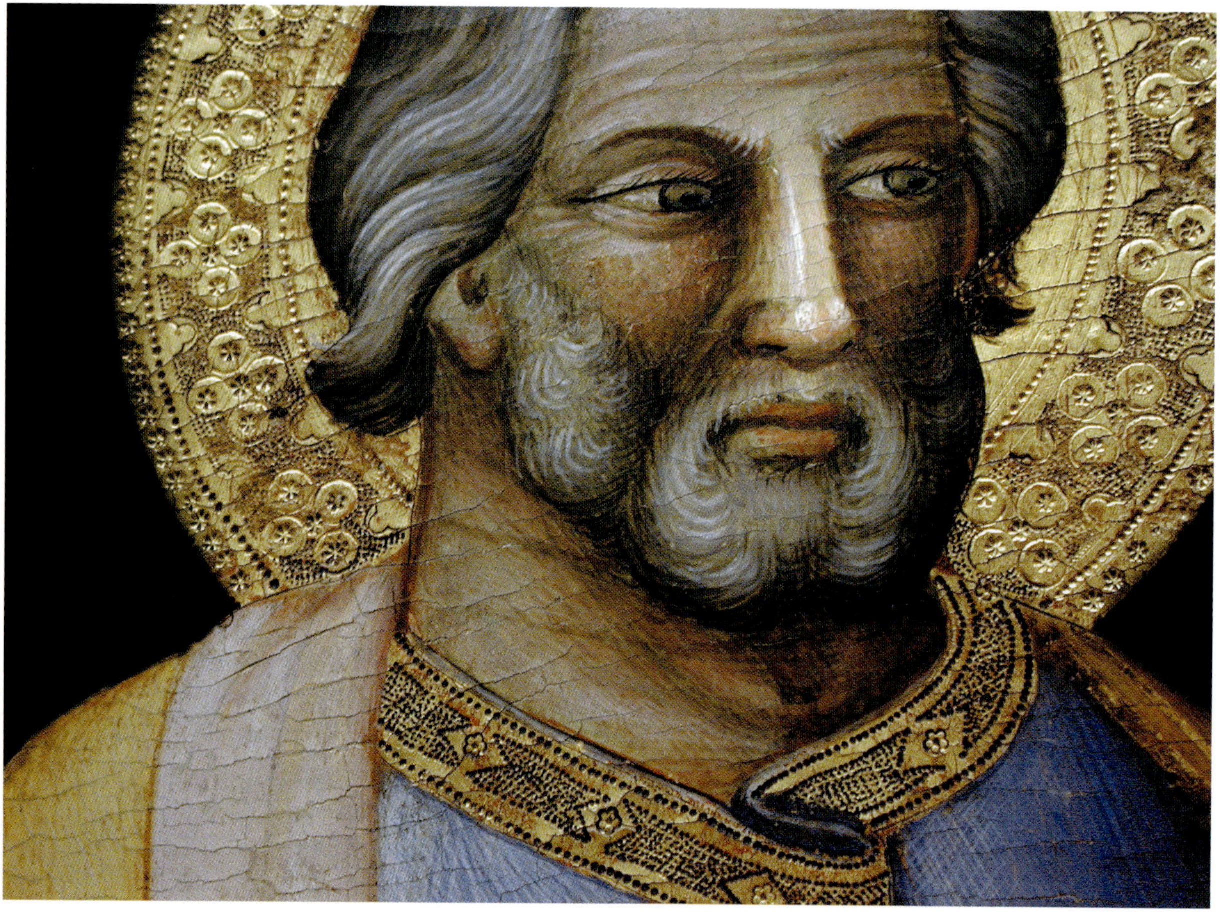

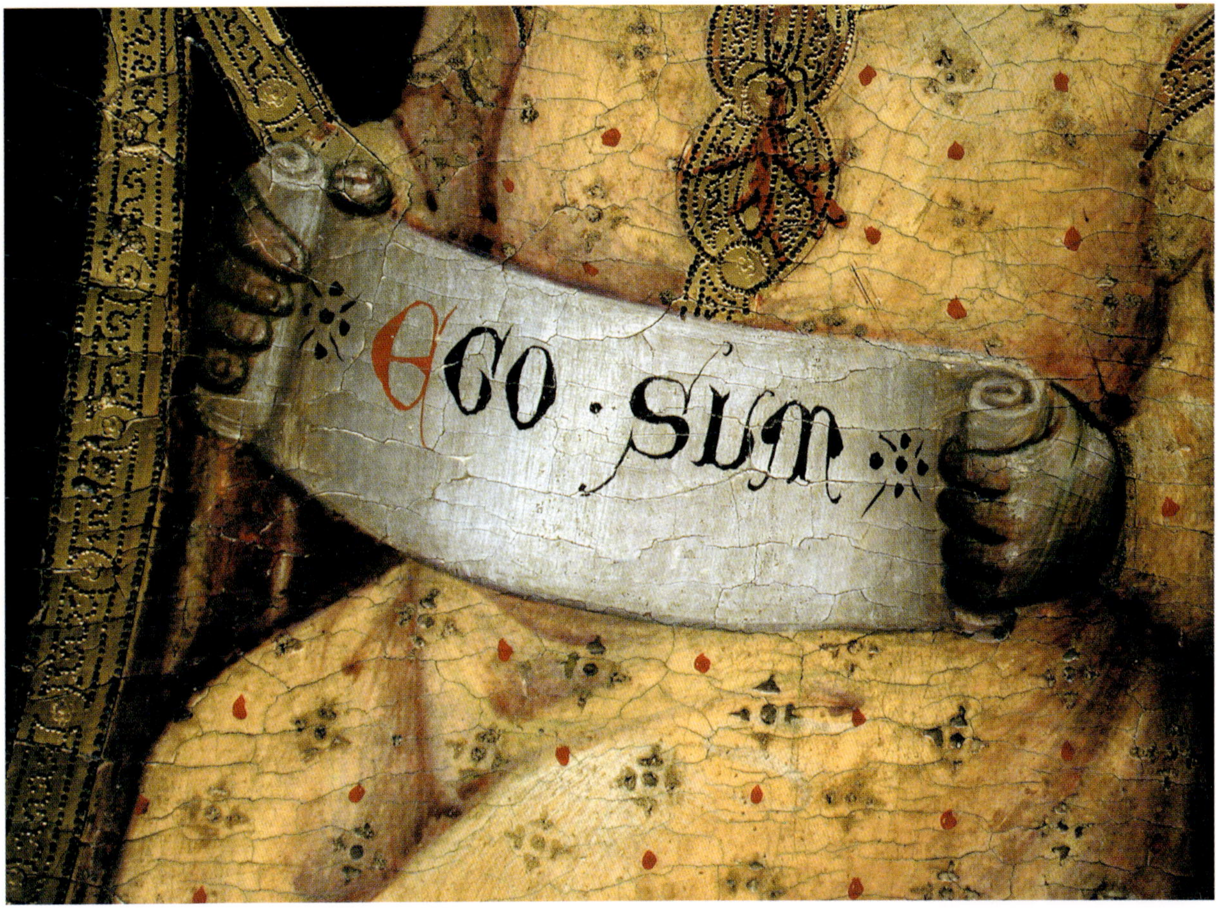
EGO · SUM

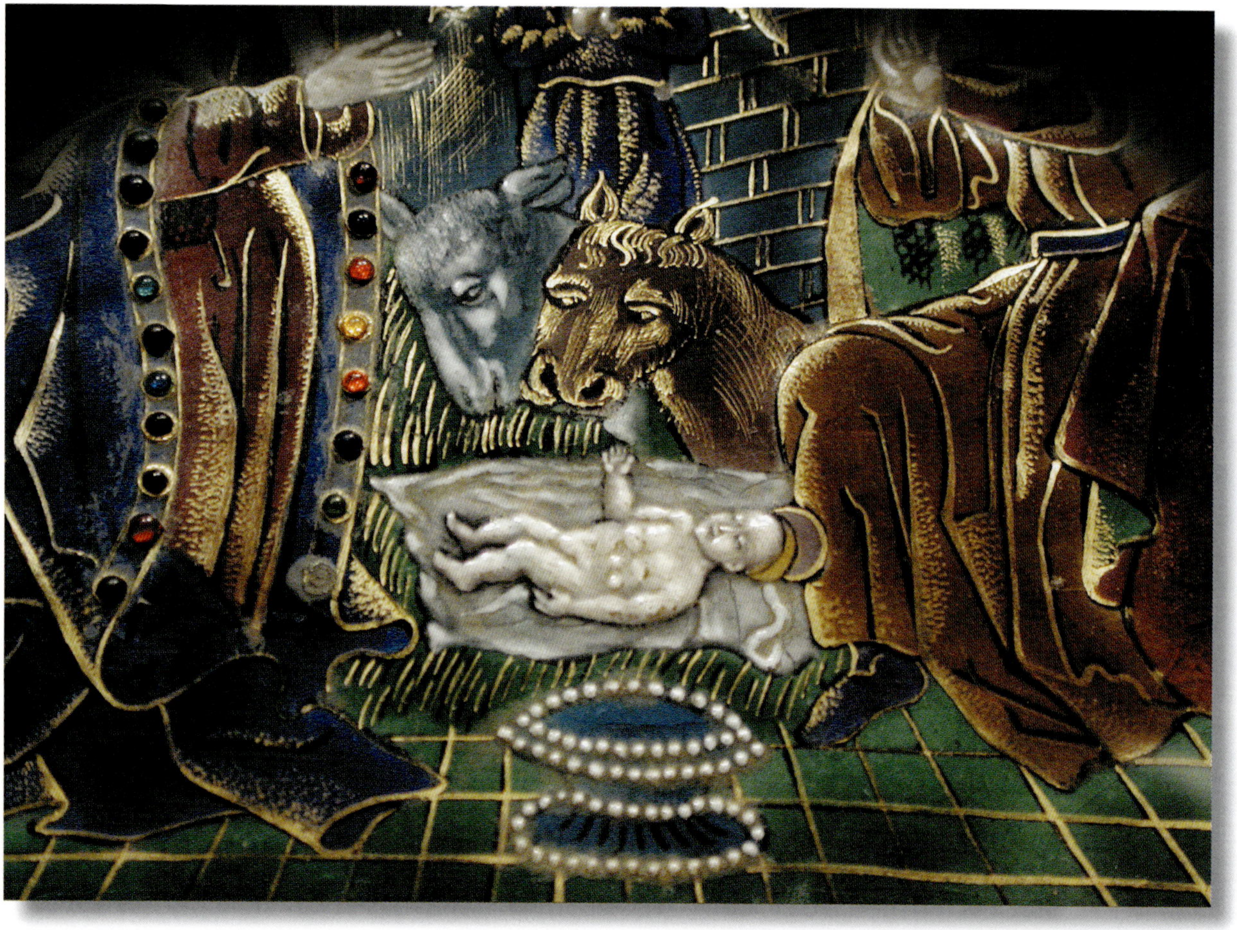

THE INDEX

Cover

M. W. Hopkins (attributed to)
American, 1789–1844

Pierrepont Edward Lacey (1832–after 1860) and His Dog, Gun, 1835–1836
American Painting
Oil on canvas
42 in. x 30 1/8 in. (106.68 cm x 76.52 cm)

Gift of Mr. and Mrs. Robert H. Dunn in memory of Ruth Hanford Munn and James Buell Munn, 78.189

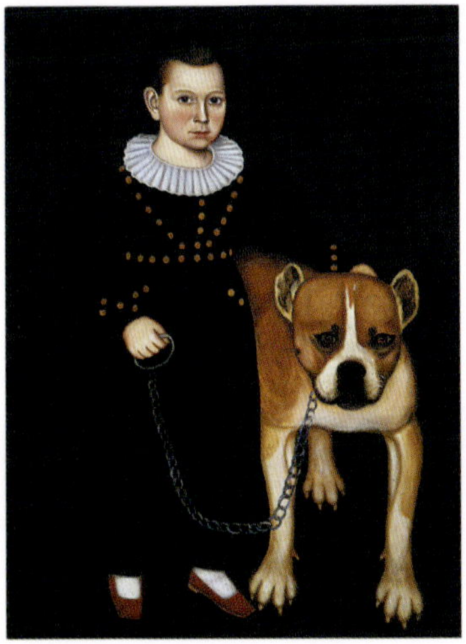

Page 9

Unknown, American

Optometrist's Trade Sign
Late 19th Century–early 20th Century
American Sculpture
Wood, iron and paint
17 3/4 in. x 30 1/2 in. (45.09 cm x 77.47 cm)

Given in honor of Isabel Herdle's 80th birthday by a group of her friends, 85.22

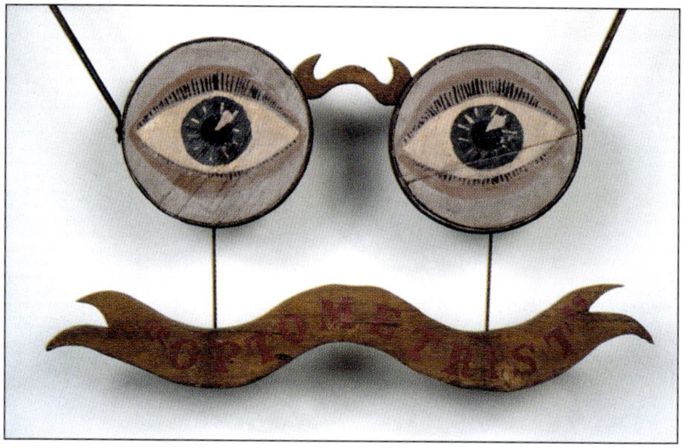

The MAG
Page 10

Frode Rambush

Zodiac Fresco, 1913
Fresco

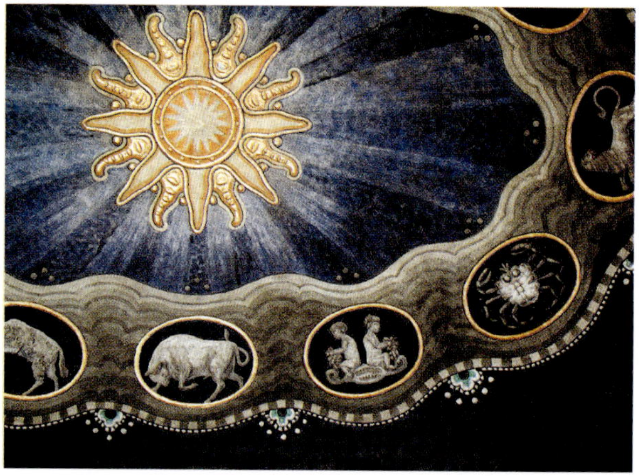

On Reading
Page 14

Ann Gennett Pixley Lacey
American, 1809 - 1841

Cross-Stitch Sampler, 1819
American Textiles
Silk thread on linen
10 1/4 in. x 10 3/4 in. (26.04 cm x 27.31 cm)

Gift of Mr. and Mrs. Robert Dunn, 78.191

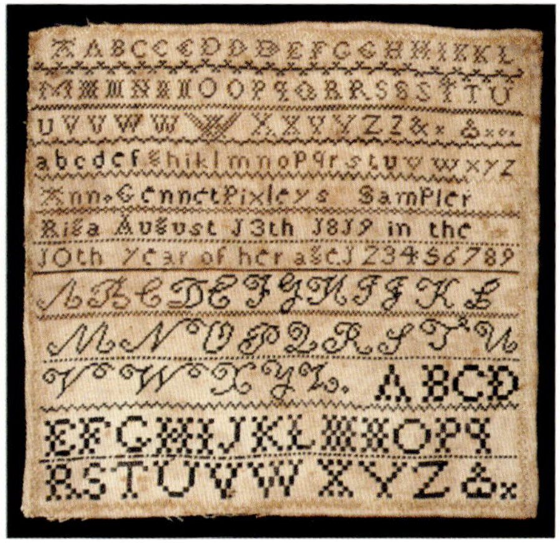

Pages 16 and 17

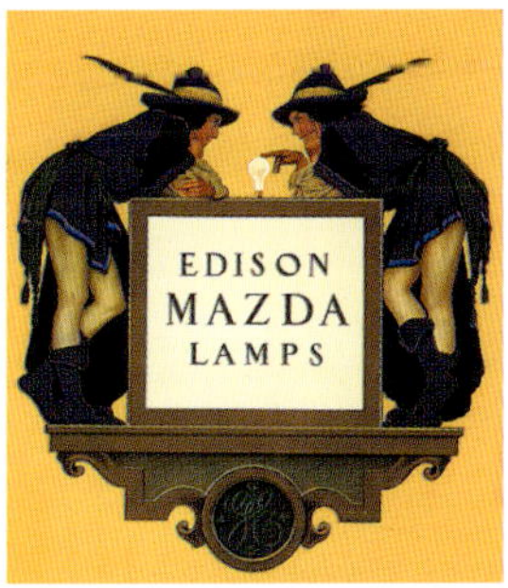

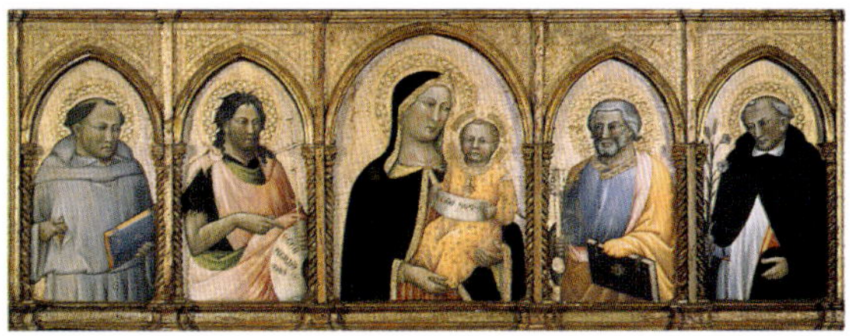

Maxfield Parrish
American, 1870–1966

Edison Mazda Lamp (Advertising Sign), after 1921
20th Century American Painting
Enamel on metal with wood
26 in. x 21 1/2 in. (66.04 cm x 54.61 cm)

Gift of Mr. and Mrs. Leo Kaplan, 70.45

Nardo di Cione (school of)
Italian, active 1343–d. 1365/1366

Madonna and Child with Saints Francis of Assisi, John the Baptist, Peter and Dominic
second half of the 14th century
Italian Painting
Tempera on panel
30 in. x 86 1/2 in. x 6 1/2 in. (76.2 cm x 219.71 cm x 16.51 cm)

Marion Stratton Gould Fund, 57.4

Pages 18 and 19

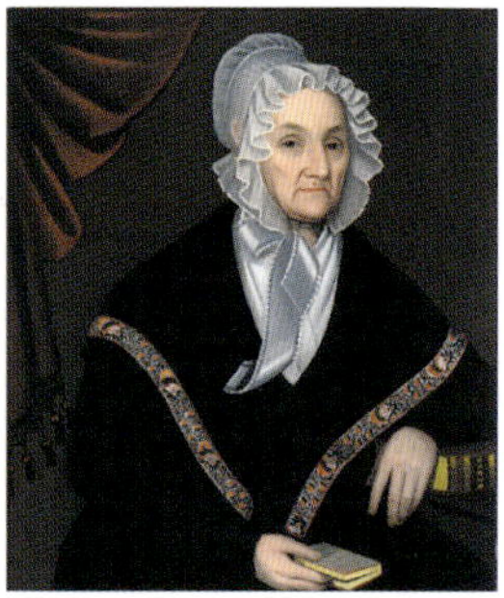

Ammi Phillips
American, 1788–1865

Old Woman with a Bible, circa 1834
American Painting
Oil on linen
33 1/2 in. x 28 in. (85.09 cm x 71.12 cm) (without frame)

Beatrice M. Padelford Trust, 84.22

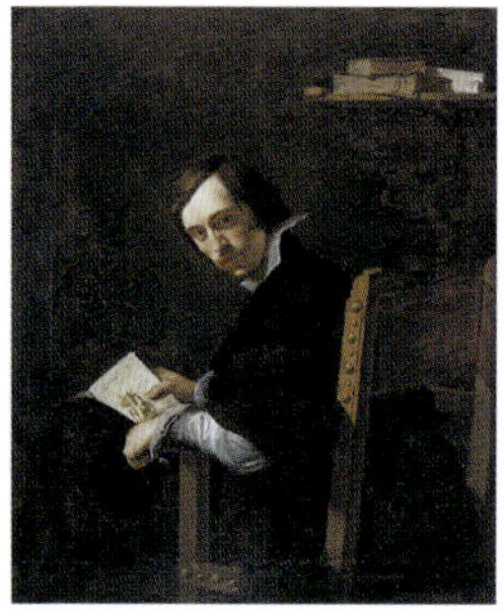

Pietro Paolini
Italian, 1603–1681/1682

Portrait of a Man Holding the Frontispiece to Dürer's "Small Passion", mid 1630s
Italian Painting
Oil on canvas
49 3/4 in. x 40 3/4 in. (126.37 cm x 103.51 cm)

Marion Stratton Gould Fund, 77.103

Pages 20 and 21

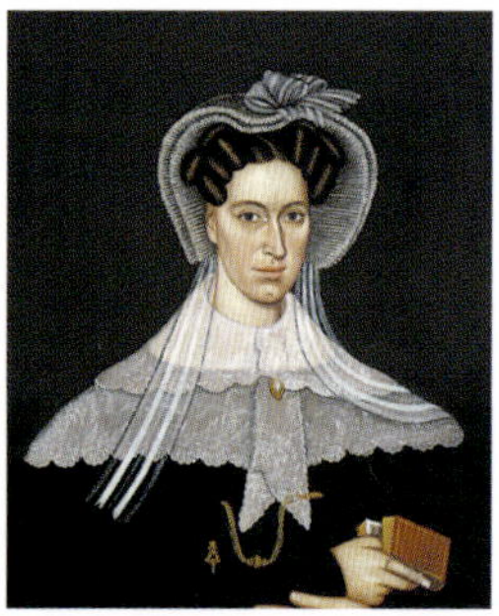

M. W. Hopkins (attributed to)
American, 1789–1844

Ann Gennett Pixley Lacey (1809–1841), 1835–1836
American Painting
Oil on canvas
30 in. x 25 in. (76.2 cm x 63.5 cm)

Gift of Mr. and Mrs. Robert H. Dunn in memory of Ruth Hanford Munn and James Buell Munn, 78.187

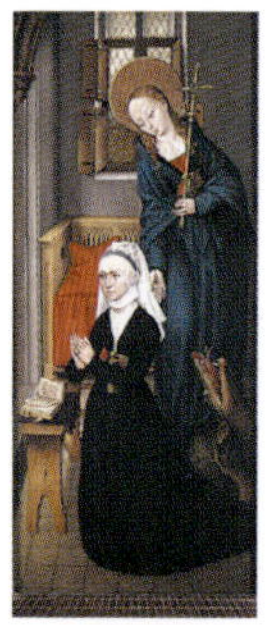

Vranke van der Stockt
Flemish, before 1420–1495

St. Margaret with Donor, circa 1444–1495
Flemish Painting
Oil on panel
18 1/8 in. x 7 7/8 in. (46.04 cm x 20 cm)

Marion Stratton Gould Fund, 44.15

Pages 22 and 23

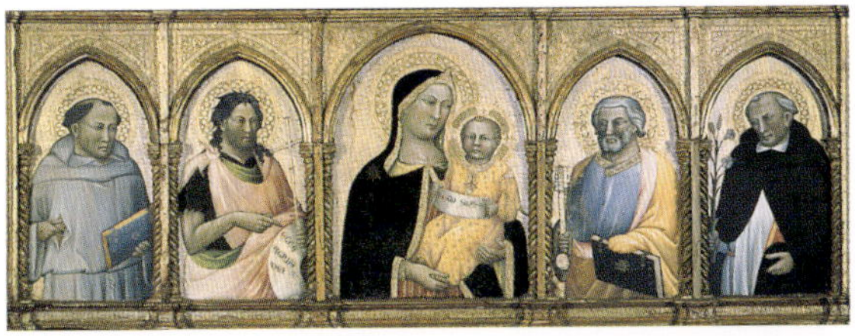

Nardo di Cione (school of)
Italian, active 1343–d. 1365/1366

Madonna and Child with Saints Francis of Assisi, John the Baptist, Peter and Dominic
second half of the 14th century
Italian Painting
Tempera on panel
30 in. x 86 1/2 in. x 6 1/2 in. (76.2 cm x 219.71 cm x 16.51 cm)

Marion Stratton Gould Fund, 57.4

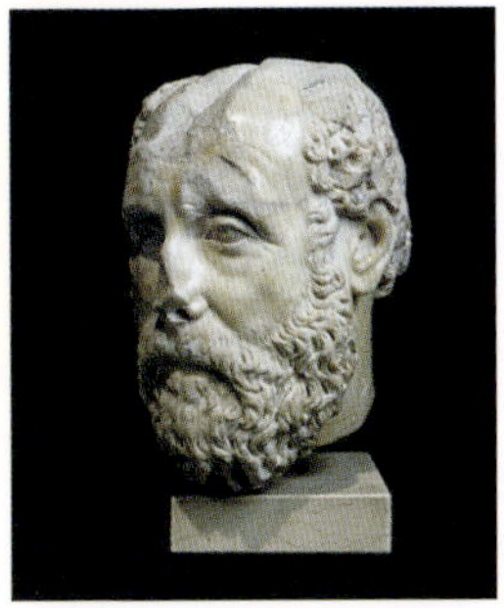

Unknown, Roman

Portrait Head of a Man with a Beard, 2nd century
Roman Sculpture
Marble
10 13/16 in. (27.43 cm)

R.T. Miller Fund, 46.39

Pages 24 and 25

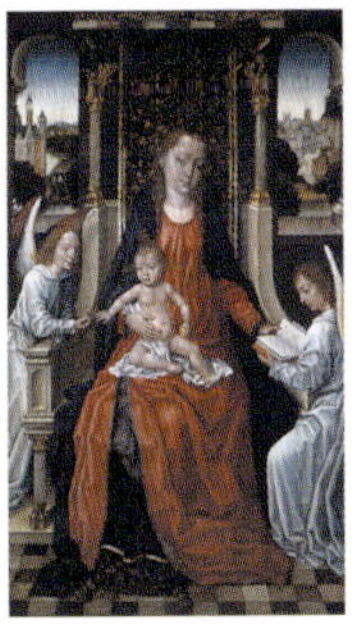

Master of the St. Ursula Legend
Flemish, active 1470–1495

Madonna and Child Enthroned with Angels
circa 1470–1495
Flemish Painting
Oil on panel
13 1/2 in. x 24 1/4 in. (34.29 cm x 61.6 cm)

Marion Stratton Gould Fund, 48.11

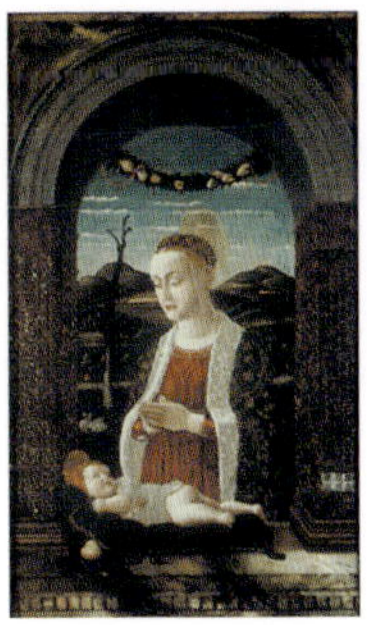

Francesco Benaglio
Italian, circa 1432–circa 1492

Madonna and Child, 1432–1492
Italian Painting
Oil on panel
26 3/8 in. x 16 3/8 in. (66.99 cm x 41.59 cm)

Marion Stratton Gould Fund, 64.21

Pages 26 and 27

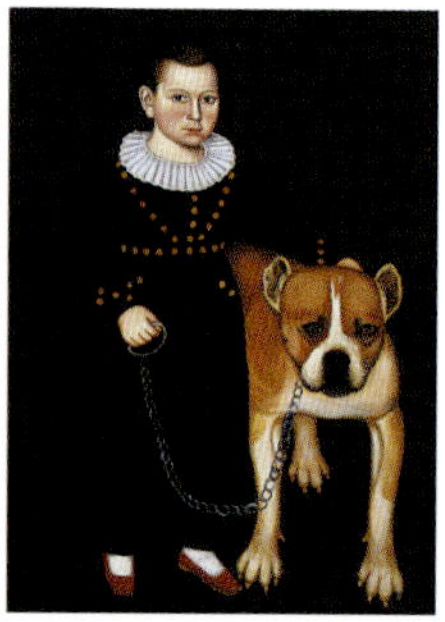

M. W. Hopkins (attributed to)
American, 1789–1844

Pierrepont Edward Lacey (1832–after 1860) and His Dog, Gun, 1835–1836
American Painting
Oil on canvas
42 in. x 30 1/8 in. (106.68 cm x 76.52 cm)

Gift of Mr. and Mrs. Robert H. Dunn in memory of Ruth Hanford Munn and James Buell Munn, 78.189

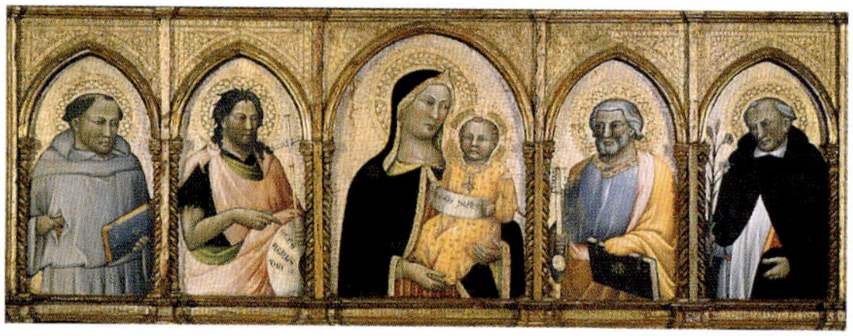

Nardo di Cione (school of)
Italian, active 1343–d. 1365/1366

Madonna and Child with Saints Francis of Assisi, John the Baptist, Peter and Dominic
second half of the 14th century
Italian Painting
Tempera on panel
30 in. x 86 1/2 in. x 6 1/2 in. (76.2 cm x 219.71 cm x 16.51 cm)

Marion Stratton Gould Fund, 57.4

On Men and Women
Page 28

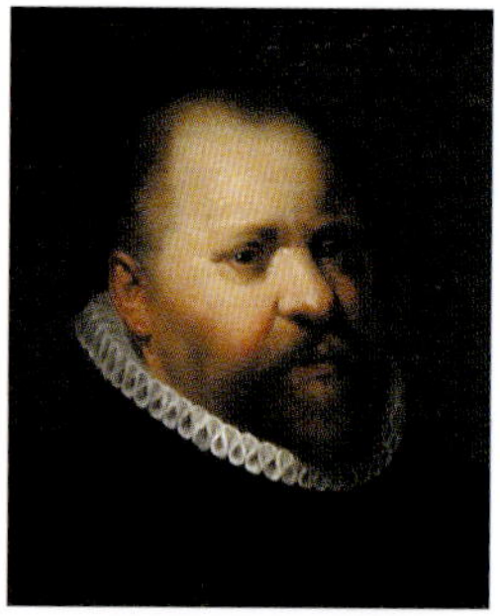

Pieter Jansz. Pourbus
Flemish, 1510–1584

Man in a Ruffled Collar
16th Century Flemish Painting
Oil on canvas
16 3/4 in. x 13 3/4 in. (42.55 cm x 34.93 cm)

Bequest of Clarence Clift, 79.69

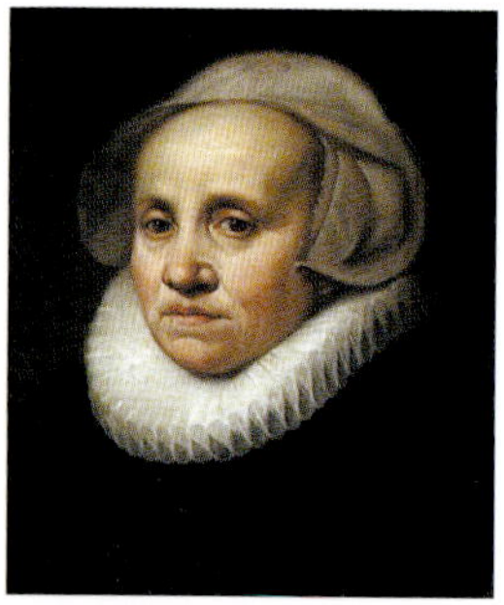

Pieter Jansz. Pourbus
Flemish, 1510–1584

Woman in a Ruffled Collar
16th Century Flemish Painting
Oil on canvas
16 3/4 in. x 13 3/4 in. (42.55 cm x 34.93 cm)

Bequest of Clarence Clift, 79.70

Page 31

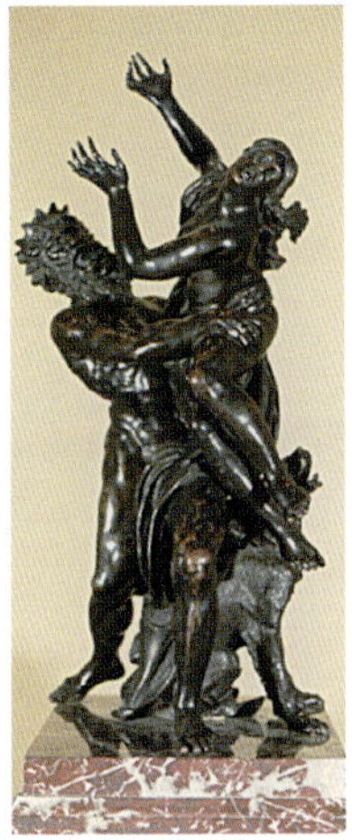

Giovanni Lorenzo Bernini (after)
Italian, 1598 - 1680

The Rape of Proserpine, 17th century
Italian Sculpture
Bronze
32 in. (81.28 cm) (overall)

Marion Stratton Gould Fund, 68.2

Pages 32 and 33

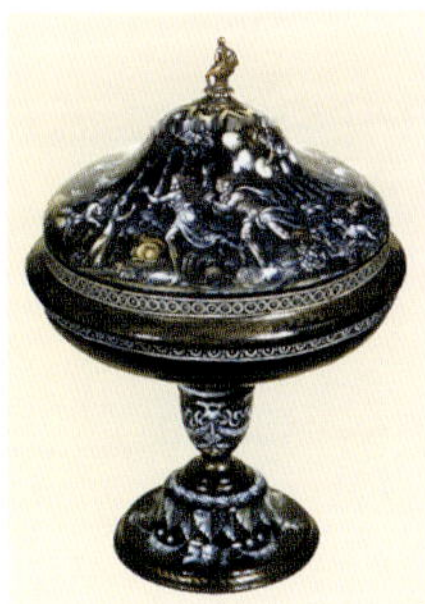

Jean de Court (workshop of)
active 1572–1585

Covered Tazza with Scenes from Genesis
second half of the 16th century
French Enamels
Enamel
11 in. x 7 3/8 in. (27.94 cm x 18.73 cm)

Buswell-Hochstetter Bequest, 55.136

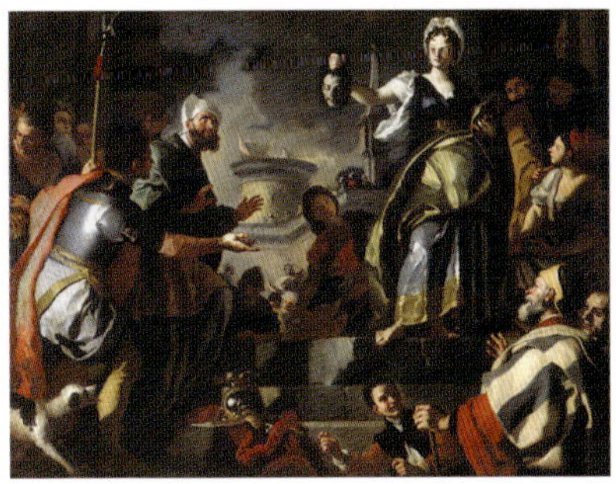

Francesco Solimena
Italian, 1657–1747

The Triumph of Judith, circa 1725–1730
Italian Painting
Oil on canvas
38 3/4 in. x 49 1/4 in. (98.43 cm x 125.1 cm) (without frame)

Gift of Dr. and Mrs. James V. Aquavella, 77.109

Pages 34 and 35

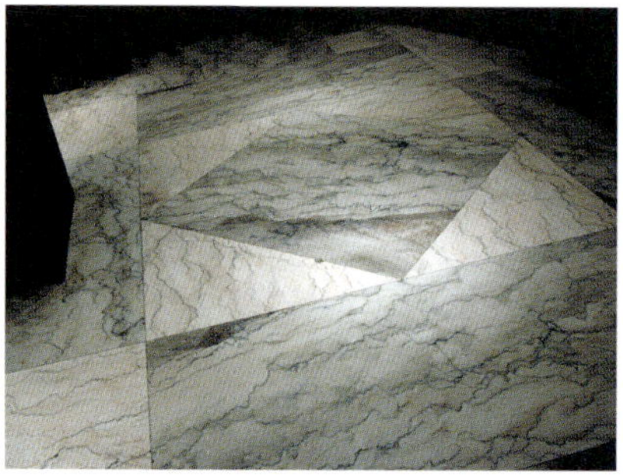

Floor of Foyer
Second floor of the original building

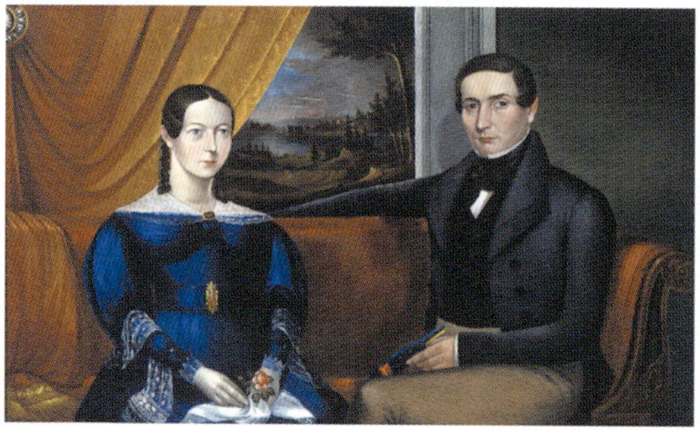

M. M. Manchester
American, active circa 1840

Judge and Mrs. Arthur Yates, circa 1840
American Painting
Oil on canvas
36 in. x 58 3/4 in. (91.44 cm x 149.23 cm) (without frame)

Gallery purchase, 41.30

Pages 36 and 37

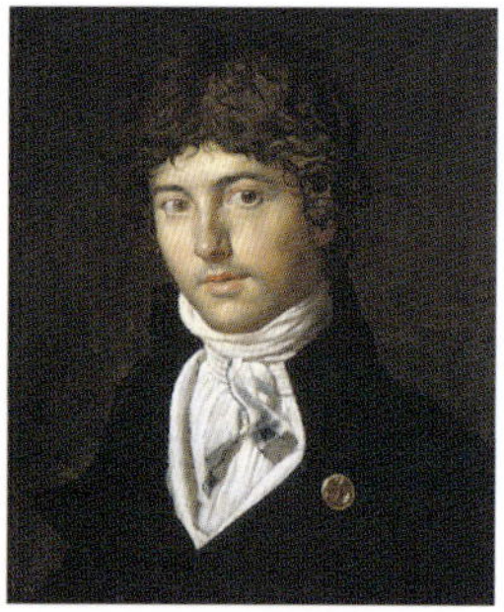

Jean-August-Dominique Ingres
French, 1780–1867

Portrait of Pierre-François Bernier, 1800
French Painting
Oil on paper mounted on canvas
18 1/4 in. x 15 in. (46.36 cm x 38.1 cm)

Marion Stratton Gould Fund, 55.176

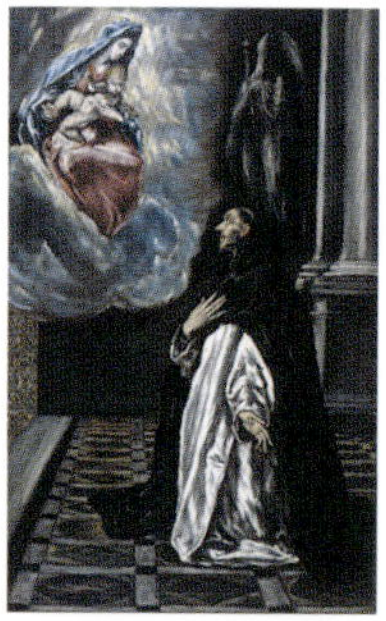

Domenikos Theotocopoulos
Spanish, circa 1541–1614

The Apparition of the Virgin to St. Hyacinth,
circa 1605–1610
Spanish Painting
Oil on canvas
39 3/8 in. x 24 3/8 in. (100.01 cm x 61.91 cm)

Marion Stratton Gould Fund, 38.28

Pages 38 and 39

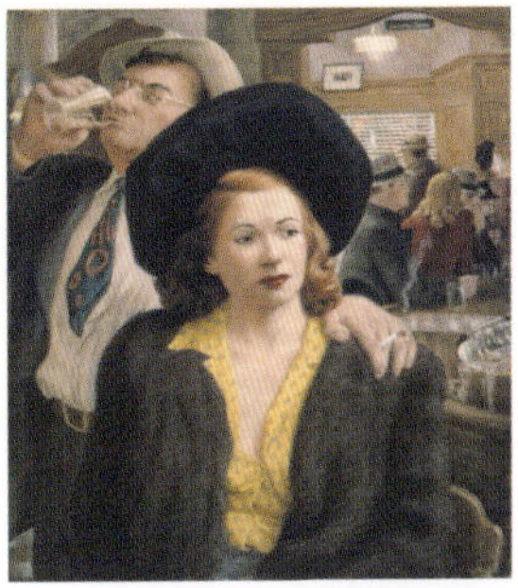

Douglas Warner Gorsline
American, 1913–1985

Bar Scene, 1942
American Painting
Oil on canvas
29 1/2 in. x 25 1/4 in. (74.93 cm x 64.14 cm)

Art Patrons' Purchase Award,1942
Rochester-Finger Lakes Exhibition, 42.19
Permission granted by Marie Gorsline

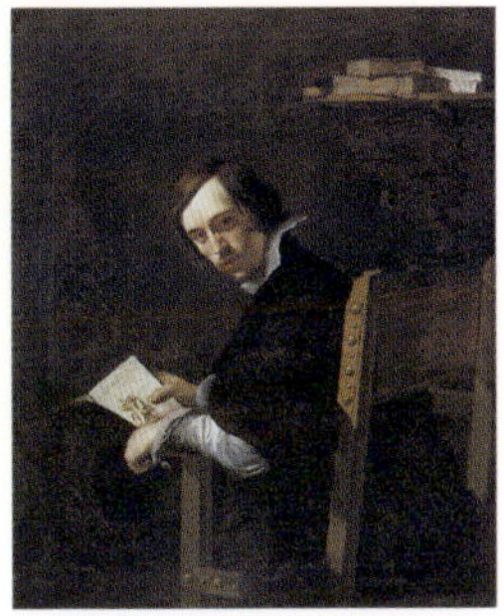

Pietro Paolini
Italian, 1603–1681/1682

Portrait of a Man Holding the Frontispiece to Dürer's "Small Passion", mid 1630s
Italian Painting
Oil on canvas
49 3/4 in. x 40 3/4 in. (126.37 cm x 103.51 cm)

Marion Stratton Gould Fund, 77.103

Pages 40 and 41

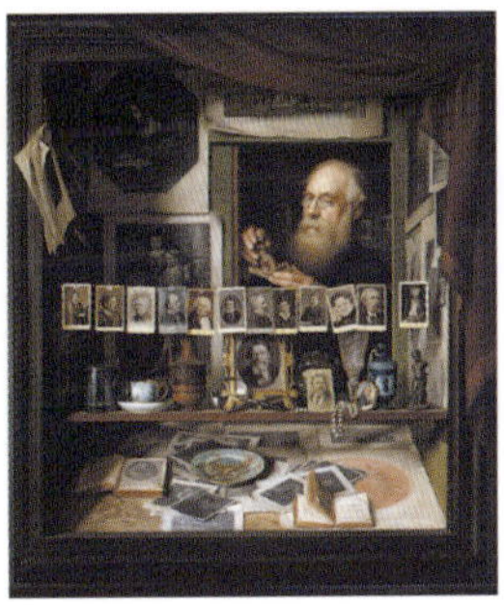

Walter Goodman
British, 1838–after 1906

The Printseller, 1882–1884
British Painting
Oil on canvas
52 1/4 in. x 44 3/4 in. (132.72 cm x 113.67 cm)

Marion Stratton Gould Fund, 98.75

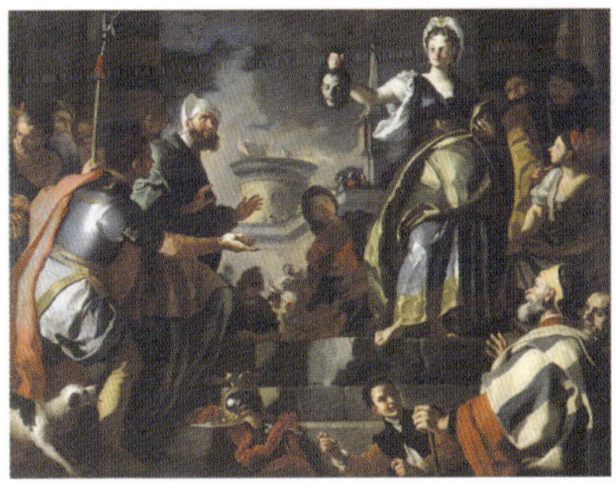

Francesco Solimena
Italian, 1657–1747

The Triumph of Judith, circa 1725–1730
Italian Painting
Oil on canvas
38 3/4 in. x 49 1/4 in. (98.43 cm x 125.1 cm) (without frame)

Gift of Dr. and Mrs. James V. Aquavella, 77.109

Pages 42 and 43

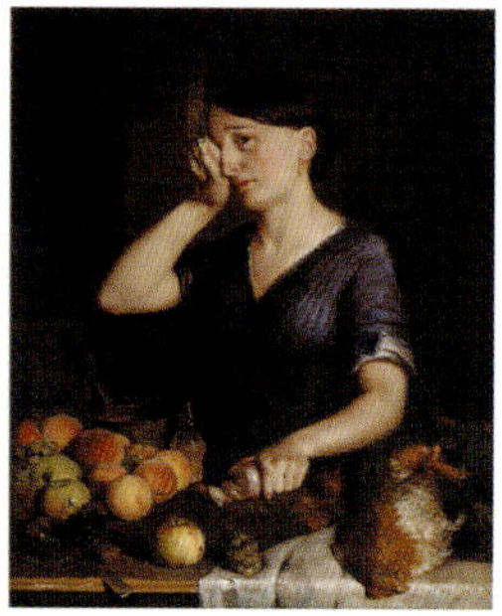

Lilly Martin Spencer
American, 1822–1902

Peeling Onions, circa 1852
American Painting
Oil on canvas
36 in. x 29 in. (91.44 cm x 73.66 cm)

Gift of the Women's Council in celebration of the 75th anniversary of the Memorial Art Gallery, 88.6

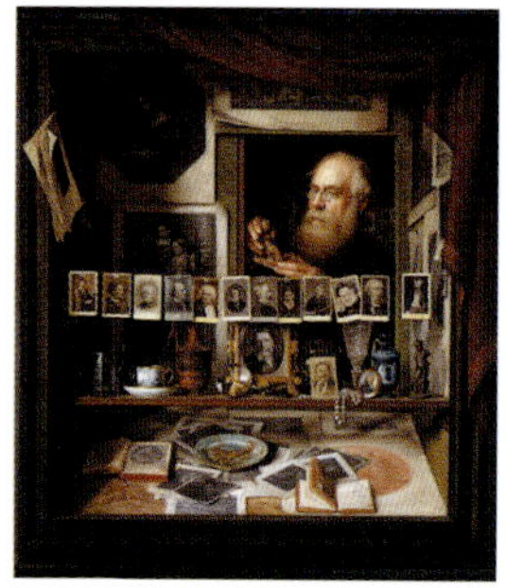

Walter Goodman
British, 1838–after 1906

The Printseller, 1882–1884
British Painting
Oil on canvas
52 1/4 in. x 44 3/4 in. (132.72 cm x 113.67 cm)

Marion Stratton Gould Fund, 98.75

Pages 44 and 45

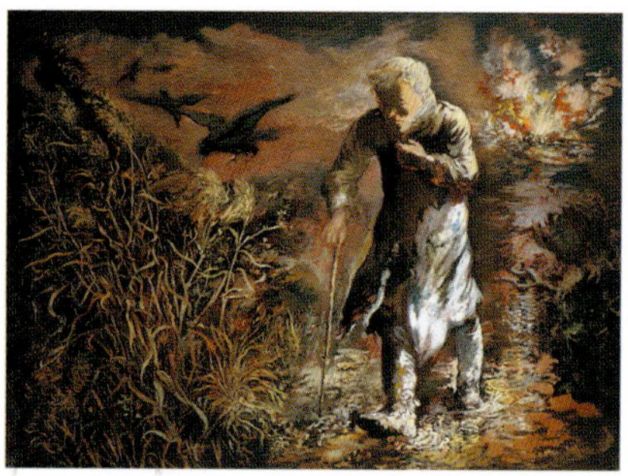

George Grosz
American, 1893–1959

The Wanderer, 1943
American Painting
Oil on canvas
30 in. x 40 in. (76.2 cm x 101.6 cm)

Marion Stratton Gould Fund, 51.6

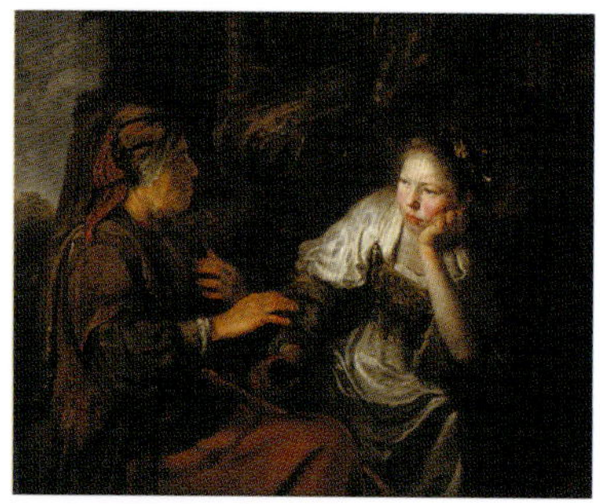

Govaert Flinck
Dutch, 1615–1660

Vertumnus and Pomona, circa 1640
Dutch Painting
Oil on canvas
38 1/4 in. x 45 1/4 in. (97.16 cm x 114.94 cm)

Gift of Dr. and Mrs. Frank W. Lovejoy, Jr., 83.10

Pages 46 and 47

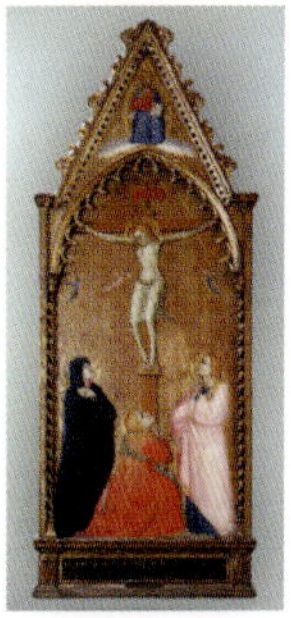

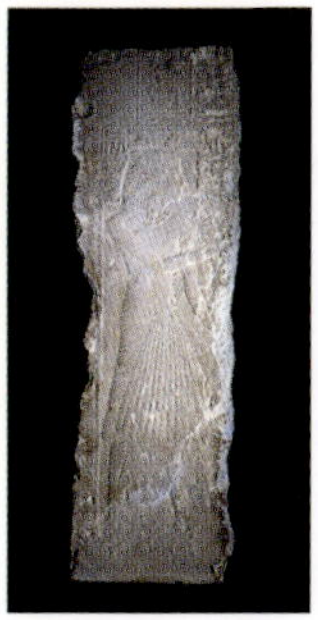

Giovanni del Biondo
Italian, active 1356–d. 1398

Crucifixion with God the Father, circa 1375–1380
Italian Painting
Tempera on panel
68 3/16 in. x 25 7/8 in. x 4 3/8 in.
(173.2 cm x 65.72 cm x 11.11 cm)

Marion Stratton Gould Fund, 51.26

Unknown Egyptian, from Saqqara, New Kingdom, 18th Dynasty, late 14th century B.C.E.

Standing Figure from the Tomb of Maya
Limestone
32 in. x 10 in. (81.3 cm x 25.4 cm)

R.T. Miller Fund, 42.55

Pages 48 and 49

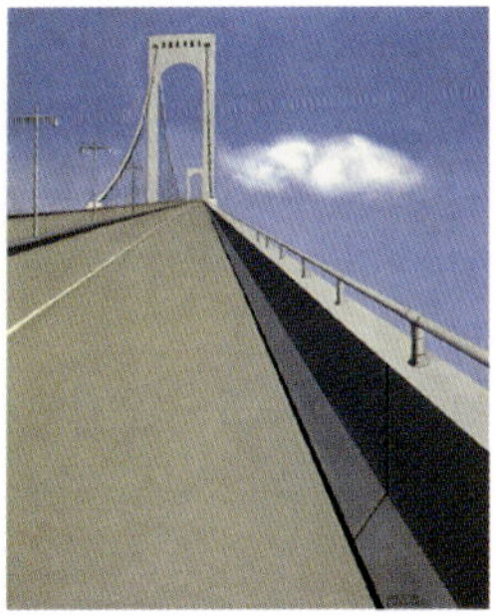

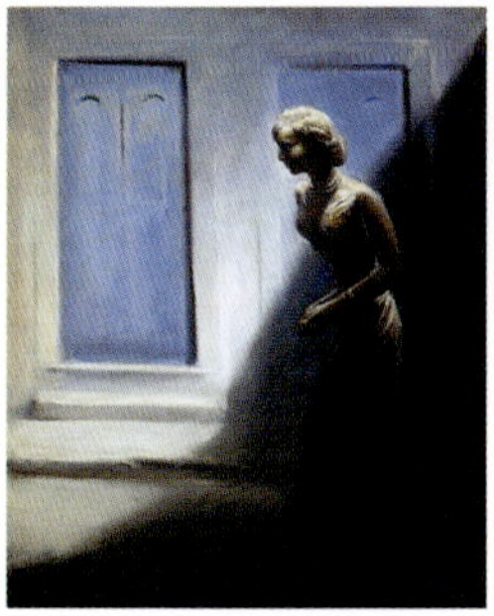

Ralston Crawford
American, 1906–1978

Whitestone Bridge, 1939
American Painting
Oil on canvas
40 1/4 in. x 32 in. (102.24 cm x 81.28 cm) (without frame)

Marion Stratton Gould Fund, 51.2
© Ralston Crawford, 1939

Guy Pène du Bois
American, 1884–1958

Jane, circa 1946
American Painting
Oil on canvas
30 in. x 24 in. (76.2 cm x 60.96 cm)

Gift of Thomas and Marion Hawks by exchange, 98.36
Courtesy James Graham & Sons, Inc. New York and the estate of Yvonne Pène du Bois McKenney.

Pages 50 and 51

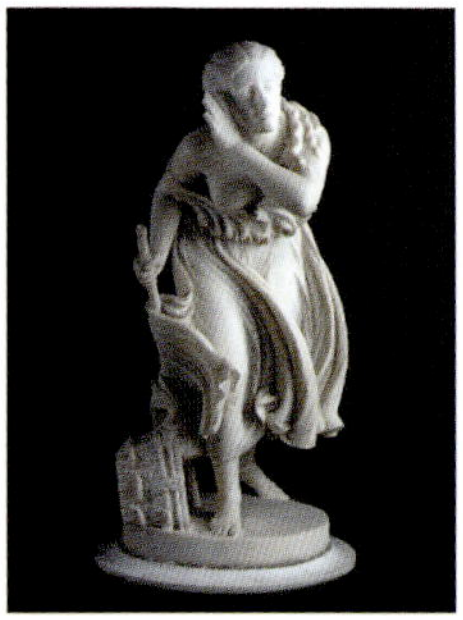

Randolph Rogers
American, 1825–1892

Nydia, the Blind Flower Girl of Pompeii, after 1855
American Sculpture
Marble
36 in. x 17 11/16 in. x 25 in. (91.5 cm x 45 cm x 63.5 cm) (overall)

Marion Stratton Gould Fund, 93.24

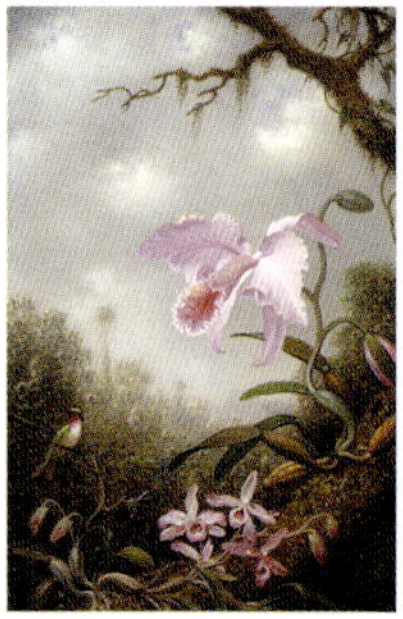

Martin Johnson Heade
American, 1819–1904

Hummingbird with Cattleya and Dendrobium Orchids, circa 1890
American Painting
Oil on canvas
22 1/4 in. x 14 3/8 in. (56.52 cm x 36.51 cm)

Harris K. Prior Memorial Fund, 76.3

Pages 52 and 53

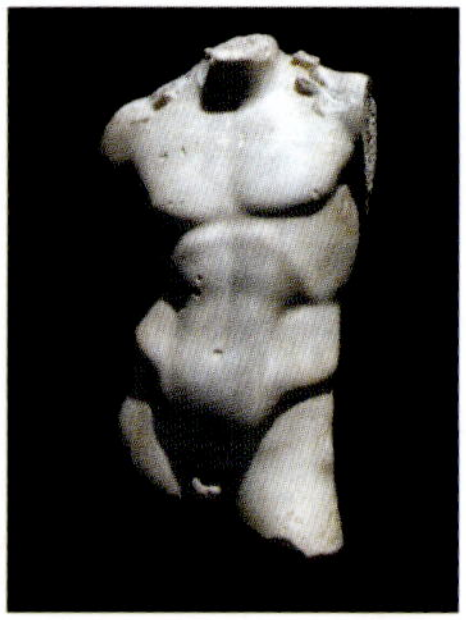

Unknown, Roman

Torso of a Young Man, 1st Century BCE
Roman Sculpture
Marble
25 in. x 14 in. (63.5 cm x 35.56 cm)

Ocumpaugh, Babcock, Dewey and Montgomery Funds, 36.53

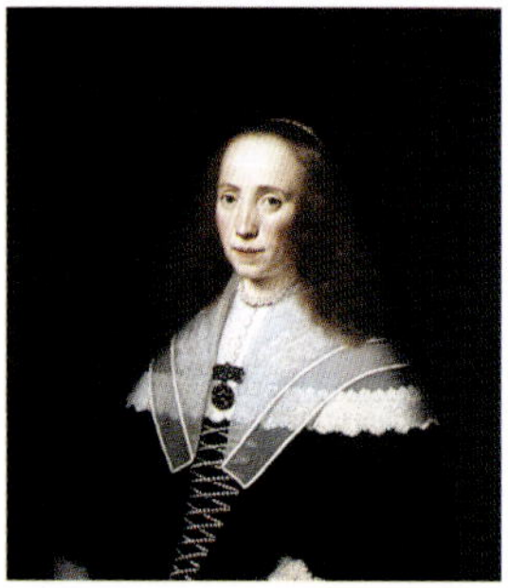

Dirck van Santvoort
Dutch, 1610–1680

Portrait of Eva Bicker, 1640
Dutch Painting
Oil on panel
27 in. x 23 1/2 in. (68.58 cm x 59.69 cm)

Buswell-Hochstetter Bequest, 55.72

On the Land
Page 54

Attributed to Augustin Pajou
French, 1730–1809

Bust of a Man
Terracotta

Marion Stratton Gould Fund, 68.3

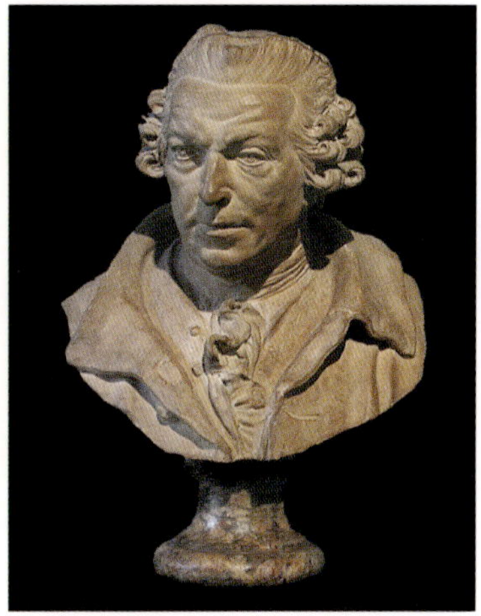

Page 57

Unknown, Spanish

Scene from the Life of St. Andrew, 16th century
Spanish Painting
Oil on panel
48 3/4 in. x 30 1/2 in. (123.83 cm x 77.47 cm) (overall)

Gift of Adolph Struber, 55.22

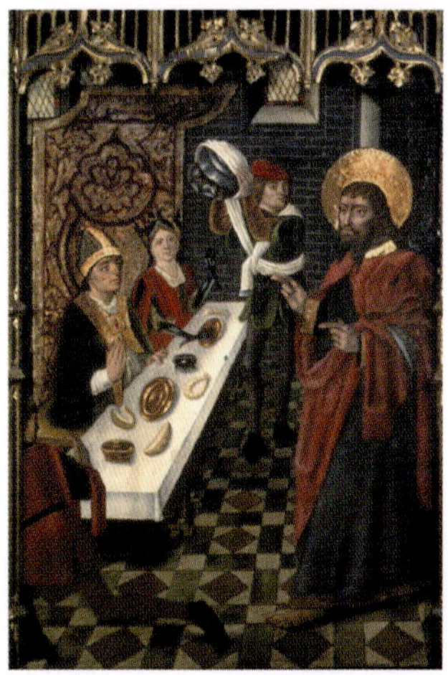

Pages 58 and 59

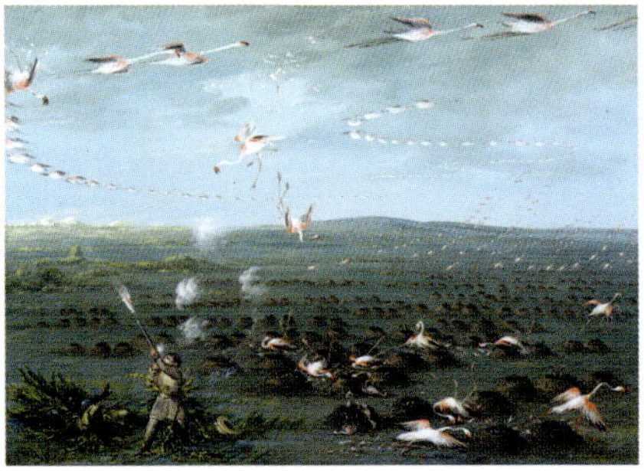

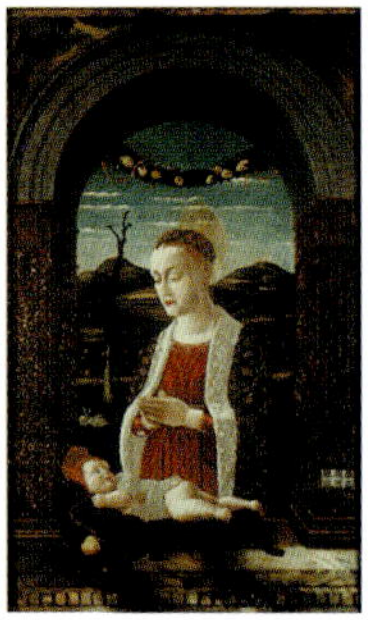

George Catlin
American, 1796–1872

Shooting Flamingoes, 1857
American Painting
Oil on canvas
19 in. x 26 1/2 in. (48.26 cm x 67.31 cm)

Marion Stratton Gould Fund, 41.25

Francesco Benaglio
Italian, circa 1432–circa 1492

Madonna and Child, 1432–1492
Italian Painting
Oil on panel
26 3/8 in. x 16 3/8 in. (66.99 cm x 41.59 cm)

Marion Stratton Gould Fund, 64.21

Pages 60 and 61

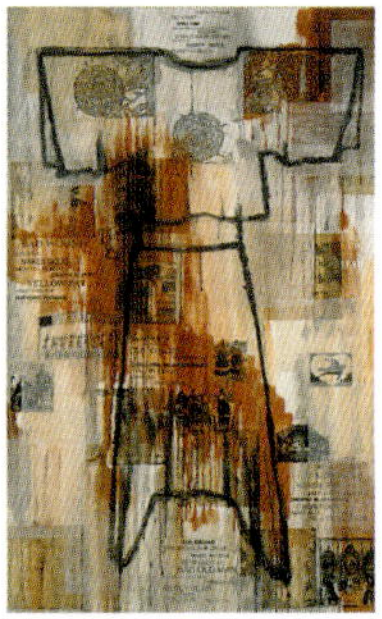

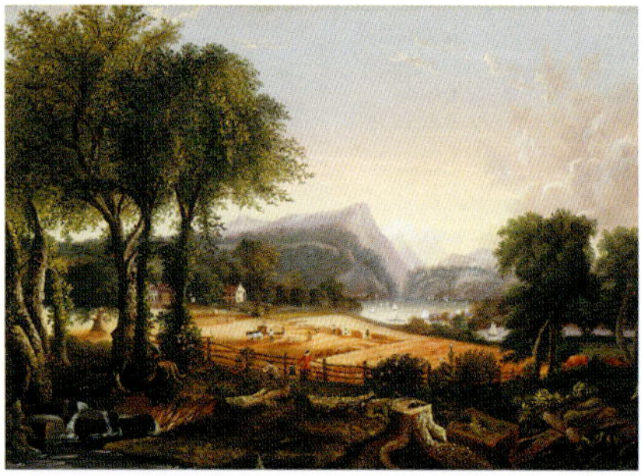

Jaune Quick-to-See Smith
American, 1940 –

Famous Names, 1998
American Painting
Oil, acrylic, collaged photographs and mixed media on canvas
80 in. x 50 in. (203.2 cm x 127 cm) (without frame)

Gift of Thomas and Marion Hawks by exchange, 98.39

Unknown, American

American Harvesting, after a painting by Jasper Cropsey, after 1851
American Painting
Oil on canvas
32 1/2 in. x 44 1/4 in. (82.55 cm x 112.4 cm)

Anonymous gift, 77.196

Pages 62 and 63

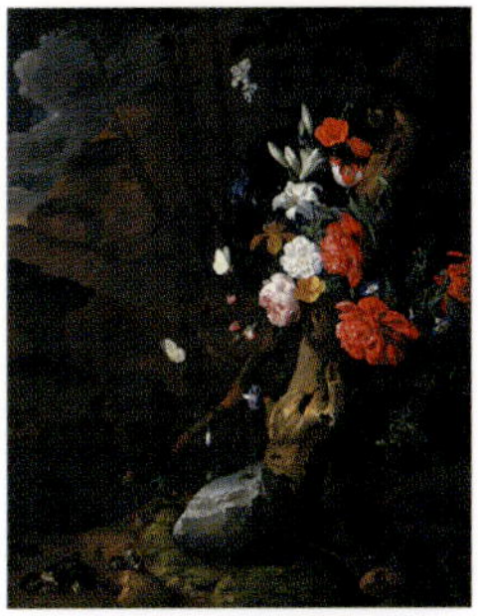

Rachel Ruysch
Dutch, 1664/1665–1750

Floral Still Life, 1686
Dutch Painting
Oil on canvas
45 1/8 in. x 34 3/8 in. (114.62 cm x 87.31 cm) (without frame)

Acquired with contributions made in memory of Brenda Rowntree by her friends, through the Acquisition Fund of the Women's Council, and the Marion Stratton Gould Fund, 82.9

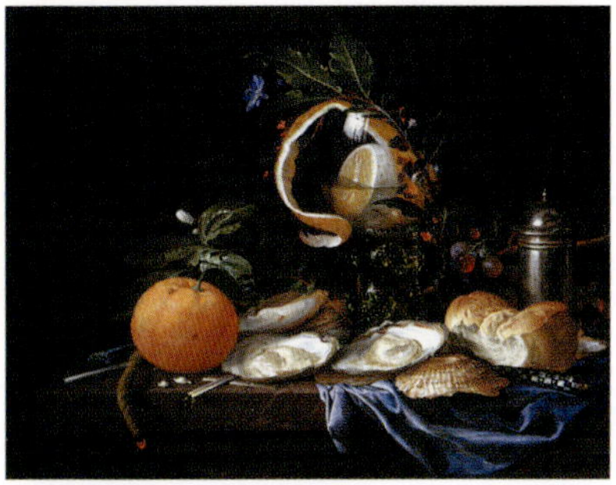

Jan Davidsz. de Heem
Dutch, 1606–circa 1684

Still Life, circa 1645
Dutch Painting
Oil on panel
14 1/2 in. x 18 in. (36.83 cm x 45.72 cm) (without frame)

Marion Stratton Gould Fund, 49.63

Pages 64 and 65

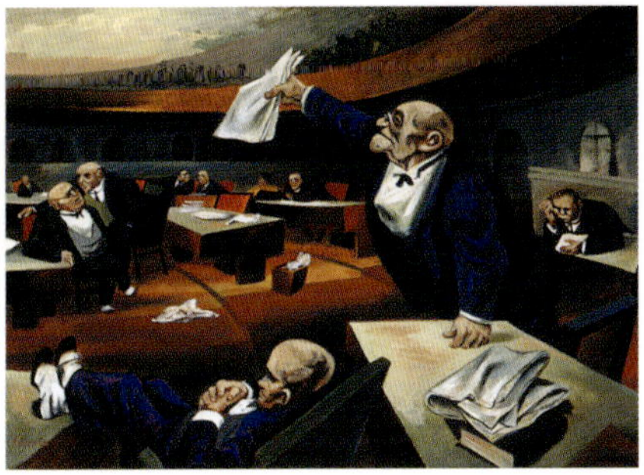

William Gropper
American, 1897–1977

The Opposition, 1942
American Painting
Oil on canvas
28 in. x 38 in. (71.12 cm x 96.52 cm)

Marion Stratton Gould Fund, 51.5
Reproduced courtesy of ACA Galleries, New York, NY

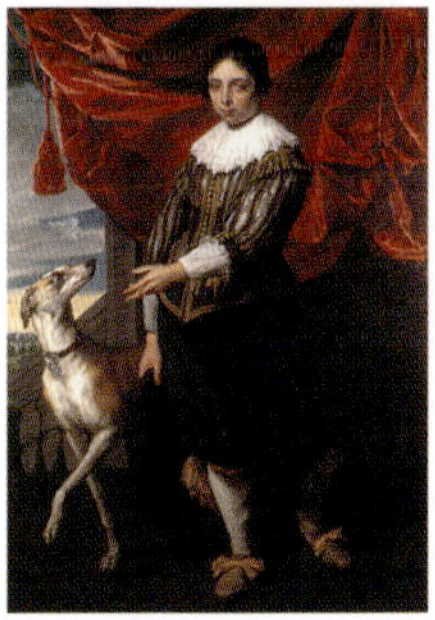

Cornelis de Vos
Flemish, 1584–1651

Young Man with a Dog, 1600–1649
Flemish Painting
Oil on canvas
57 in. x 39 1/2 in. (144.78 cm x 100.33 cm)

Bertha Buswell Bequest, 55.83

Pages 66 and 67

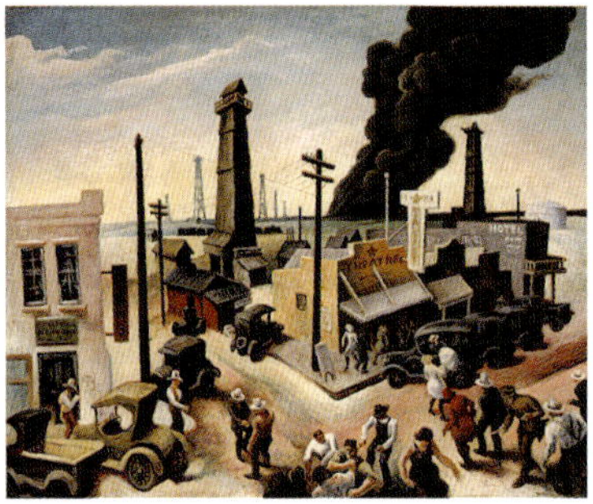

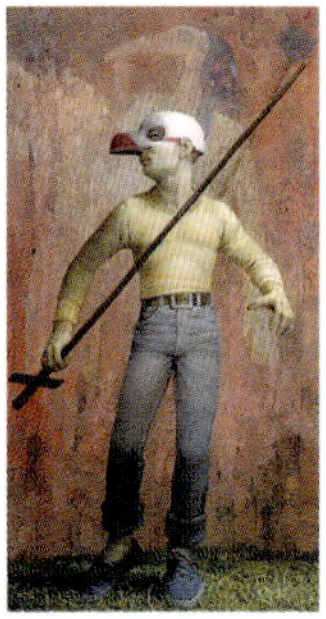

Thomas Hart Benton
American, 1889–1975

Boomtown, 1927–1928
American Painting
Oil on canvas
46 1/8 in. x 54 1/4 in. (117.16 cm x 137.8 cm) (without frame)

Marion Stratton Gould Fund, 51.1

Robert Vickrey
American, 1926–

Halloween Mask, 1953
American Painting
Egg tempera on masonite panel
48 in. x 24 1/2 in. (121.92 cm x 62.23 cm)

Gift of Earl W. Kage, 79.60

Pages 68 and 69

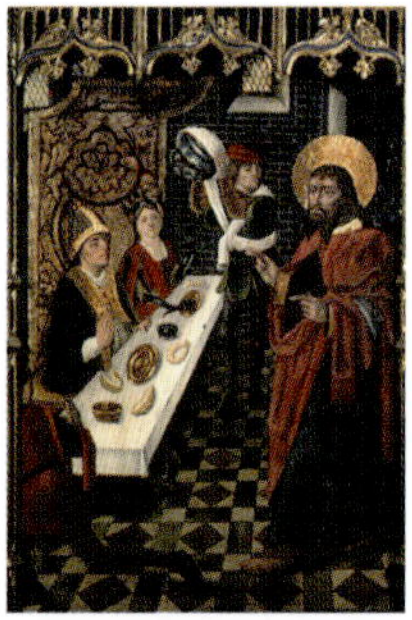

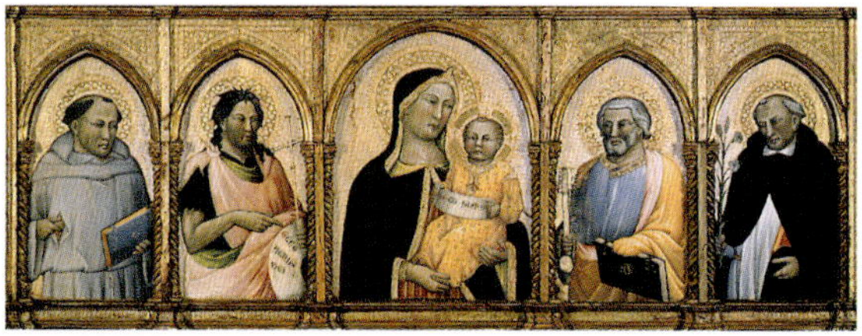

Unknown, Spanish

Scene from the Life of St. Andrew, 16th century
Spanish Painting
Oil on panel
48 3/4 in. x 30 1/2 in. (123.83 cm x 77.47 cm) (overall)

Gift of Adolph Struber, 55.22

Nardo di Cione (school of)
Italian, active 1343–d. 1365/1366

Madonna and Child with Saints Francis of Assisi, John the Baptist, Peter and Dominic
second half of the 14th century
Italian Painting
Tempera on panel
30 in. x 86 1/2 in. x 6 1/2 in. (76.2 cm x 219.71 cm x 16.51 cm)

Marion Stratton Gould Fund, 57.4

Meliora
Page 70

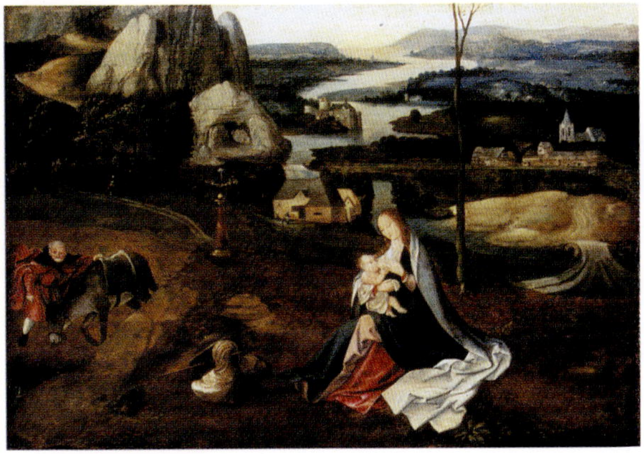

Follower of Joachim Patinir
Flemish

The Rest on the Flight into Egypt, circa 1520–1530
Flemish Painting
Oil on wood panel transferred to masonite
22 15/16 in. x 32 7/16 in. (58.3 cm x 82.4 cm)

Anonymous gift, 94.23

Pages 72 and 73

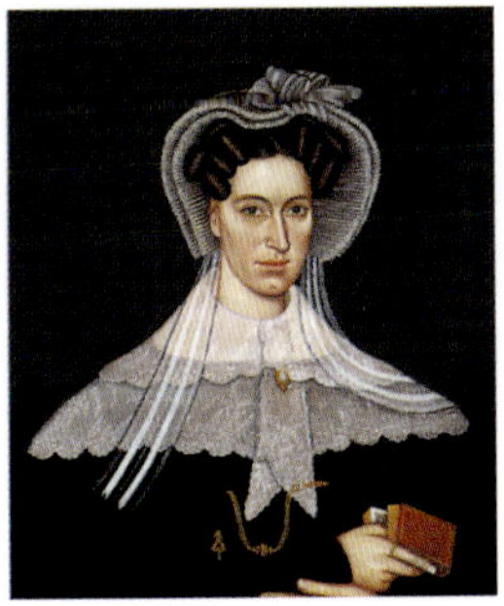

M. W. Hopkins (attributed to)
American, 1789–1844

Ann Gennett Pixley Lacey (1809–1841), 1835–1836
American Painting
Oil on canvas
30 in. x 25 in. (76.2 cm x 63.5 cm)

Gift of Mr. and Mrs. Robert H. Dunn in memory of Ruth Hanford Munn and James Buell Munn, 78.187

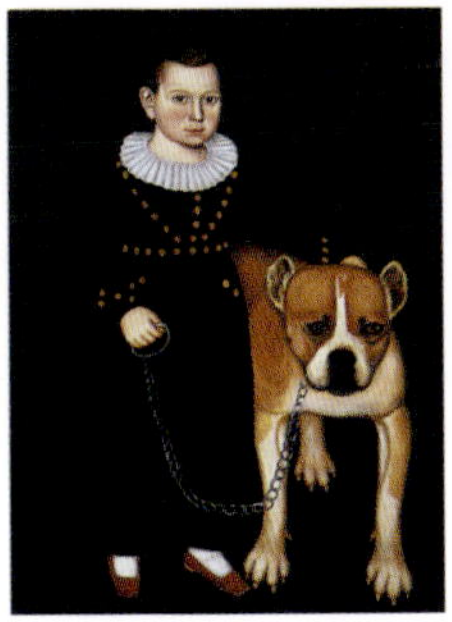

M. W. Hopkins (attributed to)
American, 1789–1844

Pierrepont Edward Lacey (1832–after 1860) and His Dog, Gun, 1835–1836
American Painting
Oil on canvas
42 in. x 30 1/8 in. (106.68 cm x 76.52 cm)

Gift of Mr. and Mrs. Robert H. Dunn in memory of Ruth Hanford Munn and James Buell Munn, 78.189

Pages 74 and 75

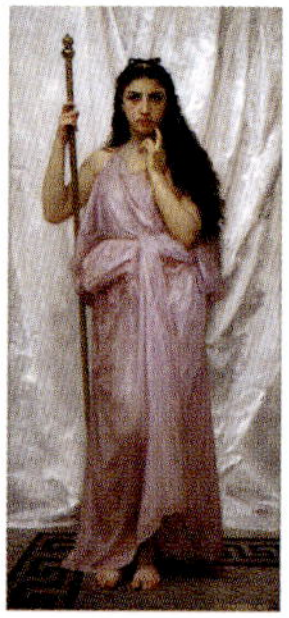

William-Adolphe Bouguereau
French, 1825–1905

Young Priestess, 1902
French Painting
Oil on canvas
71 1/4 in. x 32 in. (180.98 cm x 81.28 cm)

Gift of Paul T. White in memory of Josephine Kryl White, 73.1

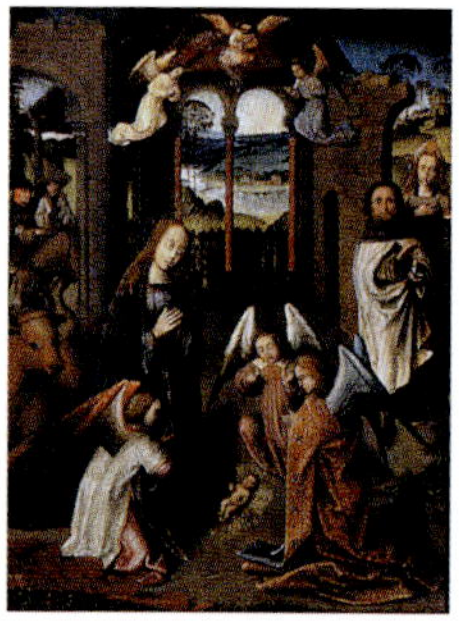

Master of Frankfurt (attributed to)
Flemish, active circa 1460–after 1505

The Nativity, late 15th Century–early 16th Century
Flemish Painting
Tempera on panel
17 in. x 13 in. (43.18 cm x 33.02 cm)

Carrie Bausch Lomb Bequest, 31.28

Pages 76 and 77

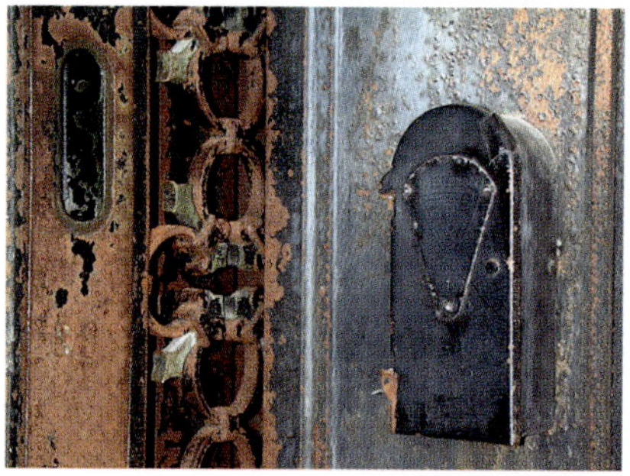

Door Lock
Front door of the original building

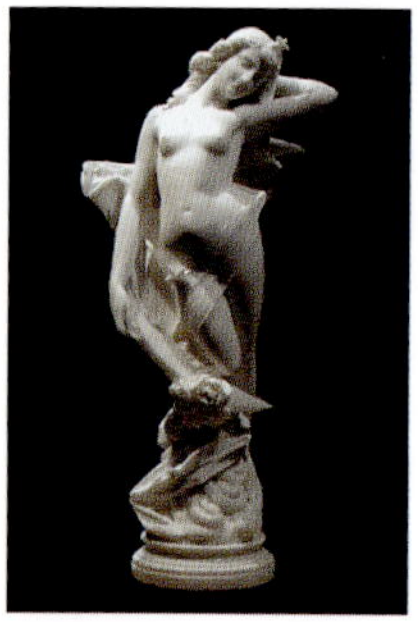

R. Battelli
Italian

Diana, 19th Century
Italian Sculpture
Marble
44 in. x 21 in. (111.76 cm x 53.34 cm)

Gift of the Leora M. Dryer estate, 68.51

Pages 78 and 79

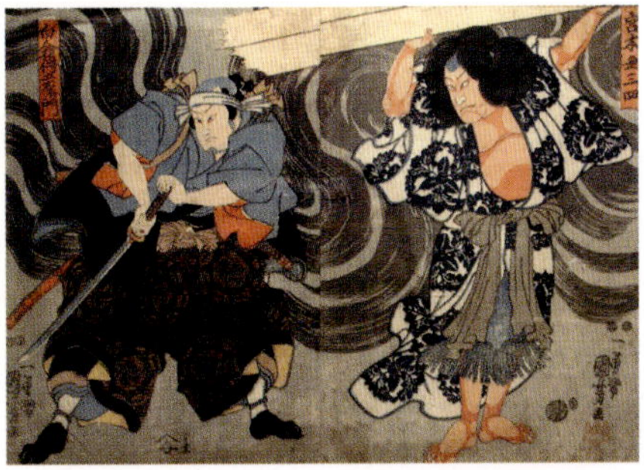

Uttagawa Kuniyoshi
Japanese, 1797–1861

Theatrical Scene, circa 1847–52
Published by Otaya Takichi
Color woodblock print
13 3/4 in. x 19 in. (35 cm x 48.3 cm)

Gift of the University of Rochester, 97.40

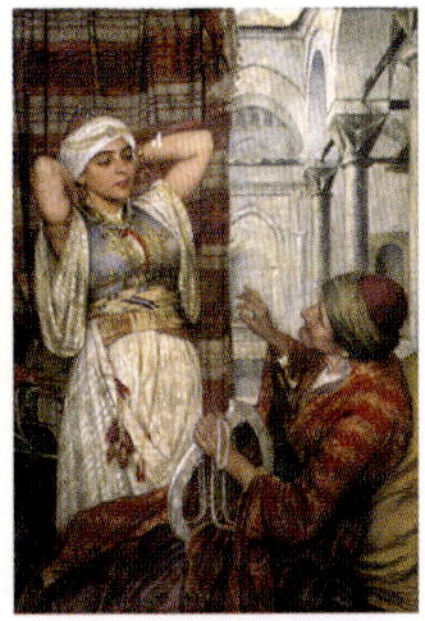

Unknown, French

Harem Scene, circa 1875
French Painting
Oil on canvas
44 in. x 32 in. (112 cm x 81.3 cm)

Anonymous gift, 91.15

Pages 80 and 81

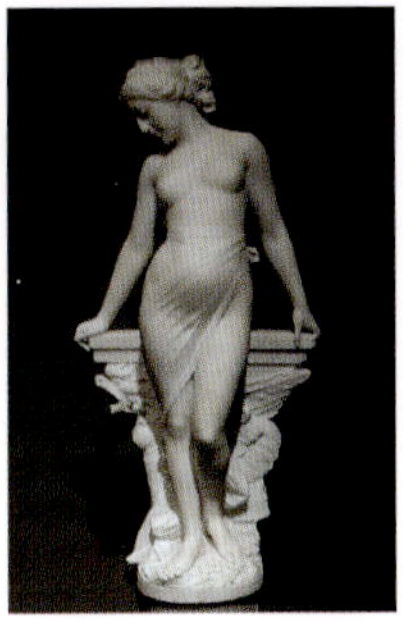

P. E. Fiaschi
Italian, active late 19th century

Standing Woman
19th Century Italian Sculpture
Marble
29 1/4 in. x 13 9/16 in. x 8 in. (74.3 cm x 34.5 cm x 20.3 cm)

Gift of James Avery, 88.33

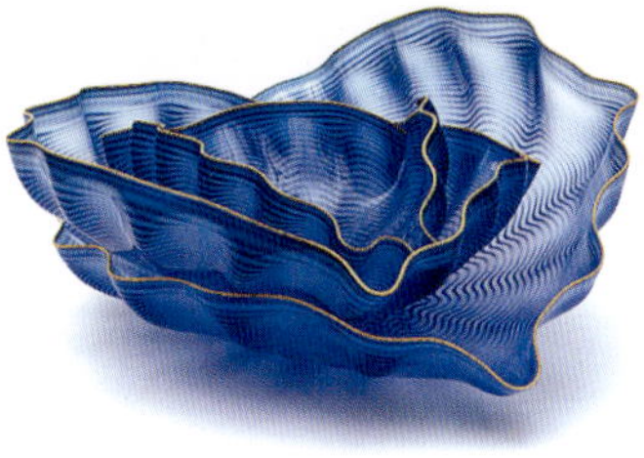

Dale Chihuly
American, 1941–

Pale Iris Seaform Set with Honeysuckle Lip Wraps, 1997
American Glass
16 in. x 34 in. x 26 in. (40.64 cm x 86.36 cm x 66.04 cm)

Maurice R. and Maxine B. Forman Fund, 98.51
Reproduced courtesy of Chihuly Studio.

Pages 82 and 83

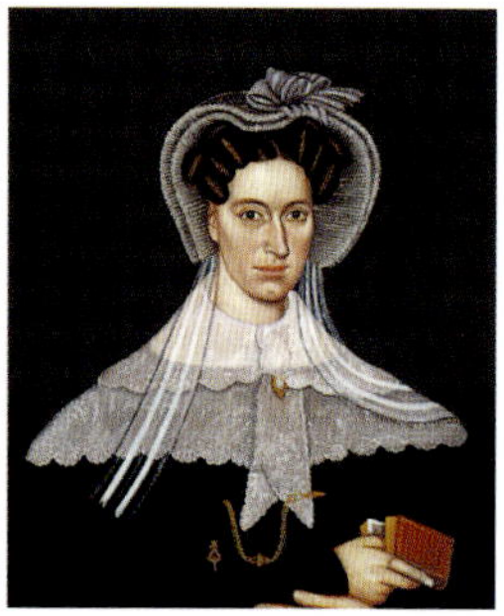

M. W. Hopkins (attributed to)
American, 1789–1844

Ann Gennett Pixley Lacey (1809–1841), 1835–1836
American Painting
Oil on canvas
30 in. x 25 in. (76.2 cm x 63.5 cm)

Gift of Mr. and Mrs. Robert H. Dunn in memory of Ruth Hanford Munn and James Buell Munn, 78.187

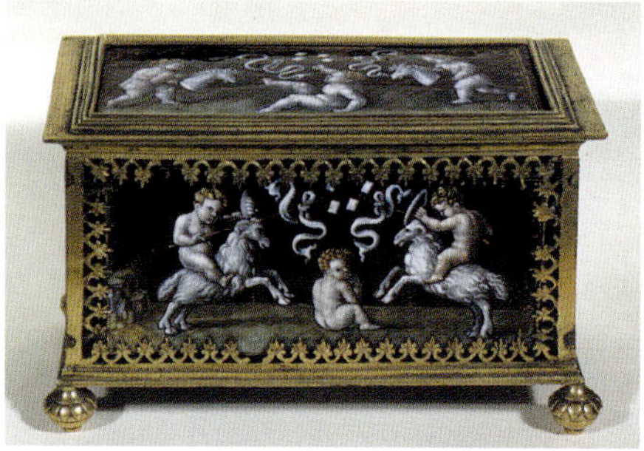

Unknown, French

Jewel Box, 17th century
French Enamels; Made in Limoges
Brass, enamel
5 1/4 in. x 4 1/4 in. x 8 in. (13.34 cm x 10.8 cm x 20.32 cm)

Buswell-Hochstetter Bequest, 55.120

Pages 84 and 85

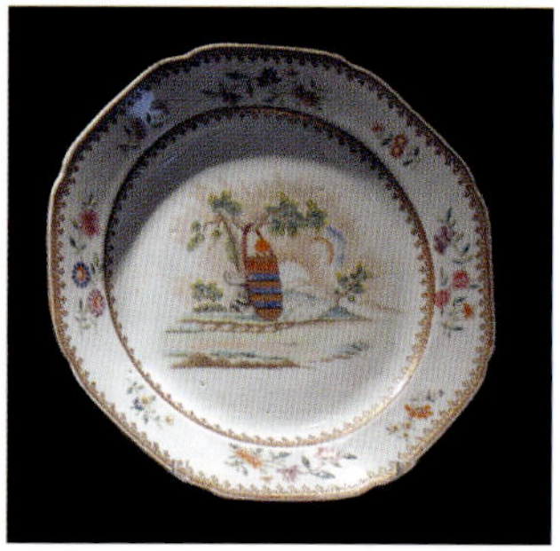

Unknown Chinese exported for the British Market

Dessert Plate, circa 1730
Oval-shaped coat of arms of the Clarke and Sandford family

Buswell–Hochstetter Bequest, 55.36

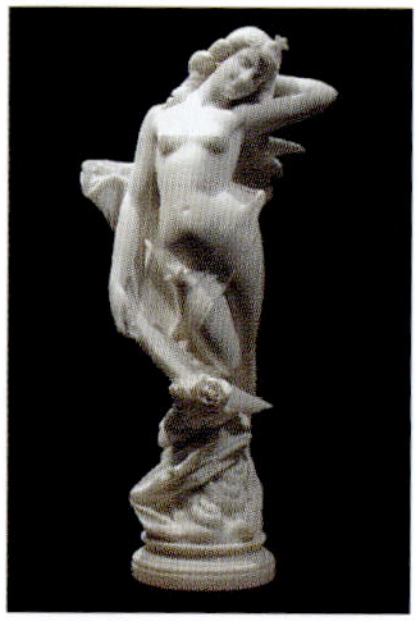

R. Battelli
Italian

Diana, 19th Century
Italian Sculpture
Marble
44 in. x 21 in. (111.76 cm x 53.34 cm)

Gift of the Leora M. Dryer estate, 68.51

Pages 86 and 87

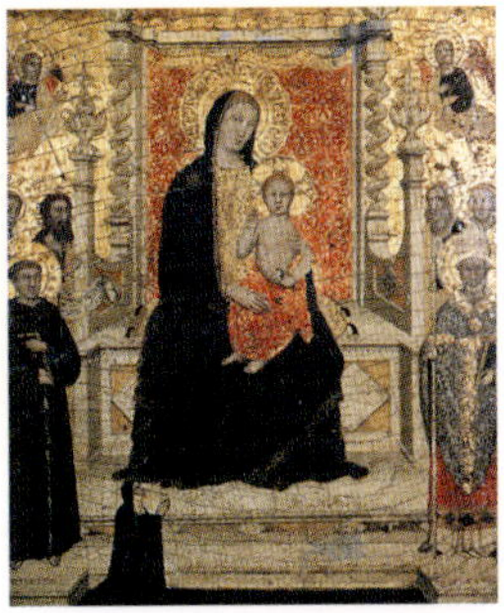

Unknown, Italian

Madonna and Child Enthroned between Six Saints and Angels, 14th Century
Italian Painting
Tempera on panel
26 1/8 in. x 22 1/4 in. x 2 3/4 in.
(66.36 cm x 56.52 cm x 6.99 cm) (with frame)

Gift of Mrs. Charles Wright Dodge and Mrs. Adrian Devine in memory of Bertha Hooker, 27.1

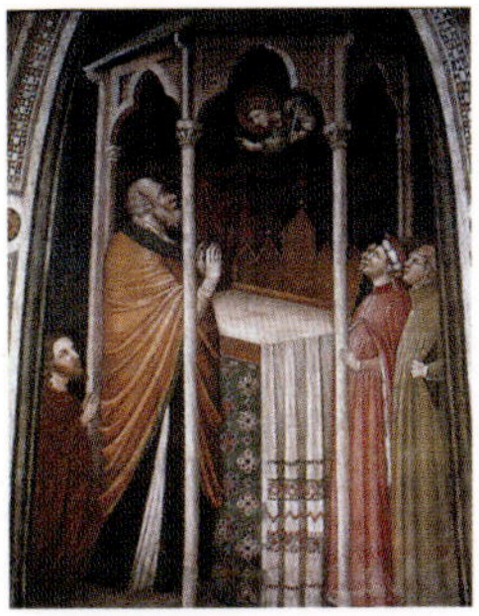

Master of the Urbino Coronation
Italian, active 1350–1375

Annunciation to Zacharias, second half of the 14th Century
Italian Painting
Fresco transferred to canvas
69 5/16 in. x 53 1/2 in. (176.05 cm x 135.89 cm)

Marion Stratton Gould Fund, 43.3

Pages 88 and 89

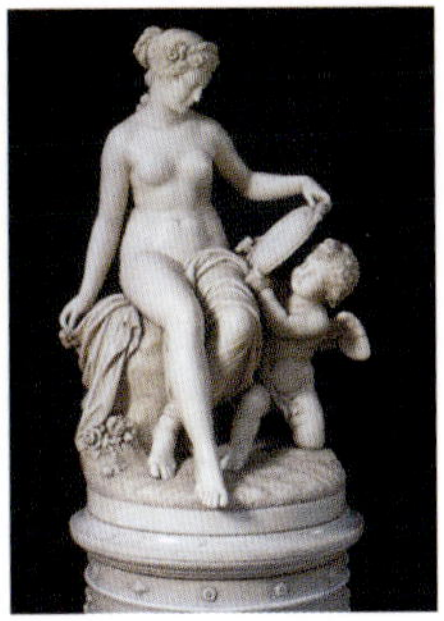

Nicola Cantalamessa-Papotti
Italian, 1831–1910

Love's Mirror, 1875
Italian Sculpture
Marble
85 in. (215.9 cm) (overall)

Gift of the Isaac Gordon estate, 66.20

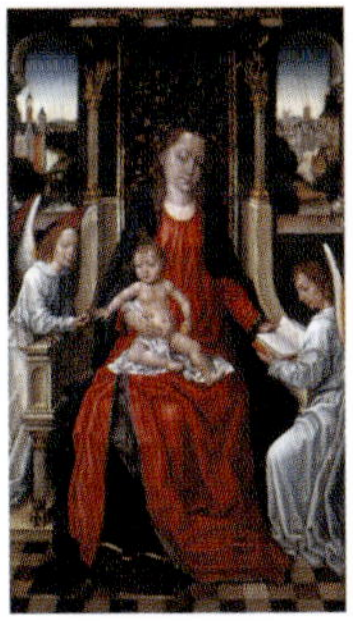

Master of the St. Ursula Legend
Flemish, active 1470–1495

Madonna and Child Enthroned with Angels, circa 1470–1495
Flemish Painting
Oil on panel
13 1/2 in. x 24 1/4 in. (34.29 cm x 61.6 cm)

Marion Stratton Gould Fund, 48.11

Pages 90 and 91

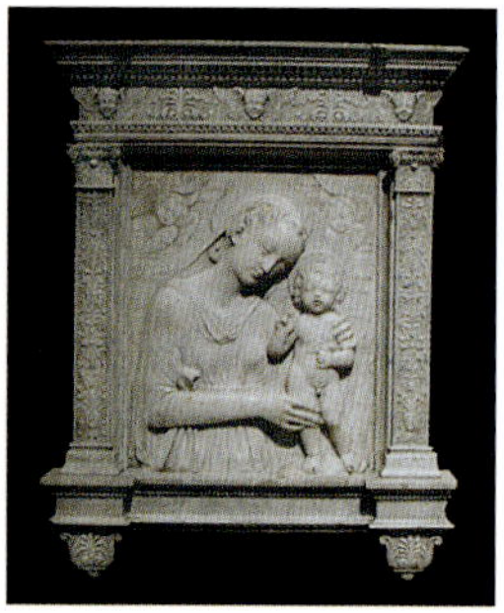

Domenico Rosselli (attributed to)
Italian, circa 1439–1497/1498

Madonna and Child, circa 1439–1498
Italian Sculpture
Marble
36 1/4 in. x 28 in. x 5 3/8 in. (92.08 cm x 71.12 cm x 13.65 cm) (overall)

Gift of the Honorable and Mrs. John Van Voorhis, 69.1

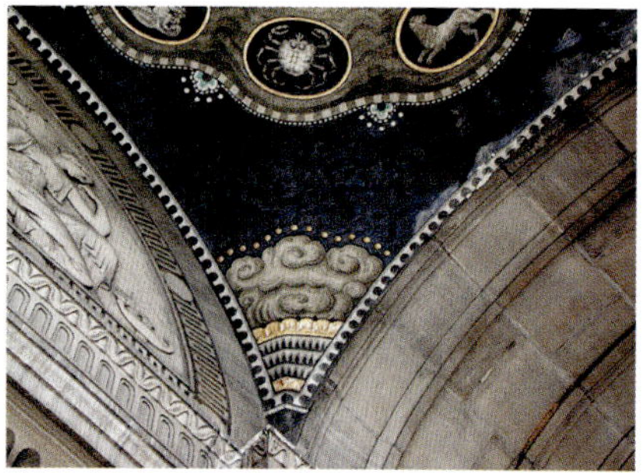

Frode Rambush

Zodiac Fresco, 1913
Fresco

Pages 92 and 93

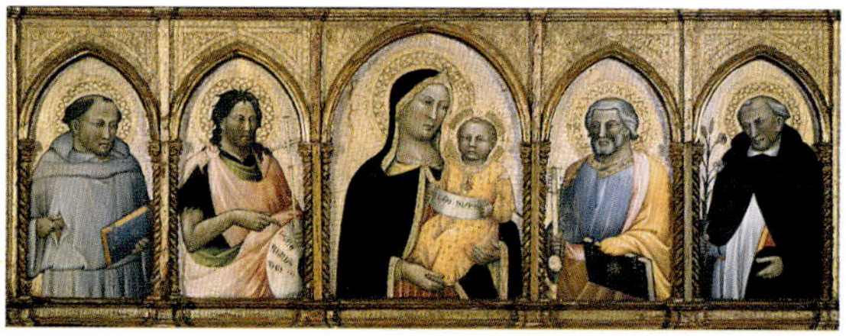

Nardo di Cione (school of)
Italian, active 1343–d. 1365/1366

Madonna and Child with Saints Francis of Assisi, John the Baptist, Peter and Dominic
second half of the 14th century
Italian Painting
Tempera on panel
30 in. x 86 1/2 in. x 6 1/2 in. (76.2 cm x 219.71 cm x 16.51 cm)

Marion Stratton Gould Fund, 57.4

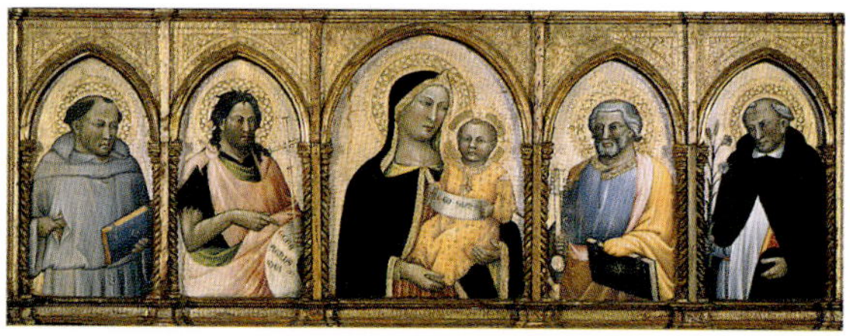

Nardo di Cione (school of)
Italian, active 1343–d. 1365/1366

Madonna and Child with Saints Francis of Assisi, John the Baptist, Peter and Dominic
second half of the 14th century
Italian Painting
Tempera on panel
30 in. x 86 1/2 in. x 6 1/2 in. (76.2 cm x 219.71 cm x 16.51 cm)

Marion Stratton Gould Fund, 57.4

The Index
Page 94

Unknown, French

Triptych, 16th Century
French Enamels
Enamel
11 1/8 in. x 12 5/16 in. (28.26 cm x 31.34 cm) (overall)

Gift of Hiram W. Sibley, 30.70

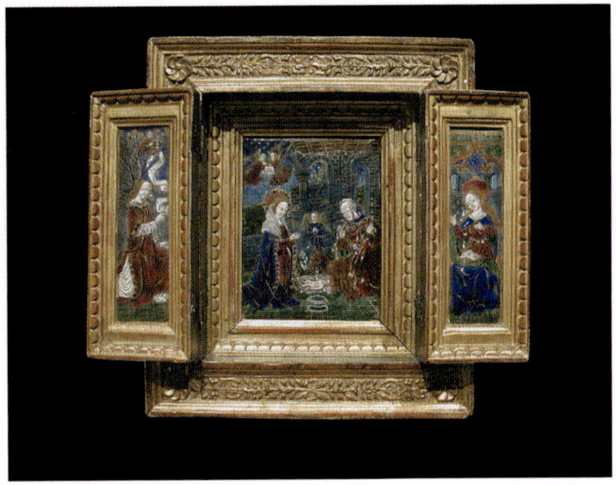

The End
Page 119

Follower of Joachim Patinir
Flemish,

The Rest on the Flight into Egypt, circa 1520–1530
Flemish Painting
Oil on wood panel transferred to masonite
22 15/16 in. x 32 7/16 in. (58.3 cm x 82.4 cm)

Anonymous gift, 94.23

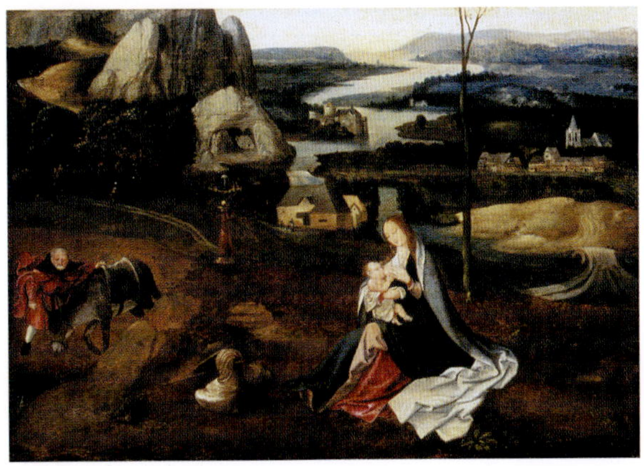

THE END

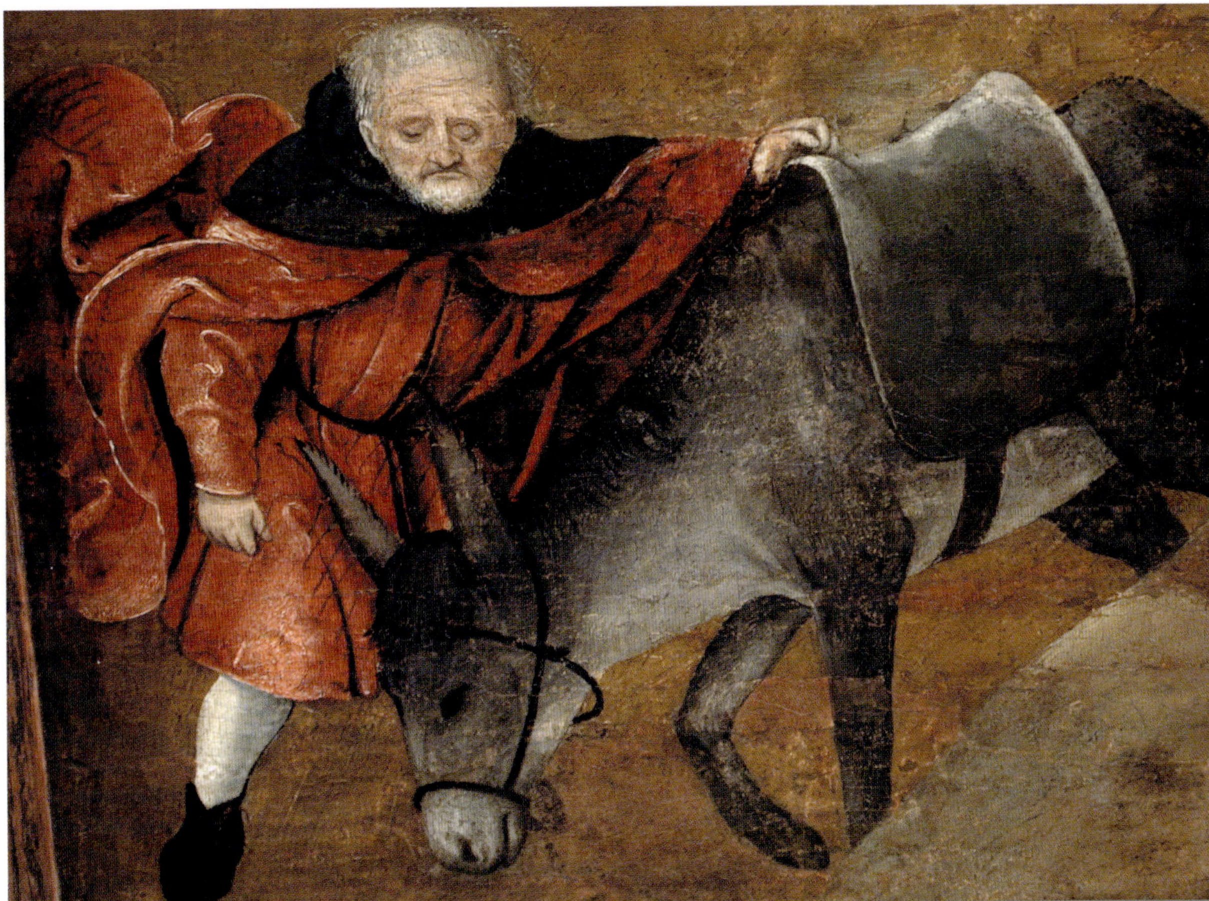